# ON YOUR OWN IN EUROPE

## A Young Traveler's Guide

*Strasbourg, France*

# ON YOUR OWN IN EUROPE

## A Young Traveler's Guide

### BY ELIZABETH McGOUGH

PHOTOGRAPHS BY STEVE MCGOUGH

MAPS BY LUCY FEHR

WILLIAM MORROW AND COMPANY
NEW YORK 1979

Library of Congress Cataloging in Publication Data

McGough, Elizabeth.
    On your own in Europe

    Includes index.
    Summary: Information for the young traveler, including tips on the best fares to Europe, what to take abroad, economical ways to get around, and places to visit in 14 countries.
    1. Europe—Description and travel—1971-      —Guidebooks—Juvenile literature.
[1. Europe—Description and travel—Guidebooks] I. McGough, Steve. II. Title.
D923.M32      914'04'55      79-13342
ISBN 0-688-27163-4
ISBN 0-688-32163-1 lib. bdg.

Printed in the United States of America.    *173846*
1   2   3   4   5   6   7   8   9   10

BY THE SAME AUTHOR
Dollars and Sense,
    The Teen-Age Consumer's Guide
Who Are You?
    A Teen-Ager's Guide to Self-Understanding
Your Silent Language

For all the travelers
who contributed their experiences to the making of this book,
and especially for Mark, Steve, and Mike.

# Contents

"Travel is fatal to prejudice, bigotry and narrow-mindedness—all foes to real understanding. Likewise tolerance or broad, wholesome, charitable views of men and things cannot be acquired by vegetating in our little corner of the earth all one's lifetime."

MARK TWAIN

# 1  YOUR FIRST TRIP TO EUROPE

How would you like to bask in the sun on the French Riviera for three dollars a day? Would you like to wander through a medieval town in Belgium, lunch on bread and cheese by the roadside of Mad King Ludwig's castle, or watch the tide rush in at Mont-St.-Michel?

Imagine this: A fisherman on Normandy's Omaha Beach invites you to share his catch grilled over an open fire, as you watch the sun's last fiery rays. Another day you walk the streets of Rome, narrow and cobbled, winding past fountains and plazas, and come upon a fountain designed by Bernini or a church with frescoes by Raphael. In Athens you walk through the cluttered flea market of leathers and copper ware in the shadows of the Acropolis. Drink a glass of wine an old farmer insists you share, in the quiet courtyard of his village home in Sardinia. "The grapes," he says with pride, "ripened out there on my own land."

A long rap session with students from Holland, France, and Germany makes you glad you came. Suddenly the world seems very small. You are surprised that they know a lot about the United States. You didn't expect them to be so friendly or concerned that you see the best of their land. You swap stories of your travel plans—where you are headed, where they have been.

Tour Europe on your own? Does this sound farfetched to you? Many students today are doing just that, and it is possible to visit Europe without holding your mother's hand or your dad's wallet. Besides, what parents want to see and do may not be what you have in mind. While few families can afford to tour Europe for a month together, a young person can easily plan and save enough for a trip on his or her own. Europe isn't so far away or so tough to get to if you set your sights on going.

There are dozens of ways to get to Europe at lower prices than you might think. This book will tell you about them, both how to get there, how to plan your trip, and what you can see and do once you get there. Getting across the big pond represents the biggest bite on any budget. But once you've arrived the rest is easier and cheaper.

## EUROPE—DESIGNED FOR YOUTH

There are several reasons why Europe is so appealing to young travelers.

• The size of Europe makes it attractive for travel. Distances are not

great, so you can get maximum exposure with little traveling time.
• You'll find many other youths traveling, just like yourself.
• Many countries are inexpensive to travel in.
• Europeans are more accustomed to foreign visitors than we are in this country.
• Europe is generally safer for young travelers than the United States.

As a once-apprehensive mother concerned about teen-agers traveling alone, I can now say wholeheartedly that the months my own teen-agers spent traveling in Europe on their own were among the most profitable experiences of their lives. They were able to ferret out and do things that would have been impossible if they had traveled with their family. Reasonable enough: two persons can see and do things better than six people. I do not think, however, that young people should travel completely alone, but rather with a friend, preferably one friend of the same sex, or with a brother or sister. More than two, unless with an organized group, could be difficult. Two people can adapt more easily to each other's whims, compromise, and help each other.

There are all sorts of other options, too. More than a dozen organizations exist to help you go to Europe, either for a summer, a month or two, or the school year. You can find a plan to suit almost any interest, from music to mountain climbing. Chapter 2 will tell you about these groups in more detail.

## IS EUROPE SAFE?

With commonsense precautions, Europe is probably safer for young travelers than the United States. In most cities you can feel quite free to walk the streets at night, and no one will bother you. But just as you wouldn't wander alone along skid row in any American city, neither would you do so in the roughest part of Paris. There are many facilities that cater to young people, from international youth hostels to student dormitories in universities that open their doors in summer to foreign travelers. Europeans are as a rule friendly and helpful to tourists. In spite of some obvious language barriers, most will go out of their way to aid a traveler.

Two American teen-agers who traveled alone for the first time got lost somewhere near Cherbourg, France, late in the afternoon on a hot July day. They were on their way to a hostel, the closest one they could find to Mont-St.-Michel, the great monastery that rises 400 feet out of the sea like a giant crown. The hostel proved too far to hike, and the thirty pounds or so they were lugging on their backs felt more like a hundred. Cab fares had already eroded their slim budget. What to do? They decided to hitchhike. A French couple picked them up, invited them home for a cold drink, then drove them all the way to the hostel, about eight kilometers away.

In Europe you will find an incredible number of accommodations and organizations whose sole purpose is to aid young travelers. The International Youth Hostel Federation was founded in Germany in 1901 by Carl Fischer, a senior student at a Berlin school. This movement eventually reached all parts of Europe. Such organizations create an environment where all people can find a greater understanding of each other through inexpensive educational and recreational travel. Many European countries attach much importance to youth interchanges with students from another country.

Females traveling in Europe are safer than in many parts of the United States. Still, a female alone may find the same problems here as in any big city, European or American, and so this writer suggests that young people should travel with another person. A dingy run-down hotel in a big city is not a good place for a young traveler, either alone or with a friend. Female travelers who wear scanty halters and suggestive clothing may be in for trouble. A young Italian told American students, "If a girl wears shorts or cut-offs to travel in Spain or Italy, we would consider her a prostitute." She would be harassed endlessly. Students told of "rescuing" several American girls who had trouble keeping males away. Blue jeans and T-shirts are perfectly acceptable clothing in most cities, and you will find young Europeans wearing them too. To ogle females or offer invitations for coffee or wine seems to be sport for many Europeans, especially in Greece, Spain, and Italy. Many simply want to talk. But a female traveler should use the same discretion and common sense in Europe that she would at home. Keep in mind, though, that many Europeans will conclude that a girl who goes alone to a disco or a bar is more than likely looking for an all-night companion.

In talking with dozens of young travelers, the one thing that emerged as nearly universal can be summed up with Mark's words, "You sure learn responsibility in a hurry." Other students said they were surprised that people everywhere were so nice. Many commented on the pangs of watching the budget and not splurging on food.

One boy bought four chocolate eclairs in a French pastry shop every day the first week he arrived. When he realized how fast his funds were dwindling, he took a second look at his spending habits. Two travelers who mapped out their tour for months in advance were startled to realize that they had not allowed time to get from one place to another. Visiting all the places they wanted to see was simply not realistic in a one-month tour. Another traveler said, "It was fantastic that I could do it on my own. I can hardly wait to go again."

Many had advice they would like to share with other young people planning to travel, from how to keep in touch with home to how to save money on food. Everyone said a traveler should learn the currency conversion in a hurry. The faster you realize you have paid $1.30 for a Coke, the faster you will find a cheaper alternative the next time. One woman who had lived in London for nearly a year forgot that fifty pence was not fifty cents. She had been tipping the cab driver almost one dollar for a seventy-five-cent fare!

While numerous travel books have been written, none give complete basic information on the many ways and means a teen-ager can use to get to and tour Europe. Your first trip to Europe will surely be exciting, and it need not be a hassle. But it will take a fair amount of advance thought and planning. To evaluate all the options you need to know first what is available. So think about a trip to Europe—on your own. Why not?

# 2 CAN YOU AFFORD TO GO?

Air fares are coming down. Transatlantic air fares have never been lower, yet they still come in an incredible variety. Normal round-trip economy air fare is about $600. In September 1977, Freddie Laker of Laker Airways in England instituted the cheapest airfare in history when he got approval for a round-trip fare from New York to London for $236. Pan Am and other international lines quickly followed suit with similar fares to meet the competition.

In order to fly Laker Airways' special no-frills Skytrain flights, you must queue up for reservations, and you learn only six hours before the flight whether you have a seat. No meals are served; no movies are shown. You can buy a box lunch on flights.

Pan Am flights cost slightly more, about $254 round trip, but you reserve three weeks in advance and pick the week you would like to travel. You are notified the exact day you will fly one week in advance. Meals are free, and movies are shown with the usual service charge of $2.00 for a headset.

Before these new fares, the best charter bargains ranged between $289 and $339, depending on the season. All the different types of fares will be explained later in this chapter.

In addition to your air fare, it will cost you about $350 to stay in Europe for one month, if you watch your budget carefully. If you have family or friends in Europe or can camp out, and if you bicycle or hitchhike, you may be able to cut the costs even lower. But $350 is a realistic figure based on student travel. How much you spend overall will depend on what countries you visit, where you stay, how you eat, what means of travel you use, and how much you spend on miscellaneous items. Of course, it will also depend on current international economic conditions and the value of the dollar, as well as the price of jet fuel.

Scandinavian countries in the following descending order of costs are the most expensive to travel in: Sweden, Norway, Denmark. Switzerland and Germany are also high. Austria, Belgium, the Netherlands, and Luxembourg are next, with France, particularly Paris, on their heels. Great Britain is reasonable, although London can be expensive. Ireland is inexpensive, but Italy, Spain, and Greece are even better traveling bargains.

Major tourist cities cost more than country villages. Posh resorts and beaches are more expensive than nearby lesser known but perhaps even better beaches and villages.

## WAYS AND MEANS

Teen-agers spend over twenty-four billion dollars annually! You may be able to earn enough money for your trip abroad in one year by stepping up the jobs you take on and cutting what you spend of your allowance. In addition, ask your parents what it costs to include you on the family vacation. They may be willing to give you that amount for independent travel once they are convinced it would be a worthwhile experience. You might also point out your individual food costs for one month (especially in the case of teen-age boys), and perhaps they will agree to supplement your travel fund with this amount.

While travel groups or university and academic programs may be expensive, the costs of a home stay with a European family are often moderate. Jobs as house-sitters or working in an *au-pair* position may be worth considering.

Scholarships are available for deserving students to take advantage of European study and travel. Ask your high-school counselor what organizations or clubs in your community sponsor exchange students or offer grants for a foreign-language session, a music seminar, or a cultural interchange. Rotary International annually sponsors hundreds of students for a one-year's stay in foreign countries. If you never thought you could afford to go to Europe, here are some more ideas to convince you that you can.

## SPECIAL FARES

*Advance Purchase Excursion Fare (APEX)* was once the cheapest possible fare available on scheduled flights. These flights are made by airlines that belong to the IATA (International Air Transport Association), and flights are standard in price and booking requirements. They can vary from one airline to another, so you will want to check around for the best deal. Such airlines include Pan American, TWA, and Air France among others.

To use APEX fares you must pay a nonrefundable deposit when you book, and reservations must be made a specified number of days before departure. You are requested to pay in full soon after flight confirmation. APEX tickets are valid for a minimum, such as fourteen days, and a maximum, such as forty-five days. These tickets are round trip, and no stopovers are permitted. However, you may fly into one city and return from another. If you change the date, or the departure or arrival city after the ticket is issued, you may be charged a penalty. Most transatlantic carriers offer round-trip peak-season (May through September) fares, if you book in advance and stay the required time. These special fare packages are constantly being reevaluated and revised, however, so conditions may change at any moment. With this type of fare you know in advance exactly what the cost will be, unlike the minimum-maximum price-range fare, which varies according to the number of seats that are sold.

Another special fare is the *Travel Group Charter (TGC)*, for which you must also book in advance, as far as sixty-five days ahead. You are considered part of a "group" but only for the purpose of receiving the fare discount. Once you get to your destination, you are on your own and not part of an actual tour group. These flights are organized by various travel organizations, and their price range depends on the number of seats sold. If the plane is not full, you may be charged an additional fee on top of the original fare. This sum is quoted at the time of booking. You must obtain a schedule of dates for departures and destinations, along with minimum length of stay required to use these flights. The Council on International Educational Exchange (CIEE) offers reliable and complete TGC-charter programs.

If you are interested in such a charter flight, write to CIEE (777 United Nations Plaza, New York, New York 10017) requesting an application and information for a flight to Europe. Choose one flight and two alternates, and mail the completed application along with your deposit of $125 in check or money order (never mail cash). The balance including taxes must be paid fifty days before departure. The charter price is subject to an increase due to circumstances beyond control of the operator, such as fuel-cost increases. If you must cancel fifty or more days before departure, you will be charged a $20 cancellation fee. If you do so less than fifty days before departure, no refunds are made unless a substitute passenger is found. A full refund is made if your seat is resold.

You should be fully aware of all these restrictions before you book a flight. Any member of the public is eligible to use these travel group charters as long as the deposit is made as required in the application. The operation of charter groups is regulated by the Civil Aeronautics Board (CAB), and passenger lists for flights are filed with the CAB sixty-five days before departure.

Icelandic Airlines is not a member of IATA and is, therefore, not bound by its fare regulations. Icelandic can save you up to 40 percent over regular coach fare on its flights, which all fly into Luxembourg. They offer youth fares and liberal booking conditions, including an APEX fare. The cheapest fare Icelandic now offers is what they call their Super-Grouper Fare, round trip New York to Luxembourg. You can save an additional few dollars by booking their Last-Minute fare forty-eight hours prior to departure and seventy-two hours on the return from Luxembourg. Icelandic flights stop in Iceland, but most thrifty travelers don't seem to mind. Compare regular-economy-class flights, youth fares, APEX flights, Icelandic special fares, and charter flights to determine which meets your travel needs best.

Most major airlines still offer a youth fare (ages twelve to twenty-one, Icelandic, twelve to twenty-three), which is higher during the peak-travel season. TWA offers a budget fare and standby fare for young travelers. These fares are lower than the regular youth fare, but there are restrictions. You must book and pay in full for your ticket twenty-one days in advance of departure, starting the first Sunday of the week in which you wish to travel. TWA then confirms the day and date of departure seven to ten days before the flight. If you do not accept the confirmed date you have to pay a $50 cancellation fee. The standby fare depends, of course, on availability of seats so there is a greater risk involved.

Remember, the greater the restrictions on flights (advance reservations, limited destinations, payment in advance, specific departure dates), the lower the price will be. Here are some other checkpoints:

• Consider taking regularly scheduled flights during the off-season, as prices are lower and charters are less frequent. Avoid peak-summer-season prices if possible. Shoulder season, between peak and off-season, is often a good time with fewer crowds and still-pleasant weather.

• Consider the countries you plan to visit abroad. If you are going to spend most of your time in England, Scotland, and Ireland, fly directly to London instead of taking a flight to the continent. Crossing the Channel adds on to your expense.

• If you plan to spend most of your time in Switzerland, Austria, Germany, France, or Holland, you may choose to fly Icelandic and take the train from Luxembourg. The train trip from Luxembourg to Paris is about five hours.

With the multitude of air fares and packages available, good professional travel help can save you money. Travel agents do not charge for their services; they are paid by the airlines so the fare is the same whether you book through an agent or directly with the airlines.

## PACKAGE DEALS

Often a package deal in which air fare, hotels, and transfers to and from the airport to hotel are offered at an inclusive rate is a better bargain than if you book only your flight. Some hotels offer special discounts to agencies that book many rooms or an entire floor for the season. Also, when you fly on your own, you must pay for transportation from the airport to city center.

I recently flew to Athens from Cologne, for one week, on a regularly scheduled airline. I stayed in an excellent, well-located downtown hotel fifteen minutes from the Acropolis, and the rate through a travel-agency package was $125 less than air fare alone. My fare included air fare, hotel, transfers, and breakfasts. Shop around for travel bargains, call the airlines for exact fares, and then compare with packages travel agents currently offer.

Swissair offers special packages for travelers, and many are geared for skiers—Europe on Skis and Student and Youth Ski packages in Switzerland. You can ski in St. Moritz for seven days, staying in a student hotel (three or four in a room), for $130 plus your air fare. This price includes continental breakfast and dinner, transfers from airport to rail station and return, train from Zurich to the ski resort, service and tax at the hotel, and the use of showers on each floor. For the two-week period over Christmas these rates increase by about $75 per week. Rates do not include lift passes or lessons. Other ski packages are available in Austria, France, and Italy through Swissair. Most of them must be booked from the United States.

They also offer Alpine Highlife packages for young people, with low-cost accommodations, teen camps, hiking schools, and a Swiss Holiday Card that gives reductions on trains, boats, cable cars, etc. Student rates per day at Emmetten, a typical mountain village near Lucerne, with full board, begin at $10. You can rent a bicycle through Swissair and the Swiss Federal Railways too. Pick up the bicycle at any station, and if you rent it for five days, it will cost you only $2.40 per day. A map showing special bike routes can be obtained from the Swiss Tourist Board or at the Zurich Airport.

You can also book a stay at a European Youth Center through Swissair. Centers are located in Vienna, Austria, Berchtesgaden, Germany, and Oberammergau, Germany. They offer varied sporting facilities and cost less than $100 for two weeks, including full board. You would stay in rooms with from two to five beds. The student hotel in Vienna, open all year, costs about $8 per day, including breakfast, and is a ten-minute walk from city center. Such centers provide a chance to meet other travelers of varied nationalities and could be a useful kick-off point for traveling in many directions.

The Swiss Student Travel Office in connection with Swissair specializes in youth travel linked with Swiss universities. You can find mountain-climbing packages, summer ski camps at St. Moritz, group tours of Europe, and foreign-language camps. For information write Swiss Student Travel Office, P. O. Box 3244, CH 8023, Zurich, Switzerland. Swissair seems to court the young traveler, and your inquiries are welcomed.

Two other unusual packages geared to special interests include a Tyrolean Tour ski package, which can be booked through American Express. The price covers only land arrangements at small Austrian ski resorts. You pay from $115 to $140 per week, depending on which hotel you choose, and it includes room, three meals a day, ski instruction four hours per day, lift pass, and special entertainment nights. No transportation is included.

Outstanding tennis packages are available at Wurzburg, Germany, for $160 per week and at Lermoos, Austria, for $115. Each includes accommodations in small pensions, two meals per day, tennis-court fees, and tennis lessons, complete with videotaped playback of you in action shown each evening. These packages are also available through American Express in Frankfurt, Germany.

Whether you choose a scheduled flight or book a charter, the Civil Aeronautics Board suggests that you ask the carrier or travel agent the following questions before you decide which is the best fare for you:

1. What is the lowest individual discount fare available between points A and B?

2. How can I qualify for this fare?

3. What are the conditions and restrictions governing this fare, such as advance reservations and ticket purchase, minimum-maximum stay requirements, prepurchase of land arrangements, cancellation provisions, blackout periods when you are not allowed to fly, period of validity, round-trip requirements, stopover privileges?

4. What other fare alternatives are available if travel plans are flexible as to time of day, day of week, season of year, length of stay, day of return?

5. Will the purchase of land arrangements or travel with a group permit a lower fare? What about group size?

6. Do I get my money back if I decide not to travel?

7. Will an alternate route provide a lower fare?

8. Does the discount fare provide for a price reduction for students or youth? What are the age limits?

**9.** What happens in the event the fare restrictions cannot be met, i.e., if illness forces an earlier or later return than the minimum-maximum duration limits?

## SPECIAL CHARTER GROUPS

In addition to getting across the Atlantic by booking your own flight, you can travel with a variety of special charter groups if you spend specific periods of time with their guided tour. The main advantage here is that most land arrangements are taken care of, sight-seeing is planned to show the highlights, and fellow travelers often share common interests, like music, art, or history. You are chaperoned during your stay in Europe, with only a few days on your own. While you pay more, you would stay in better accommodations than most budget-minded young travelers seek.

The primary disadvantage to group travel is that you do not have an opportunity to learn how to get along on your own. In addition, you would probably have more chances to mingle with local people if you are not with a large group, and you would also have more flexibility in setting your own schedule.

Organizations that offer group-travel programs:

**American Institute for Foreign Study**, 102 Greenwich Avenue, Greenwich, Connecticut 06830. This organization offers academic year and summer programs abroad, which include courses for academic credit and summer-travel programs. Here's a typical example of a summer academic program. During a course of four to six weeks at the University of Paris, plus independent travel time, classes meet for at least three hours each day, five days a week, and students are housed on a residential campus. Courses offered range from painting and sketching, a one-credit course, to French history or advanced French, a four-credit course. The cost for four weeks is about $1250 including air fare, tuition, and room and board. Generally programs are open to high-school juniors and older. Courses in business, math, music, ecology, marine biology, and literature are also available.

There are many summer-campus programs in which you can combine three weeks of study at a university with one or two weeks travel. Travel programs spend one week in each of four major cultural centers, such as London, Paris, Madrid, and Rome. These programs are guided by specialists in art, history, sociology, or other subjects. They emphasize field study, tours of galleries, museums, etc., rather than any actual classroom instruction. American high-school teachers supervise and counsel students, while foreign university professors teach classes. Students from fourteen to nineteen years old may participate in upper-level programs, and those between ten and fourteen are eligible for lower-level programs. Apply in October or November for tours the following summer.

AIFS also offers winter, spring, and summer miniprograms, educational holidays to USSR, Europe, and Mexico starting at $549 departing from New York. A deferred-payment plan is available for students. A variety of other Government and private scholarship and loan programs are applicable to most education travel. If you want financial aid, write to AIFS for more specific details.

**American Field Service**, 313 East 43rd Street, New York, New York 10017. AFS sponsors a school and a summer program in Europe, as well as Africa, Asia, and Latin America, in which American high-school students attend local secondary schools overseas while they live with local families. Students between sixteen and eighteen in their junior or senior year of high school are eligible. The school programs are from eleven to thirteen months duration, depending on when the school term begins. An AFS-affiliated agency, usually an AFS chapter in their town or school, sponsors students. Applications for academic programs are due in November for assignment the following summer. This program is assisted by the Bureau of Educational and Cultural Affairs, United States Department of State. AFS is an international, nonprofit scholarship program, formed to encourage young people to learn about another society and culture. In an AFS summer program, the student stays in the host country from mid-June to early September. Summer participation fees cost $1180, with school programs costing $2100. These fees include travel to the host country from New York, Miami, or San Francisco and a modest allowance, usually about $25 a month.

Students who have participated in such programs develop an awareness of intercultural relationships and often consider their time abroad as the most fantastic time of their lives. Kathy Davis, an AFS student who lived in Germany for a year, shared some of her thoughts. She emphasized that no one should ever think "you've lost a whole school year" by taking the time to live and attend school in Europe. "You can never say that," she repeated. While Kathy felt that she would not again take her own family for granted and that the year was not without some difficulty, she said, "I learned how much I didn't know." Decision making, thinking, and evaluating for herself were important parts of her year. "You really learn that sometimes you have to work at making friends, and you also learn more how to live alone." Kathy missed her own sister, even though she loved her German family, which included three sons.

There are no language requirements, but AFS does look for language-learning potential. Academic motivation is considered important, and a teacher and/or counselor at the student's school is asked to complete a form stating whether or not the school supports the applicant for AFS. The family and/or local AFS chapter are asked to contribute a portion of the program cost. Students who are selected to go abroad are given extensive orientation in the United States prior to departure and abroad on arrival. Volunteers on the local level and staff in AFS's national offices are available for ongoing counseling to AFS participants and their families. Interested students should contact their local chapter for specific information and application materials.

**Experiment in International Living**, Brattleboro, Vermont 05301. In addition to high-school summer programs in thirty-nine countries, the Experiment in International Living sponsors the New Dimensions Program. It offers high-school sophomores, juniors, and seniors a semester of living and study overseas. Countries involved include Germany, Belgium, Great Britain, and Mexico. The application deadline for the winter-spring program is November; for the fall program the deadline is 15 May.

In summer, groups of ten to twelve young people travel abroad under the guidance of a trained leader. For one month they stay in a community where each member lives in a private home. The rest of the summer they travel to other parts of the country, usually along with members of the host family. Interest-free loans and some scholarships are available, based on need.

This same organization also operates summer language camps of eight weeks in foreign countries, which are open to students who have completed eighth, ninth, and tenth grades.

**American Leadership Study Group**, Airport Drive, Worcester, Massachusetts 01602. The aim of this group is to help a student experience places most young people only read about. While they do not offer the experience of living with a local family, ALSG tries to give students an in-depth view of the culture they choose through the Comparative Cultures courses offered, under the guidance of teacher-counselors who accompany the group. Students who successfully complete an overseas program receive a special academic transcript, which can be used for credit through special arrangement with the student's high school. For example, one course explores the major cultural traditions in Europe, with emphasis on how the German-speaking countries helped shape the Western world. Courses are open to sixteen- to nineteen-year-olds and cost $995 for a fifteen-day course or $1500 for thirty-five days. Short programs are offered in spring or holiday seasons, with possibilities of exploring the London theater, Mozart's city of Salzburg, or its environs in the Austrian Alps. Eight-day trips cost $525.

Financial aid is available to students through ALSG, although amounts are limited and contingent upon the student's being part of a minimum-size group. Aid is administered through the teacher and is granted upon the teacher's request.

**English Speaking Union**, 16 East 69th Street, New York, New York 10021. International Schoolboy Fellowship. Isabel Carden Griffen Exchange Program for American and British Schoolgirls. These programs are offered to students from ages sixteen and a half to eighteen and a half who attend participating private schools in the United States and Great Britain. Awards cover maintenance and tuition fees for one academic year of study at a participating school in the other country.

**International Christian Youth Exchange**, 777 United Nations Plaza, New York, New York 10017. Study, lodging with a family, and service opportunities in Europe, Latin America, Asia, and New Zealand are offered for youths sixteen to nineteen years old by the INCY. Priority is given to students who have a sponsoring committee, which in turn receives an overseas exchange student. Applications are due by 1 February.

**People to People International**, 1528 Old National Bank Building, Spokane, Washington 99201. This volunteer effort of private citizens to advance the cause of international friendship was founded in 1956 by President Eisenhower. To be a High School Ambassador, one facet of this program, you need a recommendation from your principal or a teacher. Students go on a thirty-eight-day mission, with about half the time spent living with a foreign family. The program begins in Washington, D. C., with briefings by State Department officials and representatives of the Educational Travel Institute. The cost is $2285, which includes air fare, meals, lodging, and all transportation—everything except passport fees. The planned program spends time in Germany, Italy, Greece, and Austria. Students board with local families for five nights in each of three countries.

**School Exchange Service**, National Association of Secondary School Principals, Office of Student Activities, 1904 Association Drive, Reston, Virginia 22091. School Exchange Service links

American secondary schools with schools in other countries to permit regular international exchanges of groups of students, teachers, and administrators. Each school plays a dual role as both a host and a sending school and receives assistance in planning its own program. Check with your school counselor to see if your school participates, or write to the above address for information.

**World Youth Forum**, 46 East 52nd Street, New York, New York 10022. This program brings students from thirty-five countries to the United States for three months, January through March, for a program of seminars, field trips, broadcasts, family and school visits. Students are selected by foreign ministries in their home countries. A similar program is then available to American students whose schools have participated in the winter program. It is a seven-week tour of Europe during July and August.

**Youth for Understanding Teen-age Exchange Program**, 2015 Washtenaw Avenue, Ann Arbor, Michigan 48104. A one-year exchange program is offered in Europe and South America to high-school students and graduated seniors. It offers an opportunity for cultural exposure as well as a family-living experience. Summer programs are also available on a nonacademic basis for students who have completed their sophomore year.

## INVITATIONS FROM ABROAD

**British Schools Exploring Society**, Royal Geographical Society, 1 Kensington Gore, London, SW 7, England. This foundation annually takes about seventy young men between sixteen and nineteen years old on a scientific expedition for six weeks to one of the wilder parts of the northern hemisphere. Founded by one of the doctors on Scott's Antarctic Expedition of 1910-1912, the Society hopes to confirm the value of exploration—of contending with a wild and potentially hostile natural environment as a means of building character. While most applicants are British, the Society also accepts applications from American students. Cost is about $700 for the six-week trip, and financial assistance is possible, with extended payments also an option. In 1977 the expedition explored Iceland. If you are interested in such an adventure, write for details in January for travel the following summer.

**European Youth Meeting**, sponsored by Okista, Austria for Youth and Students, Turkenstrasse 4, A-1090 Vienna, Austria. European Youth Meetings are held in an Alpine resort area. Students stay in a typical Austrian inn with other young people for three weeks, full board, with a varied program of basic geology, mountain climbing, hiking, and music for $240, not including transportation to Austria. Okista also offers International Youth Sports Activities that include board and two or three meals, tennis, summer skiing, sailing, and riding. Costs for these activities run about $200 a week, including equipment, instruction, and tournaments. Okista has an international language course for students fourteen to eighteen for three weeks at $350. Rates include full board in student accommodations, about six to a room, three hours of language instruction for five days a week, with excursions related to sports, history, or culture for the remainder of the day.

**International Youth Meetings in Germany**, Federal Ministry for Youth, Family and Health, Kennedyallee 105-107, 5300 Bonn-Bad Godesberg, West Germany. Germany has hundreds of International Youth Meetings each year, with subjects as diverse as social services and language courses to botany and parachuting. You may enroll in an intensive two-week German language course and stay with local families or attend a music-and-media festival, which includes several operas and meeting European authors. A three-week painting course for $160 is open to fourteen-year-olds and over. For information and brochures with a complete listing of courses, write to the above address.

The premises of these courses is that "through mutual activities, language problems are soon eliminated and friends will be made."

The courses vary as much in cost as in content. They might include mountain-climbing equipment and instruction as well as lodging. Usually inexpensive European Youth Center or Youth Hostel lodging is provided or at least accessible. Fourteen-Day European Youth Week is sponsored in spring, summer, and winter in the Black Forest, in the Bavarian Alps, and other locations. These meetings focus on sport skills, discussions, and excursions. For details, write to the German Society of Public Utility for International Youth Exchange, Postfach 764, 5300 Bonn-Bad Godesberg, West Germany.

## MORE LANGUAGE COURSES

Under the guidance of Euro Sprachschulorganisation, Holiday Language Courses for foreigners are open to students from ages ten to eighteen. Students stay in family homes or boardinghouses, study language fifteen hours per week, and have a detailed leisure program. These courses are held at Easter and in July and August. Write to the organization at Herstallstrasse 39, 8750 Aschaffenburg, Germany, for details and costs.

Europa Sprachklub GmbH and Co., Amalienstrasse 67, 8000

Munich 40, Germany, also has three-week language courses similar to the above for about $350, including lodging with a family.

Europeans are quite serious about their sport activities and have organized training for almost any interest. Such activity is not normally a part of formal schooling, and extracurricular interests are pursued through sport clubs and other means. Music and art are also separated from the regular school curriculum.

So you can come to Europe just for fun, or with a serious and definite purpose in mind. You can travel on a student railpass and go when the moment calls you, or you can stay in well-supervised student facilities where you will find other young people, perhaps with common interests.

In any case, if you are interested in taking advantage of an exchange program or academic study abroad, begin well in advance of the time you'd like to go. Nine to twelve months in advance is not too early. Write to the organization for complete details on how to qualify, age requirements, costs, and what they include.

For your first European trip, your parents may feel more confident if you are enrolled in an organized program for at least part of your stay. Should you choose this route, do the organized part first, as an introduction to European life, then go off on your own if time and money allow.

## ARE TRAVEL-STUDY TOURS WORTH THE MONEY?

The circumstances for study abroad should be the best possible ones. Generally, these tours are expensive. But if you can earn six college credits for a summer course, as some claim, perhaps they are a good value. If you do decide to study for academic credit, the Council of Regional Secondary Schools Accrediting Commission suggests some ways to evaluate short-term study tours.

**1.** Who sponsors the tour, and what is their address? Is this agency legally responsible? If not, who is? Often the organization nominally sponsoring the tour is not legally responsible for tour arrangements. Know precisely with whom you must deal should trouble arise.

**2.** Specific objectives of the tour should be clear. The actual structure of all travel should be spelled out. How much time is spent studying, and how much in touring? The actual circumstances under which study takes place should be clear. Some tours are travel-recreation oriented; others stress instruction. Examine the program to see if it is consistent with stated objectives. Approach with caution any program that makes extreme or unsupported claims.

**3.** What are the conditions of instructions, and what are the qualifications of the teachers? If language development is a prime objective, instruction should be in the target language, preferably given by nationals of the country. Transplanting a Stateside teacher to a foreign classroom does not necessarily equip him or her for teaching there. If language barriers are not overwhelming, foreign nationals should be used as teachers.

**4.** Students should be screened and selected for the study tour. Review should include academic record, emotional stability, maturity, and suitability of student's age for this group. If instruction is to be given in another language, proficiency in the language should be considered. If a program accepts any student who can pay, you should question whether the tour would be a worthwhile educational travel experience.

**5.** No statement should say or imply that credit is granted by the home school. Credit evaluation is entirely up to the local school. A three- or four-week study experience under rather uncertain circumstances cannot be equated with formal classwork at home. While no one denies that the experience may be educational, no travel-study sponsoring agency is accredited by the regional accrediting associations. Therefore, any credits must be granted by the local school and often this decision is based on examination by the school at completion of the tour. A teacher may accompany a tour group to a foreign country, and students may be given classroom credit time for the tour, rather than being counted as absent. This arrangement does not mean students are given academic credit, even though it may enrich their understanding of language, history, art, music, drama, culture, etc.

For a complete brochure on evaluation of travel-study tours for secondary-school students, write Commission on Secondary Schools, North Central Association, 5454 South Shore Drive, Chicago, Illinois 60615.

## UNIVERSITY-LEVEL STUDY ABROAD

According to the Institute for International Education (IIE), it is recommended that United States students who wish to study abroad independently do so only after graduation from college. Foreign secondary schools provide more specialized education than high schools in the United States do, and these students enter university prepared to pursue advanced courses rather than introductory ones.

Some foreign universities do offer special courses for foreign students during the academic year. Generally, there are no academic prerequisites, and the university may award certificates of completion. But United States colleges do not then grant credit. Some foreign universities offer summer study abroad for specialized courses.

Working your way through college is not common in foreign countries, and American students should not count on finding gainful employment. Scholarships are usually available for study abroad only at graduate levels.

Some American colleges and universities have been established in foreign countries and follow the organization, credit and degree system, curriculum, and teaching methods of the home colleges. In Europe, the only fully accredited institutions of this nature are The American College in Paris and Franklin College in Lugano, Switzerland. Overseas campuses are maintained by some colleges and universities such as The Johns Hopkins University, Bologna Center, and the New England College branch in Arundel, England. Many other schools operate junior-year-abroad programs.

The University of Maryland's overseas centers admit only members of the armed forces, American employees of the United States Government, or dependents of either if they are in or employed by the European command. Further information may be obtained from University College, University of Maryland, College Park, Maryland 20742.

For detailed information on study abroad and a listing of publications on foreign study, write to the Institute of International Education, 809 United Nations Plaza, New York, New York 10017.

## WORKING IN EUROPE

Working in Europe is not the easiest thing to do considering labor laws, work permits, etc. But some students find it a great way to get the feel of the country and become acquainted with the people. Students have found employment as hotel workers, bakery-delivery clerks, ski instructors, household help, and in work camps.

Work camps can be found in many countries and may offer an interesting experience along with free room and board, leisure activities, and the company of other young people. In 1977 over eighty work camps and social-service programs operated in Germany. Young people between sixteen and twenty-five (two-thirds are foreigners) worked at building children's playgrounds, hospital service, youth and social work, or at outdoor tasks, such as flood protection, caring for nature preserves and hiking paths, and archeological work. For information on German work camps write to: International Social Service of Youth, Kaiserstrasse 43, 5300 Bonn, West Germany.

Another popular job in Europe for females is working in an *au-pair* capacity. In exchange for five hours a day of light housework or baby-sitting, girls receive room, board, and pocket money equal to about $80 a month in France and Germany, and $50 in England. In their free time these young women—seventeen or older—may attend language classes and do as they choose. The Council of Europe has recently issued Common Market guidelines to counter exploitation of *au-pair* girls. Rules stress that young foreigners should "not be used as substitutes for cleaning women and should not be asked to do heavy housework." The term *au-pair* means "on even terms," and the young women are to be treated as family members. A host family is obliged to provide the *au-pair* girl with her own room, all meals, an allowance, health insurance, and one day off each week. In Germany, *au-pair* girls are placed by Protestant or Roman Catholic agencies or by Federal labor offices in major cities.

In France most *au-pair* positions are placed through educational institutions, such as the Sorbonne and the Alliance Française in Paris. The French Government requires a work contract to insure that the family provides for the girl's needs and limits her work to a maximum of five hours a day. Some girls have complained that they have no fixed work schedule and cannot attend language classes as much as they would like.

Here are addresses of agencies to contact for *au-pair* positions in France, Germany and England:

Protestant Association for International Youth Work
   Mrs. Reich
   5300 Bonn, West Germany
Accueil Familiale des Jeunes Étrangers
   23 rue du Cherche-Midi
   Paris 6, France
Amitié Mondiale
   39 rue Cambon
   Paris 1, France
Au Pair Bureau Ltd.
   87 Regent Street W. 1
   London, England
International Catholic Girl Society
   39 Victoria at S.W. 1
   London, England

International English-language papers, such as the *International Herald Tribune*, are also good sources for job openings such as *au-pair* positions, or for secretaries and translators who can type, take shorthand, and are fluent in a second language. Should you seek employment in Europe be sure to have documents with you that can prove your capabilities.

# 3 GETTING IT ALL TOGETHER

What you want to see and do in Europe depends on your interests. If history is your bag, you can find enough history to boggle the mind. From Stonehenge to the Parthenon, history comes alive even for the student who used to find it a bore.

If you are an art buff, you can visit many of the world's greatest galleries, churches, and buildings. You'll find music, folklore, and tradition at every crossroads.

The travelers with a few months to soak up something of Europe will be able to poke around wherever their mood takes them. Their experiences may include participating in the inevitable political discussions held in sidewalk cafés and on streets. Europeans are politically aware and much involved with their neighboring countries. You may be surprised at their knowledge of the United States.

In Europe you will find plenty of people—150 to the square mile. The continent extends 3000 miles east to west, 2400 miles north to south, and within these boundaries 600,000,000 people live. Through these people you begin to see what Europe is all about: people carrying fresh, long loaves of bread under the arm, young people learning the ancient art of crystal cutting, teen-agers in sidewalk cafés sipping Coke, vendors in the daily marketplace selling their peaches and strange-looking vegetables. People are milling around everywhere, all seeking their small bit of territory.

## THE GRAND TOUR

So you begin to think, how can you make the most of the time you have to spend in Europe? What do you care about most when traveling? Sight-seeing? Touring? Sports? All of these things? You may have glorious visions of hiking in the Alps. Perhaps your grandmother grew up in Ireland, and you have a pen pal in Holland. Hold on! If you try to cover too much ground in one trip, you can get travel weary and wonder how you are going to recover from your vacation. Always assume that you're coming back. Plan realistically in line with the time you can spend traveling. Here are two actual trip routes young teen-agers enjoyed on one-month tours recently. For each trip two students traveled together. Before departure they spent several months in advance planning, writing for student identity cards, hostel lists, reading travel and encyclopedia articles about the countries, talking to friends who had visited places they wanted to see, and checking out ferry routes to places they were considering.

**Trip A**—Luxembourg–Paris–Rouen–Normandy Coast–Mont-St.-Michel–ferry Cherbourg to Weymouth–Oxford–Cork–Dublin–Chester–English Lake District around Carlisle–Edinburgh–London–Brussels–Luxembourg.

**Trip B**—Bonn–Venice–Florence–Pisa–Rome–ferry Civitavecchia to Olbia, Sardinia–ferry Olbia to Civitavecchia–French Riviera, Monaco–Barcelona–Madrid–Pamplona–Geneva–Chamonix–return to Bonn via Paris.

On trip A students spent several days in Paris, while on Trip B they merely passed through en route to Bonn. On each trip they found far more things to see and do than time allowed. For instance, they could easily have tarried longer in the Lake District and Chester, an English Tudor town. There were also many Spanish towns they could have included in Trip B had time allowed. The students were unanimous in their advice, "Never worry about having enough to do in any region. It's always the other way. So don't plan too much, too many stops." Each of the above could easily have been six- to eight-week trips.

Here's a British roundabout tour other travelers recommend: London–Oxford–Welsh coast, Swansea, Cardiff–Cork via Swansea–west coast of Ireland, Ring of Kerry, Dingle Bay–Galway–Dublin–ferry to Holyhead–Chester, Lake District–Loch Ness–Inverness, Scottish Highlands–Edinburgh–Cambridge–London.

Now that you have some idea of what you might cover on a European trek, you should begin to tackle some of the chores all travelers face.

### BEFORE YOU GO

Here are some important things you need to do before you go, no matter what direction you take.

**Passport**—First, you need a passport, which you can get by making an application before a passport agent of the Department of State at a passport agency located in either Boston, Chicago, Honolulu, Los Angeles, Miami, New Orleans, New York, Philadelphia, San Francisco, Seattle, and Washington, D.C. Look in the telephone book for the address under United States Government, Department of State, Passport Agency. You may also apply through the clerk of any Federal or state court or a postal clerk designated in certain areas by the Postmaster General. To complete the passport application, you need proof of citizenship, such as a birth certificate or if it is not available, a baptismal certificate or Jewish certificate of circumcision. You will also need identification or a witness to prove that you are indeed the person applying, and you must have two clear photographs taken within six months of application, in color or black and white, front view, and not smaller than two and one-half by two and one-half inches or larger than three by three inches. Vending-machine snapshots or full-length photographs are not acceptable. The passport costs $13 including $2 paid to the person executing the application. Passports are valid for five years and are required for traveling in Europe and also to reenter the United States. Processing usually takes two to three weeks, but be sure to allow ample time before departure.

**Visas**—A visa is an inked stamp in your passport—not the postal variety—placed there by an official of the country that authorized you to travel within its borders. Western Europe does not require United States citizens to obtain a visa for a visit of under three months. If you plan to stay in Europe longer, check with the consulate of that country before you leave the States. Visitors, including exchange students, who plan to stay in Germany for over three months must register in the town where they live and must deregister when they leave. Passports are stamped accordingly. East Germany, Czechoslovakia, Yugoslavia, Poland, and the Soviet Union all require a visa. However, if you enter East Germany on a tour or travel through Yugoslavia by train, a visa may be issued at the border. Russia and some other Eastern European countries require tourists to have confirmed travel reservations in their countries before considering visa applications. If you expect to visit a country where a visa may be required, check several months in advance of your planned departure. You may be required to apply for the visa by sending in your passport with the visa application form. Your passport may be held for anywhere from several days to several weeks for this purpose.

**Shots**—Actually, no vaccinations are now required to reenter the United States or to enter Western Europe unless you have visited a country in the previous fourteen days where smallpox was reported. Ask your local health department to make sure you can meet current requirements, for they change without warning, as during the summer outbreak of cholera in Italy a few years ago. At times a country may require a certificate of immunization against cholera or yellow fever, although none are now required.

**Identity Card**—Here's one really valuable and widely respected piece of identification you should have for European travels. The International Student Identity Card gives you discounts for train travel, allows you to use student flights, gives discounts on museum admissions, theater tickets, local transportation, and is nearly an absolute necessity for saving money. You don't need an application form. Write to one of the following addresses giving this information: dated and current proof of student status, such as a signed statement from a school counselor or principal or a Xerox copy of your school student-body card; vending-machine-size photo; birthdate and nationality; $2.50 in check or money order. Never mail cash.

CIEE, 777 United Nations Plaza, New York, New York 10017.

CIEE (West Coast), 236 North Santa Cruz, 413, Los Gatos, California 95030.

USSTS, 801 Second Avenue, New York, New York 10017.

Or ask at any local college campus if they are one of CIEE's 250 licensees who can issue cards.

**Rail Pass**—If you are planning to do a lot of train traveling, you may want to consider buying a Student Railpass or one of the other rail passes available in some countries. You must buy some of the passes before you leave the States. For further information on them see pages 57-58.

## HOW TO KEEP IN TOUCH

Suppose you plan to backpack around Europe for a month or two with no specific schedule. Short of making a transatlantic phone call, how can you let the folks back home know that you are okay, or how can they reach you in case of emergency? There are several ways, including a quick phone call using the lowest possible rates, which would be a minimum of $5 to $10. But in between calls how could they reach you? One of the most reliable is to have mail sent to you in care of *poste restante* (or general delivery) of any European city. This mail can be picked up at the central post office, where you will find the office open long hours, seven days a week, and with an efficient service. You may be asked to pay a small fee when you collect mail.

American Express has offices in most major cities, and they will hold mail for credit-card holders or for those using American Express traveler's checks. You can have your family write you in care of their offices, then check in with the American Express where you expect to have a message. They will hold messages for only one month. **Important**: Have messages sent either by telex or by mail, with sufficient international airmail postage. Amazingly enough, few people realize that international airmail goes at a different rate from domestic. Surface mail to Europe takes about six to eight weeks each direction.

Airports and railway stations usually have bulletin boards where messages are posted alphabetically when sent in care of the airline or station. At best, this a chancy way of getting news.

America Calling is the name of a message service offered by the *International Herald Tribune*, a newspaper sold in large cities abroad, usually at train stations, large hotels, and often newsstands along the street. Here's how it works. For $22.50 you subscribe to the America Calling service, which entitles you to one coded message. Extra messages cost $10 each. These messages appear at the very beginning of the want ad section of the *Tribune*, and you are given a code book to decipher your message. The only catch here is that you would have to buy (or somehow see) the *Tribune* each day to make certain you get your message. The newspaper costs anywhere from a quarter to fifty cents depending on the country. In this way you can be reached even when your only address is Somewhere in Europe. You can subscribe by writing to America Calling, Inc., 3 Hamburg Turnpike, Pompton Lakes, New Jersey 07442.

## TIME IT RIGHT

Europeans vacation in large numbers beginning in mid-July. Take your trip abroad beforehand if at all possible. Avoid traveling around the last week in July and the first few days of August, as the first group of vacationers are beginning to return while others are leaving for the one-month holiday commonly taken in Europe during August. In France roads are jammed the first week in August as this month is their national holiday period.

Avoid London's Heathrow Airport on a weekend. And never expect to find an available flight to "somewhere" out of London in summer. A freewheeling American camping family wound up going to Amsterdam—the only flight they could book in four days—when they had planned on the Bavarian Alps.

If your time is limited and your plans specific, with little margin for revamping, get your flights booked and confirmed well in advance. Fourteen people were on the wait list for a recent flight from London to Cologne. Not a single standby made the flight. While all passengers usually do not show, they may in Europe's high travel season. The early part of summer is the best time to avoid the crush of Europeans, or better still, try to schedule your trip in May or September when most other Americans are in the office or classroom.

In midsummer, many restaurants and shops in Europe simply close their doors. They go on vacation, too—whether you need them or not. In northern Italy's lake region four different restaurants recommended in the guidebook were boarded up for holiday. Theaters, concert halls, ballet, and opera have few performances in summer, except where special music fests are scheduled.

Timing, even to planning where to buy your salami and cheese for lunch, can be a factor. When you get hungry, you may find nothing open to buy picnic food. Meal hours are fixed in mid-Europe. After two o'clock few restaurants will serve lunch. At around four o'clock you may be able to order coffee and cake, but not a meal. Soon you learn to conform and plan ahead to avoid the alternative—going hungry.

## SENSORY OVERLOAD

Forty-five sights of Rome in four days! Just hearing that schedule makes me tired. But that's what two young travelers talked about after a summer of travel. One commented, "After a while it got to be like finishing your homework—a chore."

Another said, "Well, I came to Rome to see all there was to see, and so each day I dutifully checked off on the visitors' map the sights I should see." Don't feel guilty if you haven't been to every museum and monument a town has to offer. You can handle only so much. Experienced travelers usually head straight for the tourist-board office when they arrive in town. Fortunately, these offices are usually located in or near train stations and airports. There they obtain a map of the city and folders of information to help them plan what they wish to see and do. Intersperse the sightseeing with some days at the beach or time in the mountains and small villages. One boy called his objective of "seeing all there was to see" a great example of the "good and the bad planning." One day he heaved a big sigh of relief. "Well, only three more sights to go!" While you may enjoy these things when you see them, the actual physical process of getting around to them can be exhausting. If you whiz through the Uffizi Galleries in only twenty minutes, what can you possibly appreciate of Florentine art? Why not see ten things well rather than race through a mind-boggling forty-five? Repeatedly young travelers say, "The typical tourist things you see are not the things you remember."

## GETTING AID ABROAD

Reports you may have heard about the horrors of drug arrests in Europe are probably true. Under no circumstances should you take drugs to Europe, try to buy any there, or transport drugs for someone else. You may be approached and offered drugs abroad. Students say they are surprised to find how many kids come up to them and say. "You want to get high?" Hash pipes are available everywhere. The penalties for drug possession if you get caught are extremely stiff, anywhere from six to ten years in jail plus fines. Many cities, such as Amsterdam, that are notorious for widely available drugs are also notorious for undercover agents. Never accept a package from anyone in a transit station or allow anyone to share a locker with you in a checkroom, even when it's economically appealing. Some European countries have more liberal drug laws than others. Nevertheless, you are bound by the laws of the country you are traveling in. Should you be accused of a drug offense, contact the nearest United States Embassy or Consulate immediately. They cannot intercede for you or obtain preferential treatment in any way, but the embassy will provide you with a list of attorneys who can visit you, inform you of your rights, and notify your family. One counsular official remarked that some travelers think "their embassy is everything from a first-aid station to a police department." It is not. Nor is your passport any sort of license. It is only evidence of your citizenship. If you are detained by the police or other authorities in a foreign country, ask at once to be allowed to communicate with the embassy. They can also try to obtain relief for you if you are being subjected to inhumane treatment.

If you become ill abroad or require hospital or medical services, will your medical or other insurance cover the costs? Check before you leave home. If your family policy covers you abroad (not all do), be sure to take your policy identification card with you. If it doesn't, consider taking out a short-term insurance policy that will protect you.

An American consular official explained that officers can sometimes arrange hospital space for sick travelers—even charity space if necessary—but the consulate cannot pay any medical or doctor expenses.

## WHAT YOU CAN LEGALLY BUY ABROAD

According to a United States Customs Service booklet, you should know before you go just what you can bring back. Your purchases may end up costing you far more than you expect if they are subject to duty. You must declare all goods purchased abroad when you reenter the States. You have a $300 duty-free allowance, and anything over that amount may be taxed at rates ranging from 1 to 50

percent. Binoculars have a 20 percent duty, skis 9 percent, pearls 20 percent. You can ship home gifts from Europe as long as they do not exceed $10 in value, and they must be marked "unsolicited gift." Not more than one such shipment can be received by the same person in one day. If you mail a "gift" home to yourself, you may find it subject to tax and duty. You can, however, ship home your own personal goods duty-free by marking them "American goods returned." If you plan a big shopping spree in Europe, it may be worth your while to write to the United States Government Printing Office, Superinten-dent of Documents, Washington, D.C. 20402, for the booklet "Know Before You Go," stock number 4802-00039. Enclose fifty-five cents for each copy ordered.

Certain items, designated as injurious or detrimental to the general welfare or prohibited by law, are restricted for entry into the United States. These include narcotics, fireworks, lottery tickets, obscene publications, liquor-filled candies, and switchblade knives.

One final tip on buying things abroad: Personally take from the seller items you buy and mail them to your home address. In this way you will sharply reduce the chances of a misaddressed package, receiving wrong goods, or worse yet nonreceipt of goods. Nobody wants to be ripped off! One young couple bought an expensive Persian rug in Morocco, paid for it, and waited for it to arrive after they returned home. It never came.

## MANNERS AND ETIQUETTE

In your travels you may be lulled into thinking that there are very few differences between American and European cultures. Not so! There are many differences, and failing to recognize them is perhaps the greatest mistake Americans abroad can make. Some differences seem slight, yet they count for more than you may think.

You will find European manners are more formal. Not with other teen-agers, you think. Nonetheless, if you understand the pattern of courtesy expected in the adult world, you will be a better ambassador for your country. And, of course, you won't meet only teen-agers in your travels. Some of the following information applies more to situations involving adults. You will have to judge for yourself how informal you can be when with your peers.

Most European teen-agers pay more respect and consideration to adults than American teen-agers consistently do. While you may know that you should stand when an adult enters the room, you may not know that you should never address European adults by their first name. Even adults who have known each other for years and have daily contact may still address each other as Mr. (or Herr or Señor or Monsieur) so-and-so. Neither should American adults address European adults by their Christian names at first meeting, as this usage implies a friendlier basis than initial meetings have in Europe.

Handshaking is very commonplace in Europe. Everyone shakes hands when they are introduced, women with women, women with men, etc., including teen-agers. When they leave, they shake hands again, all around the room. Expect to extend your hand often. In some offices, as in many homes, the handshake ritual takes place on the initial meeting each day.

While at home you may be just as polite to the mailman as you are to the mayor, in Europe you will find a more status-conscious culture. A duke, however far away from his castle, will not consider you his equal. He would expect to dominate the conversation, and "inferiors" in his presence would defer to his status. A medical doctor does not consider himself on the same plane with a local tradesman.

American friendliness, our open ways that we enjoy on home ground, may not serve us so well when traveling. Be yourself, of course, rather than stilted and reticent, but take your cues from your host. Americans are accustomed to asking personal questions. We want to know what people do for a living, what their favorite pastimes are. How else would we get acquainted? Yet such personal questions are often considered too forward in Europe.

Let others steer the conversation until you can gauge the tone of it. Teasing and jokes made in one language rarely translate the same as they are intended. Sarcasm and slang are also difficult to handle when you try to explain what you mean. The slang of other languages may embarrass you if it is literally translated into English. Quite likely you will hear a joke or two that doesn't seem at all funny, no matter how acute your sense of humor is. Even when the joke is explained you won't think it's funny. The easiest way out is to smile and let it pass.

If you're looking for a topic of conversation that seems fairly safe, remember that Europeans are, in general, very proud of their heritage—the history of their countries and historic sites. The modern tower of glass you find pleasing may be scorned by the townspeople who prefer the ancient Romanesque fortress, where the town was defended from invaders in 1300, or the tiny Pest Capella erected in thanksgiving when the bubonic plague stopped at a certain corner in 1600. Be careful not to criticize old things, like the tourist who commented loudly, "What this old monstrosity needs is some new paint and a good heating system. Who would ever want to live in a place like this?"

Remember, too, that many Europeans are multilingual. What you say is likely to be heard by someone who understands English. Confine your negative comments to private conversations, and keep your voice down in public places.

In England especially and in many other European countries, you must queue up in order to be served. Do not be afraid to push forward in line. You'll quickly learn to be aggressive in defending your place in a ski-lift line, or you'll be trampled in the mob.

You should also know something about nonverbal communication, or body language, of other cultures. One anthropologist said that any American sent abroad to represent our country should have extensive training in nonverbal language as well as the spoken word. For example, a closed door means just that in most European countries, particularly Germany, Austria, and Switzerland. Knock before you enter. If you are invited to sit down, sit in the chair offered. Don't move the chair closer. The distance between the chair and the other person's desk is intentional. While some cultures prefer to keep distance between people, others stand very close. Polish, Italian, and French people, along with other southern Europeans, may stand so close to you that you think they are breathing down your neck. Watch where others stand and don't back away.

At home, when you attend a public event and something pleases you, you may cheer and whistle. A long, low wolf whistle is taken as appreciation. Not so in Europe. A whistle is considered a jeer, a sign of displeasure.

If you are a guest in someone's home abroad, it is always considered good manners to give flowers to the hostess. In fact, in some countries it is almost mandatory to take a small gift of chocolates or flowers. It is, however, less common to write a note of thanks after spending an evening in someone's home in Europe. Should you stay overnight or longer, you would be expected to thank your host in writing.

The offering of food in European homes is not simply a meal; it is a way of extending the hand of friendship. You should, therefore, greatly compliment your hosts on their home and the food and for the trouble they have gone to. If the foods offered do not appeal to you, take some anyway. If you are unaccustomed to drinking wine at meals, sip a small glass, but never taste the wine before the host offers the first toast.

The American manner of keeping one hand in the lap while eating, or at least not on the table, is not the usual way in Europe. Both hands are expected to be seen at the table, usually holding the fork and knife, or with wrists resting on the table when you are not eating. This custom dates back to medieval times, when it was important to show that you were not bearing weapons or concealing one under the table. Unlike Americans, Europeans cut meat with the right hand and do not transfer the fork to the right hand to bring food to the mouth. They may also use the knife to place food on the back of the fork tines. You need not adopt this fork-and-knife usage, but you should recognize the custom of keeping your hands visible when seated at the table.

Europeans are also generally more careful about their property and possessions than many Americans. At the American Embassy Club in Bonn, Germany, I heard a teen-ager ask the receptionist if anyone had found a sweat shirt. "Take a look in there," she said. "There's a room full of things American kids have lost. They never come back to look for them. There are all kinds of things—towels, gym bags, swimsuits, warm-up suits, new soccer shoes. When German kids lose something, they are here for days, searching everywhere. Their mother comes; they don't give up." While I initially resented the tirade, I later came to realize some truth in what she said.

Europeans are careful to turn off lights behind them. Shops may even look closed at midday, since lights are not always used. European goods often cost more, but they are well made to last for years. We discard and replace things more often, to the point of being called a "throw-away society."

Travelers new to Europe should not be alarmed to find a female attendant in a men's rest room. Often she will unlock the WC (water closet, i.e., toilet) for you after you have paid her. Facetious travelers sometimes call this woman, who expects a small tip for keeping the room clean, the "toilet troll."

This look at some differences in customs and manners is only a brief one. But in recognizing that neither way—yours or theirs—is right or wrong, merely different, you will be better able to appreciate your travels and you will become a better representative for your country.

# 4 PACK YOUR BAG

Student travelers say, "Never travel with a suitcase. A backpack is a must." A pack is efficient since both hands are free to handle items like passports, tickets, maps, and coins. However, if you go to Europe for a school year or the entire summer, you will need conventional luggage. But for the summer traveler on the move, we would agree that a backpack is a necessity. One traveler found his hands blistered and sore after a few weeks of toting a conventional suitcase. A kindly Swiss woman made a special padding out of potholders to ease his tired hands.

## CHOOSING A BACKPACK

Buy a backpack before you go, preferably well in advance. American manufacturers produce good-quality packs, and your best place to shop for one is a sporting-goods store or one that specializes in camping equipment, not a department store or a surplus store. Packs come in either nylon or canvas waterproof fabric. Nylon is lighter; canvas may be more durable, though heavier when wet. A brightly colored, orange or yellow pack can be easily spotted and is safe to wear when walking along roads. Lighter colors, of course, will show soil faster.

Buy a pack with a good frame, either of aluminum or magnesium. If your pack will simply serve as your suitcase and you intend to travel by trains or other commercial means, we suggest a frameless or an A-frame backpack. These packs are less bulky than ones with an exterior frame and you will be comfortable as long you don't hike for long periods. If you plan to walk a lot, a pack with an exterior frame is best for comfort. For either type you should have easily accessible pockets and zipper closures rather than cumbersome buckles. For a large pack, get one with two main pockets and about four smaller ones. Some travelers say main pockets should be in two sizes, one larger than the other to hold items you may want to bring home without folding and rolling them up. Look for welded joints on a bag rather than sewn ones. Straps should have reinforced metal fasteners and not merely be sewn on. Also look for rubber feet on the bottom of the pack frame. It can prove very annoying if your pack won't stand upright while you fish around for something buried inside. Look for well-padded shoulder straps and a comfortable waist belt.

Get a salesperson who knows the merchandise, then ask to load the

pack with twenty to thirty pounds. Try several on to find the right one for you. Have the salesperson demonstrate where you can carry various things, such as sleeping bag, tent, etc. Look for some small outer pockets where you can stash a paperback book or a snack you'll want to be accessible in a crowded train compartment. Put your swimsuit, towel, soap, toilet articles in the larger outer pockets. You won't want to undo the tied-down pockets everytime you need something. Pack your gear so that you'll only have to undo the main pockets at night. A small day pack is great for city touring, bike trips, and overnighters, and it costs only about $6.

## SUGGESTED PACKING

Your packing list will vary depending on when you travel and on the parts of Europe you plan to visit. If you spend most of your time in high mountainous countries, pack warmer clothing than you would for Greece, Italy, and Spain. Central Europe, the British Isles, Ireland, and the Scandinavian countries can be quite cool and rainy, even in summer. The layered effect, using turtlenecks, sweaters, and windbreakers, works well for travel. You can peel off clothing for warmer midday hours and add on for chilly evenings or rain.

If you are moving to Europe for the school year or a summer session, your packing will naturally be more extensive than for touring students. You would need: coat, raincoat, folding umbrella, and more formal dress clothes (sport jacket or suit for males; velvet suit or long dress for females). You may want to invest in a good-quality camera to record your travels and more equipment for your own special interests.

Here's a suggested packing list for a one- to two-month trip for moderate weather:

**Male:**
good-quality walking shoes
sandals or sneakers, good quality
2 pairs pants
4 shirts
5 changes of underwear
5 pair socks
2 large handkerchiefs
swimsuit
sweat shirt
jacket with several pockets
rain poncho, lightweight
plus what you are wearing

**Female:**
sturdy walking shoes
comfortable sandals for city (not platform heel)
2 pair pants or jeans
T-shirts, blouses, turtlenecks
1 packable dress
1 jacket with several pockets
5 changes underwear
5 pair socks
handkerchiefs, cloth and disposable
pantyhose
sweater
swimsuit
headscarf
plus what you are wearing
**Both male and female:**
passport
money
traveler's checks
reading material
camera, film
towel
**Toilet bag:**
toothbrush, toothpaste, dental floss
small soap
washcloth
toilet paper
Bandaids
12 aspirin
12 antidiarrhea tablets (Lomotil, available by prescription)
needle and thread
pocket knife, or folding all-purpose gadget
combination bottle and can opener, simple type
shampoo
tube detergent for laundry
shaver, not electric
notebook, pen, envelopes
address book
matches (needed for cooking in hostels)
map
Females may wish to carry a small supply of sanitary napkins or
tampons, which are sometimes hard to find in small villages.

## FOOTWEAR

Ever have tired, aching, and blistered feet? This misery can ruin your trip almost as fast as eight days of downpour. Sturdy, lace-up walking shoes, always worn with socks, even for females, or lightweight hiking boots will keep your feet comfortable a lot longer. If you have to sacrifice looks for comfort, do so. You won't regret it. Sandals make a good change of pace for city or travel wear, and they can also double as a dress shoe. You can buy good-quality sandals in Europe, and you will find excellent buys in hiking boots in Switzerland, Austria, and Italy, particularly in the Dolomites. But don't rely on the new ones you may buy abroad as your only good walking or hiking shoes. Bring along an old, broken-in pair.

## ELECTRICAL APPLIANCES

Most European countries operate on 220-volt alternating current, which can pose a problem for the American 110-volt hair dryers, shavers, record players, etc. Buy or borrow a small currency converter before you leave home. You can usually find one in a large hardware store, luggage shop, or department store. One student blew out a brand-new electric typewriter the first time he used it on a Munich campus. Do not plug in any 110-volt appliance to a European outlet. The outlets are round rather than rectangular, so this difference should be enough to make you stop and think a moment. Hotels do not provide currency converters or transformers.

## LAUNDRY

Laundromats are not common in many European cities—almost unheard of in Germany—and they can be both time-consuming and expensive. Your best bet is to plan to suds out your dirty clothes in a sink every few nights. Bring along a tube of liquid detergent, or buy one in Europe. You can purchase a good-quality detergent called "Rei—in der tube" in Germany. It costs about seventy cents and is the size of a large tube of toothpaste. It works well and gets perspiration out effectively in warm water.

It's a good idea to pack permanent press or at least wrinkle-free clothes. If you choose dark-colored clothing and things you can mix and match, you can stretch your wardrobe pretty well. Darker clothes make a neater appearance and are more often seen in Europe. In fact, you can spot the bright-pink-polyester-clad American rather quickly among Europeans. Denim jackets, pants, and skirts, both plain and embroidered, are seen everywhere.

# MONEY

Traveler's checks are without doubt the safest way to carry money. You can get them from major banks, credit unions, and other agencies, including American Express. American Express charges 1 percent to issue these checks. But some banks will issue them free. Traveler's checks from major banks or American Express are readily recognized, and you will be able to cash them easily. Don't expect a small grocery store in an out-of-the-way village, however, to accept a traveler's check. Have checks issued in American dollars rather than in foreign currency, and get them in denominations of $20 and $50. Hotels, restaurants, and shops will take the smaller checks, but may not want to accept the larger ones.

The best place to cash traveler's checks is in a bank, preferably not on weekends. Hotels will also cash traveler's checks, but sometimes only for their own guests. Exchange rates are not as favorable in hotels as at banks, and there is usually a surcharge. If the rate of exchange is posted, ask if there is a surcharge in addition. Airports and railway stations usually have a change booth operated by a branch bank, and exchange rates there are about the same as you find in town—if the booth is indeed a bank branch. If the booth is merely a change station at a subway, avoid it like the plague. Recently in London on a Sunday, when normal banks were closed, we tried to convert dollars to pounds at an Underground (subway) change booth. The fee, or surcharge, for changing our $200 transaction was $10, a whopping 5 percent. We asked for our dollars back and did not complete the changing process. The difference between this change booth's rate, plus surcharge, and the bank rate we got the next day was $11.90. Always ask if there is a surcharge if you are forced to use an exchange other than a bank. Traveler's checks are exchanged at a better rate than cash, strange as that may seem.

Be sure to record the numbers of your traveler's checks, and keep copies in different safe places, perhaps one with a traveling companion and one with you but apart from the checks. If you lose the checks, knowing the numbers will make replacement easier. If your American Express traveler's checks are lost or stolen, go to the nearest American Express office to ask for help. Or ask the telephone operator for the number of the nearest office; there may be a toll-free number you can call to report lost checks. Lost checks are replaced as quickly as possible, usually the same day reported if you have proper identification when you go to the nearest American Express office.

Change your foreign bills back to American dollars when you leave each country if possible. If you wait until you return to the United States, the rates will not be as good. Coins will not be changed for you, so try to use them up for last-minute purchases.

Pay for purchases as closely as possible to the exact amount, since getting change in some countries is a hassle. You also avoid being cheated. Quickly learn what the local currency is worth; then you won't be surprised by the rate at which your money shrinks.

If you are stranded without funds, call home collect and have them wire money to you in care of American Express. A good idea is to tuck aside $50 of your traveler's checks for an emergency. Don't expect to spend it, and keep it separate from your normal travel funds.

One of the best ways to carry your money is in a money belt. It is simply a rectangular packet with a zipper or Velcro closure that either buckles or ties around your waist. Money belts are made of canvas or nylon and can be purchased in surplus or camping stores and luggage stores for about $3. Your passport and traveler's checks and other valuable cards should be carried in one. Each day put in your wallet the money you expect to use, with the remainder safely in your belt. You can also sleep on the train or in a hostel with the money belt loosely fastened around you. The worst place for males to carry their funds is in a hip pocket of their jeans. Doing so is an open invitation to a thief.

Females who carry shoulder bags also need to take extra precautions. Never carry your passport and all your funds in a shoulder bag. As you walk along a street, it's not unusual for thieves to try to grab your bag. Worse still, they sometimes do so from a passing car. If you carry a shoulder bag, keep a firm hold on it, particularly in crowds. You might consider carrying a pouch-type purse with a strap that runs around your neck and under the arm. While they are usually small and cannot substitute for a larger handbag, you could carry tickets, money, and a few valuables in one. Or wear your shoulder bag diagonally so that it's by your hip.

When you arrive in a new country, you should have coins in that currency. Plan ahead and obtain some at an earlier stop if possible. In some train stations and airports you may be able to buy a "tip pack," an assortment of small coins, at a change booth or in a vending machine. You will need coins for local transportation, such as undergrounds, to make a telephone call, or for countless other unforeseen reasons, especially if you arrive late at night or early in the morning before change banks open.

# 5 GETTING AROUND IN EUROPE

Once you've made it across the big pond, how do you get from one place to another? There are special flights from city to city, and surprisingly few young travelers take advantage of them. It depends, however, on your specific travel plans whether they are a practical way for you to go. If you plan to visit only two or three major cities, and then go on to small towns by train, the flights are definitely worth checking. Do a cost comparison of the time consumed en route using air and other modes of travel, figuring in the meals and hotels required, and decide which is best for your needs. Student flights are available through student-travel centers in major cities, and you can get advance information on them by writing to CIEE, 777 United Nations Plaza, New York, New York 10017.

## STUDENT RAIL PASSES

By far the most popular way to travel in Europe for students, as well as for many Europeans, is by train. There are many types of special tickets for European train travel. To begin with, there are three lower-cost special rail passes. They are InterRail Pass, Student Railpass, and Eurailpass. Other tickets, such as BritRail, are available in the more popular tourist countries.

The Student Railpass is an extremely popular one for Americans. It offers unlimited second-class travel on any train in the fifteen participating countries: Austria, Belgium, Denmark, Finland, France, Germany, Greece, Holland, Italy, Luxembourg, Norway, Portugal, Spain, Sweden, and Switzerland. This pass cannot be purchased in these countries so you *must* buy it before you leave home. For two months of unlimited travel you pay $250 if you are a full-time student under the age of twenty-six. To buy this pass, you need an International Student Identity Card, which can be obtained from the United States Student Travel Service, Inc., 801 Second Avenue, New York, New York 10017, or any student-travel center.

For both Student Railpass and Eurailpass, you may ride as many trains as you wish as often as you wish within these fifteen countries. However, you must have a reservation on any TEE train (Trans-Euro-Express, first class only) and on *all* Spanish trains. If you ride a TEE train and have a Student Railpass, you will have to pay an additional fee. Your ticket covers fare only, with any stopovers you choose, but sleepers and meals are extra, and so are reserved seats.

Most students get by quite nicely without seat reservations and rarely have a problem finding a seat.

Eurailpass operates much like Student Railpass, except that it is designed for travelers over twenty-six years old and is for first-class travel. Rates are: One month, $260; two months, $350. To purchase either of these tickets, write to Eurailpass, 610 Fifth Avenue, New York, New York 10020, or ask your local travel agent. If you write, state which pass you want, include your passport number, and your address. The pass is issued with an open date. When you present it at any European railway station within six months of purchase date, it will be validated.

InterRail Pass, available at any European railway station, includes unlimited second-class travel in thirty countries (including the British Isles) for one month for $144. You must pay half fare for travel in the country where the pass was purchased, so buy it in the country you will travel in least. The InterRail Pass also allows you discounts on ferry services between France and Corsica, Germany, Norway, and Sweden, Italy and Sardinia, England and Denmark, and Spain and Morocco. Sea-link ferries between France and England, and Holland, Belgium, and Ireland also give a 50 percent discount to InterRail Pass holders. Your pass will expire at midnight one month after the first day of your trip. You must have your passbook stamped at the ticket window every time you go to board a train. Reservations are not included in the price. You can board any train that has a second-class section (nearly all do, except for TEE trains). You can also use your pass on the Rhine for some boat trips. When you buy an InterRail Pass, ask for an inter-rail brochure that contains a map of the rail lines and ferry routes covered by the pass. For advance information on these passes, you can write to Deutches Bundesbahn, Bahnhof Strasse, Bonn, West Germany. When you request information from abroad, be sure to include two airmail international-reply coupons, available at all post offices, and send your inquiry by airmail only. Surface mail takes six to eight weeks for each direction. Don't forget to turn in your InterRail Pass in the country where you bought it within one month after it expires for a refund of about $5.

## OTHER BARGAIN FARES

Austria offers a special bargain valid for unlimited travel on rail and bus, which you can buy from any Austrian travel agent. It's called the Austria Ticket and costs $35 for eight days and $48 for fifteen days, both in first class. A second-class ticket costs $26 for eight days and $36 for fifteen days for those under age twenty-three. Rates are slightly higher for those over twenty-three. A season ticket (*carte d'abonnement*) costs $90 for one month, second class only.

The one disadvantage of both Student Railpass and Eurailpass is that they do not include travel in England or Ireland. England offers BritRail Pass and Youth Pass for travel in the United Kingdom. Youth Pass for economy class only, fourteen to twenty-two years old, costs $50 for seven days, $80 for fourteen days, $95 for twenty-one days, and $120 for one month. You must verify your age by passport to purchase these passes.

BritRail introduced a Sea Pass in 1977, through which you can make two one-way ferry trips by hovercraft on Sealink or Seaspeed service, for $22 over your rail-pass price.

These passes can be purchased from British Rail Offices in Paris, Brussels, Basel, Rome, Milan, Frankfurt, and other major European cities, or by writing to British Rail Travel Information Office, 270 Madison Avenue, New York, New York 10016. These passes are not sold in England.

Germany offers a junior pass or youth fare, for $41, which gives those between twelve and twenty-three a 50 percent discount on all travel in Germany for one year, either first or second class. You can buy this pass in Germany. It would be especially useful if you stay for a school year or an entire summer.

Italy has a Go-Anywhere Ticket, where you can travel second class for eight days at $45; $55 for fifteen days; $79 for thirty days. These tickets are validated at the first Italian boarding place. You can buy the ticket through a travel agent or at any Italian rail station.

Spain requires that you must make a seat reservation no matter what kind of ticket you use. You may be forced off the train or dropped off at the first stop if you do not have a reservation. Much of what you have heard about Spanish trains is true. Some students who rode a train called Rapido claim they covered 100 kilometers (about 60 miles) in four hours!

Switzerland offers unlimited travel on their rail system, including Swiss mountain trains and lake steamers, with a Holiday Card. Second-class travel costs $45 for eight days; $63 for fifteen days; $88.50 for one month. You can buy this pass only through the Swiss National Tourist Office, Swiss Center, 608 Fifth Avenue, New York, New York 10020. Write to them giving your passport number, date of birth, and expected date of travel.

You can consider kilometer tickets if you travel 3000 or more kilometers in one country. They offer 20 to 50 percent discounts.

Another alternative to rail passes is the student trains that run between major European cities about once a week during the summer. For information and schedules write CIEE, 777 United Nations Plaza, New York, New York 10017.

## HOW TO MAKE THE MOST OF RAIL TRAVEL

When you travel on a rail pass, you must normally present the passbook to an employee at the ticket window before boarding the train. However, many students just hop on and write in the point of departure and the destination. Technically, though, you are expected to have the pass approved at the ticket window to insure that it is valid for the train you intend to board, since an express train would cost you an additional amount. If you want a seat reservation you must also make it at that time, since the pass allows you merely to board the train. One student found himself aboard a TEE with only coins left in his pockets. The kindhearted conductor allowed him to pay the fare in pesetas, Swiss francs, Austrian schillings, French francs, and some stray German marks.

Use overnight trains to make the most of your time, unless you are traveling through truly scenic country. Taking overnight trains is also a good way to save money on a night's lodging. A popular overnight accommodation is the *couchette*, or *Liegewagen*. They are simple sleepers designed like bunks, three on each side. You are given a blanket, towel, and pillow. *Couchettes* are more comfortable than sitting up overnight, and the gentle rocking of the train lulls you to sleep like a baby. But don't worry, though. You won't sleep past your destination. The conductor who collects your sleeper ticket also takes your passport, and then returns it to you in the morning about thirty minutes to one hour before you arrive at your stop. Such trains, of course, have toilets and washrooms in each car. *Couchettes* cost $7.50 on German trains, slightly less on most others. Make *couchette* reservations in advance. A private sleeping compartment costs more and offers the privacy needed to change clothes.

### Meals on Wheels

Bring your own food on board is the unanimous advice of student travelers. Even well-off Europeans often take a sack lunch for train travel, since meals in dining cars are expensive, space is limited, and the menu often includes only full-course dinners. There are buffet cars, in which you can buy sandwiches, fruit, and beverages. Vendors sometimes push carts through the aisles selling coffee, tea, chocolate, or soft drinks. Often, though, a soft drink or orange juice may cost as much as a dollar. On train platforms and in the stations you can buy food—a fresh orange or a snack—to take on board. But generally you have more choice and pay less for food in town. Student travelers tell of being fed well by generous passengers on trains, of having huge loaves of French bread and salami offered to them in Italy and France by fellow vacationers. The universal custom on European trains seems to be to share when food is brought out.

Water on trains is not drinkable and is clearly marked as such in three languages, including English. One traveler thought *Not Potable* meant you could not fill pots from the tap.

## At the Station

When you arrive at the station, first check one of the large wall boards to find from which platform your train leaves. If you can't find your destination listed (and only the final destinations are listed on some trains, while others list many of the stops but not all en route), go directly to the information desk. Information desks are marked clearly with a large *I* with a circle around it, and employees there speak English. The word *information*, or *informacione*, is uniformly used. Don't go to a ticket window, for most rail employees do not speak English.

In large cities the information line may be a busy one, so have your questions clearly in mind and be prepared to write down the answers. Allow enough time to take care of your inquiries, and you will find plenty of helpful people ready to look up schedules, arrival times, and show you how to make connections to your ultimate destination.

Information desks are not the same as a tourist desk or an accommodations service in a train station. They are for matters concerning train service and schedules exclusively. Tourist and accommodations services are organized to give you a map of the city, a list of accommodations, a tour guide, or perhaps even make hotel reservations for you.

When you arrive at your destination, get the necessary train information for the next leg of your trip in order to avoid making another trip to the station simply to learn departure times, etc. Plan ahead. Write down the exact time the train leaves, so you won't waste time arriving early—or worse, ten minutes late. In addition to the information desk, you may also need to go to the ticket window to make a reservation or to have your rail pass checked. And remember, even though you are on vacation, Europeans are still commuting to the office. Commuters buy their monthly tickets the first and last few days of each month, usually early in the morning or late in the afternoon. So plan to take care of your ticket-office business between the hours of nine and twelve o'clock and two and four o'clock to avoid long lines.

While pictograms are used to indicate locations of many services, such as toilets, washrooms, food counters, etc., you should learn a few key words for efficient train travel. One student complained that he waited at the *llegadas*, or arrival, platform for nearly thirty minutes in Spain, when he actually wanted *salidas*, or departure. See pages 244-245 for a key to some important terms listed in four foreign languages.

When a train stops on your platform, be ready to board quickly. Most trains stop for exactly one minute only.

## On the Train

Along with your food, you should bring a liter of water or juice, available in lightweight, plastic bottles in grocery stores. Wear comfortable travel clothes, and have a sweater or jacket ready for sleeping. Most important of all, wear comfortable shoes, not clumsy platform shoes or high-heeled ones that could make running for a train a nightmare.

If you have a ticket in addition to your rail pass, don't destroy it once it has been checked or punched. You may have to show it in the station or later during the trip.

Once you are settled in on the train, stow your luggage in the overhead rack or under the seats. Put food where you can get at it without disturbing others. Do not leave the train to hop off for a quick candy bar at a platform. Stay with your baggage, or take it with you. There will be another train along should you get left behind. But if your baggage has gone on ahead of you, you could have considerable trouble tracking it down. If you need fresh air, open the window or stand on the platform between cars. Keep your money, passport, tickets, and camera with you at all times.

Many expensive cameras have been stolen on trains. One boy stowed his in the luggage rack overhead en route to Venice from Rome, then fell into an exhausted sleep. A few hours later it was gone. Another slept with his camera on a wide strap around his neck. Only the strap remained when he woke up.

Stow valuables where they cannot be seen, and where they could not be stolen without alerting you. Pack them inside your backpack, rolled in underwear or a towel, and place the pack, securely fastened, in such a way that someone trying to open it would have to disturb you.

## PEDALING ACROSS EUROPE

Some parts of Europe are ideally suited for bicycle touring. Cycling is extremely popular and offers one of the best ways to get off the beaten path and meet local people. But you should be in good physical shape to spend long hours traveling by bicycle. Most major rail networks have bicycle rental points, where you can rent a bike for a modest charge and drop it off at some other stop. You need not have a train ticket to rent a bicycle, but you will need your passport. In many countries you can also take a bicycle on the train for a small charge. Typically, you can rent a bicycle for about $1.50 to $3 for a day, pick it up at one station, where you get a map showing all the drop-off stations in that country, then tour the countryside as much as you like before heading back to a train again. You can also take the bike on board when you tire of cycling or when the terrain is too rough. When your legs feel fit enough, you can get off the train and resume cycling.

The Swiss Tourist Board offers special bicycle tours, which include maps showing suggested routes, hostels along the way, drop-off

points, etc. They call it the Rail-Bicycle Service, and the location of these points are marked with a red-and-white placard at information offices in main train stations. Although the stations usually have more than 100 well-equipped three-gear cycles in stock, you should reserve one about two days in advance. You can rent the bicycle for two hours, twenty-four hours, or for five days or more. The longer you rent it, the cheaper the cost per day. The one-day rate is 8 Swiss francs (about $4.24), and on long-term hires the rate is 6 Swiss francs per day.

Cyclists are common in Holland, and the country is ideal for bicycling because it is so flat. Even members of the royal family are cyclists. Major Dutch cities have bicycle lanes, so you won't have the harrowing traffic experiences you may encounter in some noncycling countries. The provincial tourist board in Oveerijssel (as in nearly all Dutch provinces) in eastern Holland organizes several unguided bicycle tours. They can be booked to include meals, a sturdy one-speed cycle, travel insurance, maps, and a written route description. Your luggage can also be transported by another means from place to place on these tours. Still, the limit to the luggage you take on your bike is a factor when considering bicycle travel. You can stow much of your gear if you plan to return to your point of departure. Specific addresses for bicycle rentals are given for Denmark, England, Ireland, and the Netherlands under the listings for each country.

## Buying A Bicycle in Europe

If you have your heart set on buying a bicycle in Europe, check out prices before you leave the United States. You may not actually save any money by buying abroad. An American dealer can usually quote you the European prices. If you buy a European model, you may not be able to buy parts for it readily once you return home. Ask for an American model, or stick to British ones, whose parts are interchangeable with American ones. And also consider the duty you will have to pay if your purchase exceeds $300.

One student spent many hours poring over consumer magazines to find just the right ten-speed bike. When he finally did buy it in Europe, at a good price, he was chagrined later to find his European Peugeot required tires he had to order from France. The tires were not available at many European Peugeot dealers in Germany. The result was he waited six weeks to change a tire!

## BEHIND THE WHEEL

You can rent a car in Europe from major rental agencies for about $115 per week with unlimited mileage, but you pay for the gasoline.

Gasoline costs about three times the Stateside price, or about $1.80 per gallon. For groups of three or four traveling together, car rental may be economical. It does offer the advantages of getting off into the countryside and exploring villages you might not have discovered in any other way. European driving is not to be attempted by the fainthearted and definitely not by inexperienced drivers. For one thing, there is no speed limit on German *Autobahns* (freeways), and German drivers are as a rule extremely aggressive. Cars roar up behind you at ninety miles an hour, flicking their lights off and on for you to pull over and let them by. The experience can be unraveling. The highways are in excellent condition, but dangerous and crowded.

While German *Autobahns* intimidate the tourist driver, city driving can be worse. Streets are narrow, full of bicycles, mopeds, moffas, trucks unloading, and cars that suddenly leap up onto the sidewalk to park.

Usually you need an International Driver's License, which can be obtained through AAA for $3 and your photograph, to drive abroad. Some countries, however, will accept your Stateside driver's license. You must be at least eighteen years old for some rentals, twenty-one for others.

## HITCHHIKING, THE CHEAPEST WAY

While often the slowest, hitchhiking is certainly the cheapest way to travel. Good friends from Ireland recommend hitching as the best and quite acceptable way to see the wild, untamed western shores, where trains and buses are either infrequent or nonexistent. Nonetheless, hitchhiking has some risk, no matter what country you visit. A single female may get a ride the fastest, but she also runs the most risk. We do not recommend hitchhiking for lone females *anywhere*. Two girls hitching together are safer, but the practice is still not recommended, especially in southern Europe. A boy and girl can hitch with some success and run less risk. Three people will have a hard time finding a ride together. When hitchhiking, travel as lightly as possible, and keep your gear in good order, not scattered along the roadside. Dress neatly, and make an easily visible sign showing your destination. If there's little long-distance traffic coming by, you may choose to forget the sign and take a shorter ride in the right direction. If you are too close to a town, consider accepting a ride to a nearby major highway, or take public transportation to a more convenient hitchhiking spot.

Find a place to stand where drivers can see you well in advance, so they can slow down and pull over safely to let you in. Put a fair distance between yourself and the next hitcher. At the entrances to superhighways and *Autobahns* you may find a large group of hitchhikers. Sometimes you can distinguish a queue, although some hitchhikers resent having to queue up for anything. They may push and shove, so you'll have to size up the situation and determine where the last hitcher to arrive should stand. Don't worry! You will find out soon enough if you've infringed on someone's territory.

## FERRY CROSSINGS

Your train pass may entitle you to a discount on certain ferry crossings, and ferries can be a boon in saving travel time. The maps on pages 67-68 show some major ferry crossings you may consider in planning your trip. Costs vary with the length of the journey. If you take a night ferry, you will, of course, economize on hotel fees. For high-season crossings, book in advance. Two students crossed from Rome via Civitavecchia to Sardinia and then returned to Italy the same way, at considerable time savings over retracing their train route up the boot of Italy.

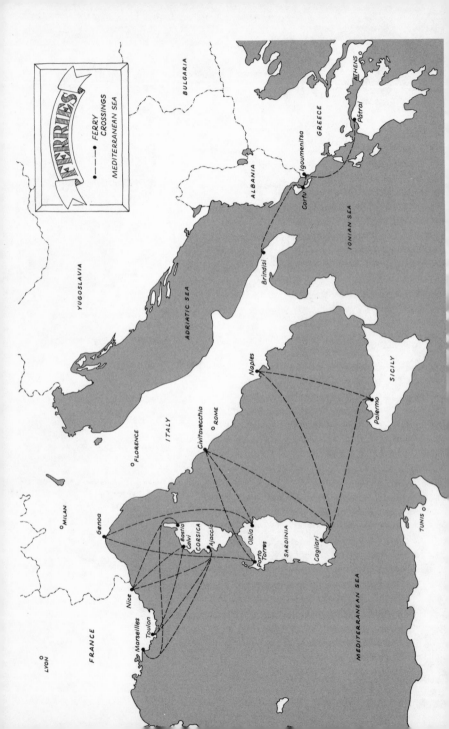

# 6 CHEAP PLACES TO STAY

European countries do an exceptionally fine job of catering to young travelers. All sorts of accommodations abound where you can stay cheaply. Most of them are designed with youth in mind, and they are lively places filled with other "birds of passage," travelers who hope to see more of the countryside than is possible on a train or plane.

## YOUTH HOSTELS

By far the most popular type of place to stay for the budget-minded are the several types of youth hostels, including those operated by the International Youth Hostel Federation (IYH). The IYH movement was originally called *Wandervögel,* which means "birds of passage" in German. The name Youth Hostelers is actually a misnomer, since membership in the organization is open to everyone regardless of age. Children under fourteen may use a hostel outside their own country if they are with an adult. Most associations do give priority to younger travelers and those over thirty may be excluded from making advance reservations.

In order to stay at a hostel, you need a hostel membership card, which is issued by the recognized youth-hostel organization in your own country. It costs $4.50 for students under eighteen, and you can apply for a card by writing to American Youth Hostels, Delaplane, Virginia 22025.

Of course, the basic appeal of hostels is their low price, their abundance (more than 4500 in fifty countries), and generally good locations. They cost anywhere from $1 to $3 a night for a clean, safe place to stay, including washing and toilet facilities. They are not hotels and do not have the same standards of comfort and service that hotels offer. While most travelers report good experiences staying in hostels, the quality does vary. Most are clean and well kept, but some are not. Some travelers report that in Greece and Italy hostels were not up to the expected standards. Each hostel is supervised by houseparents, or wardens. Most hostels prohibit drinking and smoking on the premises.

Some hostels have strict curfews, and you are usually not permitted to stay more than three consecutive nights at any one hostel, unless you are booked with a special ski party or other travel group. Hostels often close during the day, from about ten o'clock until three or four o'clock, so you may not be able to check in then.

Hostel guidebooks state that you should have a clean sheet with a pocket in which you insert the pillow. You buy them from youth-hostel national offices or at large hostels. The student travelers who did so much research for this book say that most hostels will accept a sleeping bag in place of the clean sheet. In some countries you are required to rent the sheet even if you have your own. In Italy the sheets are included in the price. None of our student travelers had previously purchased the special sheet and encountered no problems without one.

Here's what to expect in a hostel: Rooms are generally very clean, sometimes Spartan, and there are about four to ten beds in a room, with men and women separated by floors or even separate buildings. (Some dorms are as large as a gymnasium!) A common room is provided for rap sessions or music, games, etc., at night. Toilets, showers, and washbasins are provided, and you may find a place to hang out some laundry, although no actual washing machines or dryers are available. You will usually be able to buy a few items at a hostel, such as soap, Kleenex, aspirin, yogurt, cereal, milk, and snacks. Most hostels serve breakfast (for a modest fee), if only the continental one of hard rolls and hot beverages.

Many hostels have cooking facilities, complete with pots, pans, and utensils. You may cook breakfast or evening meals, and you are, of course, required to clean up after yourself. Refrigeration facilities are not available. We are told that you should bring matches for hostel cooking since gas-burning hot plates are sometimes provided. If cooking facilities are not available, you will be able to buy inexpensive meals that are staff prepared. Our student researchers say the hostels are uniformly the best place to find a good, cheap meal. They even found some great bargains in France.

In their location, hostels vary a lot. Many are well situated, on or near beaches and resort centers, in towns popular with tourists. Others are out of town and relatively difficult to get to, short of hitchhiking or walking for several hours. If you are carrying a backpack, you may opt for finding an inexpensive hotel in town rather than trekking ten miles on foot to the hostel. If you plan to travel in Europe for any length of time, buy a copy of the "International Youth Hostel Handbook for Europe and the Mediterranean," which costs about $1.25 at major hostels or at the AYH headquarters in Virginia. This book lists hostels by country, with a coded guide to exact location, facilities, number of beds, fees, average cost of meals, nearest train stop, and local transport. Write ahead for reservations if you have a fixed schedule at any point. You should have reservations in major cities during the peak season. Don't forget to use the correct international-airmail postage, and enclose two airmail international reply coupons for confirmation.

Aside from the low cost and wide availability of hostels, students say one of the best things about them is that they meet other kids there. "They are a great source of information. There's a sort of unity, like we're all out here together, on our own." They like the feeling of camaraderie, the sharing of information on where each has been and where he or she is going. So hostels do afford memorable times and foster communication among young people of many countries. An occasional hostel has a disco, Ping-Pong, and laundry facilities, such as the one in Luxembourg City. In general, young travelers find that staff at hostels are cooperative and willing to offer help or advice within the framework of the hostel regulations.

You may not leave your bags at a hostel for the day if you are not staying there at night. A safe place is provided for check-in of valuables—camera, moneybelt, etc. The staff cannot be responsible for your belongings, so do not leave them scattered throughout the hostel. They may be gone when you return for them. Laundry left hanging in a washroom might also disappear. Students advise that if you keep your gear assembled around your assigned bed, no one will be likely to bother it.

### Student Hostels and Private Hostels

These lodgings are similar to youth hostels, except that they are often located at colleges and may be open only during summer when classes are not in session. You do not need a membership card, and the overnight levies are modest, from $1 to $6, although sometimes more than youth hostels. You'll find other young people to talk to and perhaps even a kitchen or cafeteria. Privately owned hostels (often state-subsidized) also have low-cost accommodations for young travelers.

### CAMPING

You can expect a wide variation in campsites, from lovely, peaceful spots along a scenic river to places that look like a traffic jam of vacationers. Camping out frees you from the need to make room reservations in advance and from the austerity that often accompanies cheap hotels. You would, however, have to carry a small tent and a sleeping bag, and you should buy a copy of "Europe Camping and Caravaning Guide," published by Europa Publishers in Clay Center, Kansas. Tourist centers at border crossings and at train stations also offer advice on the nearest campsite and how to reach it. A campsite will offer a grassy spot to pitch a tent, showers, toilets, laundry facilities, a small store to buy provisions, and perhaps a place to get together with other campers in the evening. Several students stayed almost exclusively at campsites last summer on a tour through southern Europe. This mode of travel worked out very well for their needs, in spite of one lightweight sleeping bag, which was easy to carry, but too light for a cool night, even on Spanish beaches. Campgrounds in Europe are marked with a pictograph, a large *C* encircling a tent or a square with a tent on a black or blue background. Expect to pay from 50¢ to $1.50 a night for a tent site.

## PENSIONS AND GUESTHOUSES

Other cheap places to stay in Europe include pensions and guesthouses, hundreds of which dot the landscape and line the streets of resort towns and small villages. Pensions and guesthouses may have a few rooms, or they may have twenty or more. Many Europeans and seasoned American travelers stay only at pensions because they are cheap, relatively easy to find, and the owners are usually friendly and helpful. They can tell you the interesting, out-of-the-way places to see in their hamlet or city, how to get the most out of a ski pass, and where not to buy things.

A pension costs more than a hostel but less than a hotel. Pensions in Germany, Switzerland, and Austria have the well-deserved reputation of being immaculately clean and usually offer an enormous down quilt, with breakfast included. Prices vary, but range from about $6 a night in a ski town in February to about $16 in higher-priced cities, such as Vienna. Frequently in Europe these rooms have no private bath or toilet, although each floor has several baths you may use. You are sometimes charged more to use the bath facilities, perhaps fifty cents, and you may have to ask the owner for a key. Breakfast is included, but may be only *Brötchen*, jam and butter, and coffee or chocolate. Sometimes breakfast includes cheese, cold meats, and a boiled egg.

*Gasthaus* and *Zimmer Frei* are common terms you will see used all over German-speaking Europe to indicate rooms for rent. A *Gasthaus* resembles a local tavern, with rooms upstairs, and may be located in the center of town. *Zimmer Frei* is a German phrase meaning "rooms free (vacant)," and the sign with these words hangs out on the gaily painted balcony of many Alpine homes where the owners rent out a few rooms. You will also find these signs on roads leading into the town itself.

## BED-AND-BREAKFAST ACCOMMODATIONS

In the British Isles and Ireland, Bed and Breakfast, or B and B, is the equivalent to the *Zimmer Frei* of Germany, Austria, Switzerland, etc. B and B's are so abundant that many a veteran traveler would not hesitate to set out on a tour of Britain, Scotland, or Ireland without a single reservation, even in high season. Typically, they cost about £ 3.50 a night, including a full Irish or English breakfast of eggs, bacon and sausage, toast, tea, and sometimes juice. Even if the English sausage sometimes has the texture of ground sawdust, the breakfast is hearty enough to get you through nearly to dinner.

Never feel reluctant to ask to see the room first before deciding to take it. And if you're low on funds don't hesitate to say, "Do you have anything cheaper?" You may be offered the very same room for less.

The symbol △H△ on the maps in this book indicates accommodations suitable for youth.

# 7 FOCUS ON AUSTRIA

Population: 7,507,000          Language: German
Capital: Vienna                Currency: schilling (AS)

## THE LAND AND THE PEOPLE

Austria is a baroque land that sings in every sense, alive to the
sounds of music everywhere, with glittering music halls and
incredibly beautiful mountains and pastoral villages. Austrian cities
have concert halls where audiences dress with the elegance of another
era, where girls in beautiful, long, rustling taffeta dirndls, men in
velvet-trimmed suits, and Old World manners are commonplace.
When you enter a shop or a café, you will be welcomed by *Grüss
Gott!* (Greetings!), and you should return some kind of general
greeting. When you leave, say good-bye, or *auf Wiedersehen,* as they
will say to you. Generally Austrians are a dignified people, reserved,
yet cordial and helpful.

Traveling in Austria is not cheap, but the Austrian Government
makes an effort to help visitors stretch their budgets.

This is a land for people who enjoy the outdoors—about 70 percent

of Austria is mountainous. Come to Austria for skiing from November through May, then for hiking in the summer. Alpine huts—more than 600 of them—exist to service hikers along the mountain trails. You can hike with a group or go on your own, although you should be experienced in Alpine hiking first. Proper clothing and well-broken-in hiking boots are a must. Maps and advice can be obtained in hiking areas and villages.

Several places you can write to for more information on mountaineering are: Young Austria Touring, Alpenstrasse 102, Salzburg, Austria; Österreichischer Alpenverein, Wilhelm Greilstrasse 15, A-6020 Innsbruck, Austria; Deutscher Alpenverein, Praterinsel 5, Munich 22, Germany.

## TRANSPORTATION

Austrian trains go through most all the scenic areas, particularly the ski resorts. Such routes include Vienna to Basel, through Salzburg, Tyrol, and Vorarlberg. Their trains are in excellent condition—fast and on time.

City transportation is also very good, and tickets can be bought in vending machines. You usually punch your own ticket when you enter a tram or bus. Taxis are expensive.

## FOOD

Austrian food tends to be very hearty, and large portions are the norm. Breakfast is light, *Brötchen* (rolls) and a beverage. The main meal *(Mittagessen)* is served at noon, and a lighter meal in the evening *(Abendessen),* although in restaurants you can usually order a large meal in the evening as well.

Specialties include *Leberknödl Suppe,* a meat broth with liver dumplings; *Gulasch,* a hot, thick soup with meat chunks; Wiener schnitzel, large slabs of pan-fried, breaded veal cutlet; schnitzel, tender veal of any kind; *Schwein,* pan-fried pork cutlet; *Rehrücken,* beautifully prepared venison usually served with a berry sauce, such as cranberry. Definitely try *Tafelspitz,* which is boiled beef with chive-sauce potatoes. Noodles and dumplings are a national institution, as are the famous Viennese apple strudel and various tortes, particularly Sacher torte, coarse-crumbed, chocolate cake glazed with apricot and glossy, black chocolate. And there is the inevitable *Schlagsahne*—whipped cream—heaped over sinfully rich pastries.

The basket of *Brötchen* placed on your table at restaurants is there to tempt you. For each roll you eat you will be charged; breads are not routinely served as part of the meal price.

Tip (15 percent) and the tax are included in the prices shown on the menu. You may leave an additional small tip *(Trinkgeld)* if you wish, although local people seldom do.

## SHOP HOURS

Usual hours are 8 AM to 6 PM, Monday through Friday, with lunch closing from 12:30 PM to 2 PM, give or take a half hour either way. Saturday hours are 8 AM to 12 noon.

## SHOPPING

In Austria you will find an enchanting selection of dirndl dresses, all with a matching apron, from everyday cotton styles to rustling taffetas for formal wear. They will look even better when you get them home. *Lederhosen* are found all over Austria, as well as woolen sweaters with Bavarian-style trim. Capes and coats made of loden, a heavy cloth that's waterproof, are also good buys. Sporting goods, from skis and ski boots to hiking shoes, are sensibly priced, with special prices in summer. Give your sales receipt to the border guard to receive a 16 percent refund for purchases you take out of the country. Ask for the special receipt in the stores where you make your purchases. Petit-point handbags are a speciality of Austria, as are the fragrant spiceballs, bouquets made to hang in doorways and on walls. You can buy them in the marketplace, wrap them in tissue, and mail home for a sweet-smelling gift. They cost $5 to $10, depending on the size, and since they're so light the mailing costs are low. Check the **Salzburger Heimatwerk** on the Residenzplatz in Salzburg for handmade wares; the **Lanz** shops in Vienna and Salzburg for exquisite (but expensive) dirndls and other ladies wear; and **Leopold Kosch** in Vienna for ski wear.

## VIENNA

Vienna and the Blue Danube (Donau) seem almost synonymous, yet the famous river only touches the northern edge of the city. Vienna is a quiet, easygoing city, lightly moving in three-quarter time. Its parks and streets are full of strollers, for the Austrians, like the Germans, are enthusiastic walkers. Children in *Lederhosen,* short leather pants, and old pensioners, men and women, dressed in green loden coats, everyone is out walking.

**Important Addresses**

- **United States Embassy**, Boltzmanngasse 16, Tel. 346611
- **Police emergency**, Tel. 133
- **American Express**, Kärntnerstrasse, 21-23, Tel. 520544

- **Visitors Information Bureau,** at the Westbahnhof (west train station), open 6 AM to 11 PM; at Südbahnhof (south train station), 6 AM to 9:30 PM; also at Opernpassage, 9 AM to 7 PM.

_____**Where to Stay**

Vienna hotels are expensive, but there are many reasonably priced student facilities, and a good **Student Accommodations Service** at Fuhrichgasse 10, near the Opera House, Tel. 529247. Rates for these hotels run from about 80 to 90 AS ($4.80 to $5.40) per person per night.

In Austria, as well as in Germany and Switzerland, people who have rooms available may go to the train station and approach travelers. Rather than recommending specific names of such persons, the Austrian National Tourist Bureau states that travelers should know that this practice is common. But be sure to check out their offer with the tourist desk. You may be pleasantly surprised and encounter a gracious host. However, the tourist bureau cautions that many odd characters loaf around train stations. Any legitimate person offering a room would not object if you want to verify the arrangements with the tourist desk.

**Internationales Studentenhaus,** Seilerstätte 30, Tel. 528463. Some single rooms, doubles and triples mostly; free hot showers on each floor. Well located near city center. 110 AS including breakfast.

HOSTELS

**Pötzleinsdorf,** Geymüllergasse 1, Tel. 471312. About 45 AS per night with breakfast.

**Turmherberge Don Bosco,** Lechnerstrasse 12, Tel. 731494. Men only.

**Hostel Wien IX,** Pulverturmgasse 11, Tel. 340517. Women only.

**Hutteldorf Hostel,** Schlossberggasse 8, Tel. 821501. Take subway lines WD or GD to Hutteldorf. Open year round.

**Hostel Ruthensteiner,** Robert-Hamerling-Gasse 24, Tel. 834693. Near the Westbahnhof. Singles, doubles, and triples. Dorms as low as 52 AS. Singles 107 AS.

The hotel-finding services of the city are called the **Wiener Verkehrsverein,** with a main office at Schubert Ring 6, and a service called the **Zimmernachweis** is located at the airport and train stations. They can find a room for you in a specific price range. Renting out a few rooms in a private home is commonly done, and the _Zimmer Frei_ sign in front of a house means that a room is available for rent. Generally you will find these rooms to be immaculate, with hospitable people to serve you a continental breakfast. You may have to ask for a key to the shower or bath facility.

PENSIONS, HOTELS

**Hospiz Hotel,** Keyongasse 15, Tel. 931304. Nice management, we're told. About 140 AS for singles with breakfast.

**Pension Reimer,** Kirchengasse 18, Tel. 936162. Singles for 150 to 200 AS.

TOURIST-CLASS HOTELS

**Hotel Gloriette,** Linzer Strasse 105, Tel. 921146.

**Hotel Alsegg,** Bergsteiggasse 14, Tel. 488839.

**Hotel Kugel,** Siebensterngasse 43, Tel. 933355.

_____**Where to Eat**

**Wiener Rathauskeller,** Rathausplatz, in City Hall, has four different rooms, local-style cooking, schnitzel specialties, and a wide menu and price range.

**Student Mensa,** Fürichgasse 10, Monday through Friday, 9 AM to 7:30 PM, weekends 11:30 AM to 2 PM.

**Restaurant der Tabaks Pfeife,** Goldschmiedgasse 4. Hearty meals, popular with the local young crowd.

**Zum Laterndl,** Landesgerichtsstrasse 12. Recommended for students.

**Trzesniewski Buffet,** Dorotheergasse 1, near St. Stephen's, for lunch.

**Lehmann** and **Aïda Konditoreien** (confectionaries) offer pastries served _mit schlag_—topped with thick cream—at reasonable prices and good quality. These spots may be slightly below the famous top-quality establishments Sacher and Demel, but they are nonetheless quite good.

**Wienerwald,** a chain (nine restaurants in Vienna), specializing in roast chicken _(Backhendl)_; also features onion soup and goulash.

_____**What to See, What to Do**

At the Opera House, daily from 9 AM to 7 PM, there's a visitors' information booth, where you can get information on current attractions, concerts, cultural events, streetcar trams, and the metro.

**Opera House,** the center of town for most visitors, has musical performances except in July and August. In June there's a Vienna Festival; September has preseason concerts.

**Spanish Riding School** features the famous Lippizaner horses in Sunday-morning performances. Tickets are difficult to come by, but you can attend rehearsals from 10 AM to noon Tuesday through Friday, for 6 AS. Your best bet is to get tickets through a travel bureau in the city, where often a few tickets have been set aside.

**St. Stephen's Cathedral** holds free concerts on Wednesday at 7 PM and has an extensive collection of medieval sculpture.

**Freud's apartment,** Berggasse 19, for a peek at the famous psychiatrist's home.

**Schönbrunn Palace,** a summer castle where theatrical performances by the Vienna Kammeroper are presented in the **Schloss-theater** during July and August.

The Vienna Philharmonic and the Vienna Symphony present concerts in various halls such as **Musikverein,** located at Dumbastrasse 3, and **Konzerthaus,** at Lothringerstrasse 20. Each house has its own ticket office, and even if you are told the performance is sold out, be insistent and ask to queue up for standing-room tickets. Or say that you would like to buy any tickets that are unclaimed. Better yet, find an usher, and tell him you want a seat. He'll ask you to wait off to the side by the coatroom, and when a season-ticket holder doesn't show, he'll charge you $4 to $6 for their first-class seat. The usher pockets your money, but you're in for a fine concert at a bargain price.

**Grinzing** and the **Vienna Woods.** Grinzing is an appealing village where small *Weinstuben,* or wine cellars, hang a garland of green boughs and vine leaves over doorways to announce the new wine— and to welcome you. Sit at long tables with many others, indoors or on inviting patios, and order wine and cheese. You can also bring your own bread and cheese. To get to Grinzing, take trolley 38. To continue on to the Vienna Woods (Wienerwald), take bus 21 from Grinzing to Kahlenberg. You can walk back through Nussdorf, then catch a D tram back to city center.

## SALZBURG
_____ **Important Addresses**

- **United States Consulate,** Franz-Josef Kai 1, Tel. 43705.
- **American Express,** Mozartplatz 5, hours 9 AM to 5:30 PM Monday— Friday, 9 AM to noon Saturday.
- **Police emergency,** Tel. 133.
- **Visitors' Bureau,** Auerspergstrasse 7 and Mozartplatz 5, next to American Express.

Salzburg, the home of Mozart and his glorious music, is a baroque jewel in an exquisite mountain setting along the banks of the Salzach River. Various architecturally ambitious churchmen through the years set out to make Salzburg rival Rome. You can see buildings in Romanesque, Gothic, and baroque styles all in one moment if you

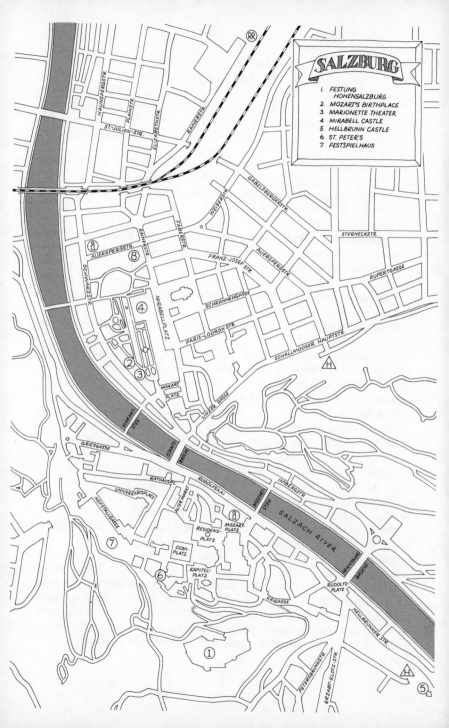

climb high above the city to the magnificent Festung Hohensalzburg, a twelfth-century fortress that once guarded the city.

## Where to Stay

There are several youth hostels, and the visitors' bureau has an excellent room-finding service for tourists. The information bureau at Mozartplatz 5 has a very capable youth-information center.

HOSTELS

**Jugendgasthaus,** Nonntal, Josef-Preis-Allee 18, Tel. 42670. Take bus 2 or 3 from central station; 42 AS including breakfast.

**Jugendherberge Glockengasse,** Glockengasse 8, Tel. 76241. Bus M or D. 40 AS including breakfast.

Three others not quite as central:

**Jugendherberge Walserfeld,** Salzburg-Walserfeld, Tel. 84553.

**Haus der Jugend,** Franz-Hinterholzer Kai 8, Alpenstrasse.

**Jugendherberge Salzburg,** Eduard-Heinrich Strasse, Tel. 46553.

## Where to Eat

**Student Mensa** of Salzburg University, Hellbrunner Strasse 30. Dinner about 30 AS, lunch 24 AS.

**Wolf-Dietrich Heim,** Wolf-Dietrich Strasse 16. Lunch only, in the University area.

**Stieglkeller,** Festungsgasse 10, home of the Stiegl Brewery, on the way up the hill toward Hohensalzburg. This *Hofbrauhaus* has open-air dining, as well as indoor. Popular with the student crowd; very reasonable, about 50 AS for a meal.

**Stiftskeller St. Peter,** in courtyard of St. Peter's Abbey, a traditional place to eat after concerts, less crowded before concerts. Austrian menu, also supper platters, cold cuts with cheese and salami.

**Glockenspiel Café,** on Mozartplatz by the Glockenspiel, is a very large outdoor coffeehouse, with superb pastries and coffee.

**Sternbräu,** Griesgasse 23, self-service garden and half-covered garden restaurant, for lunch, snacks, coffee, beer.

**Weinhaus Moser,** Wiener Philharmonic Strasse, near the Festspielhaus. Food okay, modest cost.

**Zur Bastey,** Kaigstrasse 7. Expensive, fine food.

## What to See, What to Do

**Residenzplatz,** located in the heart of the city, a lovely square with a forty-foot-high fountain and sidewalk cafés, only five minutes from the Old City. There are horse-drawn carriages and carillon concerts in the Glockenspiel tower. Located on the square is the **Residenz,** once the seventeenth-century palace of archbishops. Palace hours, 9 AM to 4 PM daily.

The **Cathedral,** at Domplatz, the first and one of the finest baroque buildings north of the Alps. Hours, 10 AM to 5 PM.

**Abbey Church of St. Peter,** begun in 847, cemetery, chapel, catacombs, early-Christian prayer cells. Hourly tours, 9 AM to 6 PM in summer.

**Festung Hohensalzburg,** which you can tour for a 10 AS student rate. Taking this thirty-minute guided tour is the only way you can get inside the walls of the fort. Armor and torture chambers are the highlights here, plus the view. You can reach the fort by funicular, which costs 14 AS, up and down, or you can save 6 AS by walking down. Hours, 9:30 AM to 5:30 PM in summer.

**Mirabell Castle,** near Congress House, a convention-meeting hall, has manicured flower gardens, pleasant walks, and benches for enjoying a picnic.

**Hellbrunn Castle** has trick fountains and a natural setting for an Alpine zoo, where animals live in what look like caves in the side of the mountain. Take bus H for this fifteen-minute trip out of the city. Hours, 9 AM to 4:30 PM.

**Festspielhaus,** a magnificent concert hall, which seats 2400 people, has the world's largest stage. The Vienna Opera performs here. The visitors' bureau can provide you with information on concerts. Hours, 11 AM to 3 PM, in summer, except during Summer Festival.

**Mozart's birthplace,** in the Old City, at Getreide Gasse 9, is a typical Old Austrian, middle-class house. It includes a small Mozart Museum. Hours, 9 AM to 6 PM. In summer, 8 AM to 8 PM.

**Marionette Theater,** Schwarzstrasse 24. From April through September you can see a unique marionette show set to Mozart's music; 90 AS with a student ID card. Daily performance at 8 PM. Closed Sunday.

As you walk the streets of Salzburg you will hear lovely sounds of musicians at practice, particularly near the University section and buildings near the Festspielhaus. Truly, the whole city seems to be set to music, from classical to jazz.

There are **concerts** literally everywhere, from Youth Concerts in Salzburg, seven in springtime (inquire at Danreitergasse 4, Tel. 22544), to free concerts in Mirabell Gardens every Wednesday, to Europe's largest, most important music festival, **The Salzburger Festival,** held each year from the last week of July to the end of August. Tickets for it are sold well in advance, and they are expensive, as are hotel accommodations at that time.

There is a superb **Youth Information Bureau** in Salzburg that can provide you with all sorts of information, including a special folder called "Salzburg for Youth." It gives reduced rates, lists of concerts especially for youth, places to stay, places to meet other young people, sporting events, and just about anything you can think of. You can pick up a brochure at the information bureau on Mozartplatz.

_____**Side Trips**

To visit the **salt mines** at Dürnberg, near Hallein, take a bus from city center eleven miles to Hallein. A cable car to the mines costs 360 AS, mine entry an additional 60 AS.

If you're interested in **hiking,** Untersberg, a cable railway, will take you up the mountain for 64 AS round trip. This area is a great spot for hiking. Trails are mapped and well marked.

The **Salzkammergut lake region** and the nearby **Berchtesgaden area** (across the German border), where Hitler lived in his famous Eagle's Nest retreat, are about fifteen miles from Salzburg by bus. You can explore these areas on foot once you get there. Many middle-aged Austrian and German hikers come here for a holiday, and they are the best-dressed hikers you may ever see.

## SALZBURG-ANIF

Salzburg-Anif, a personal favorite much preferred over downtown Salzburg, is only twelve minutes by bus from city center, yet light-years away in solitude. Caution: City buses are not cheap, 6 AS per ride (half price if you are under fifteen), so buy the ten-ticket booklet.

If you have an opportunity, try to get out into the countryside of Austria. Walk the village streets, and poke your head into a doorway. You might see an old man weaving beautiful wool gathered from the Alpine flocks. Down another street in another village, perhaps in Ehrmoos, Austria, you may find a woodcarver whose father and grandfather before him also learned to carve at Oberammergau. By the churchyard watch for a small deer munching dandelions in a small enclosure. There are local food stores, where you can buy yogurt and cheese for a picnic by the stream.

Let me tell you what I found away from the city noise. I walked one early morning toward what I thought to be the river. The road narrowed, then forked into two small ones. I took the less traveled, tree-shrouded one. Not 500 meters from the main road, a tiny castle appeared out of nowhere totally surrounded by water, complete with drawbridge and moat. A weeping willow in fresh spring green framed the picture. Two swans floated by. I stood there breathless, sure that it was all a dream.

I later learned that the castle belonged to the duke of Anif, who lives there now. I had stumbled down a private road totally invisible from the highway. But don't visit my castle. Have fun looking for your own. It won't be the same if you know where to look!

_____**Where to Stay**

These pensions are the typical whitewashed houses with wood shutters and balconies that seem to be the uniform style for Alpine villages. All rates include continental breakfast.

**Pension Alpenblick,** Fr. Wallner. Singles 100 AS, doubles, 160 AS. There are flowers everywhere and tiny tables on lawns and patio. Typically Austrian, very cozy with a wonderful view of surrounding mountains and meadows.

**Pension Wiesenberger,** 90 AS single.

**Pension Gallnhof,** newer, set in fields of dandelions and wild flowers.

**Haus Hammer,** 100 AS single.

**Pension Eibenhof,** Herbert von Karajan Strasse, near Hotel Friesacher, singles 110 AS, doubles 180 AS without private bath.

_____**Where to Eat**

In Anif the **Hotel Friesacher** has excellent food at modest prices, including venison with cranberries *(Preiselbeere)* and game specialties. Dinners run about $6. There is also a disco, the **Stadl,** in the rear of the hotel.

**Gasthof Zufaren,** special menus, 40 AS for soup, Wiener or *Schwein* schnitzel, potato, salad, and dessert. Or you can order soup, goulash, and salad for 25 AS.

## SKIING

Austria's Tyrol, one of the best skiing centers in the world, has more than 200 ski schools at major resorts and hundreds at lesser-known villages as well.

**St. Anton am Arlberg** is the famous resort in the western edge of the Tyrol, with St. Christoph, Lech, and Zürs, lesser known, adjacent. Same snow, same mountains, but not the same prices. In the stunning Alpine village of St. Anton, where over the Christmas holidays you will hear more American voices than European, expect top prices, long lift lines, and delays in getting a table for dinner—if you can find a restaurant not fully booked. Plan on spending about $12 per day for lift passes if you buy on a weekly basis, more for single days.

Move over the mountain a bit to Lech, and you will find cozy Alpine houses, small pensions at lower prices, and thinner crowds.

**Innsbruck,** site of the 1976 Winter Olympics, and its neighboring villages can easily accommodate thousands of skiers on more than a thousand miles of mountain slopes. Hotels are expensive, but Innsbruck has student centers and several hostels. Like nearly all Alpine ski areas, *Zimmer Frei* signs are posted on houses everywhere. You can find a room through the visitors' bureau by writing ahead or by taking your chances when you get there. Never, though, go over the Christmas or Easter holidays without a reservation. Nearly all pensions require you to stay a minimum of two weeks at these two high-season periods, and you usually must take your meals there.

**Kitzbühel,** Austria's oldest resort, is well developed and tame. Its four cable cars, eighteen chairlifts and thirty T bars will loft you to 2000 meters.

**Ehrwald,** at the foot of the Zugspitze (Germany's highest mountain), gets a super amount of snow until June. Beginners and intermediates will love it here.

Solden, Hochgurgl, and Obergurgl (the highest village in Austria), Stubai, and St. Johann are other ski areas less well known but with good runs, pleasant villages, and lower rates. Write to the visitors' bureau for a list of moderately priced lodgings within walking distance of a lift. Ask also for a map of lifts and runs.

# 8  FOCUS ON BELGIUM

Population: 10,000,000
Capital: Brussels

Language: French and Flemish
Currency: Belgian franc (fr.)

## THE LAND AND THE PEOPLE

*Quaint* and *lovely* are the words to describe Belgium. Take your time in this country. Some of Europe at its best is tightly packed in this second most densely populated European country. But Belgium is tenacious and sprightly, too, with a share of ethnic competition from its two "halves," the Flemish and the Walloons. Each speaks a different language, and in some schools children must learn both. Suspicion and rivalry are common between the two peoples.

The Belgian people are industrious, as befits a country that has recovered from two military occupations in thirty years. In just a few years after World War II this postage-stamp-size country brought its exports to a level exceeding imports, while larger neighboring countries looked on in wonder.

SHAPE and NATO are headquartered in Brussels, the capital, a cosmopolitan and expensive city. Brussels is also the base of the EEC, European Economic Community.

In Belgium's past lies much of its beauty, and its art heritage is something to behold. The Flemish School of painting is the special art form of Belgium, dating back to the early fifteenth century. From peasant portraits by Pieter Brueghel to the great canvases of Peter Paul Rubens, Belgium can justifiably be proud of its artists. There are also lush, green forests and mist-shrouded castles in Ardennes, as well as forty miles of splendid golden beaches. Although not as well known as others in Europe, Belgium's beaches offer good summer camping and low-cost accommodations.

## FOOD

Though not as famous for their cuisine as the French, Belgians cherish their cooking and rightly so. They are even more lavish with butter and cream than the French. Pastries are inviting, but *moules* (mussels) are the real specialty of Belgium. They are served in over thirty-five different ways and always in ample quantity.

Most restaurant prices include a 15 percent service charge. This charge is always stated on the menu, so check to be sure.

Breakfast usually consists of hard rolls or French bread and a hot beverage. The main meal may be served at noon.

## SHOP HOURS

Usual hours are 9 AM to 6 PM or 6:30 PM, although supermarkets may remain open until 7 PM. Shops must close for twenty-four consecutive hours once a week, and they post a notice announcing which day this closing will be. Banks are usually open from 9 AM to 3:30 PM, a few until 4:30 PM.

## BRUSSELS
#### Important Addresses

- **United States Embassy,** boulevard du Régent 27, Tel. 5133830
- **American Express,** 24 place Rogier, Tel. 2190190, hours 9 AM to 5:30 PM, Saturday 9 AM to noon.
- **Police emergency,** Tel. 906.
- **Belgian Tourist Information,** rue Marché aux Herbes (Grasmarkt) 61, Tel. 5138940, open daily from 9 AM to 9 PM. Information and money-changing service.

#### Where to Stay

**International Youth Hostel,** 1030 Brussels, Postraat (or rue de la Poste) 911, Tel. 2178655. Get off at Gare du Nord; the hostel is five minutes from the station. 240 beds.

**Centre International des Étudiants,** 26 rue de Parme, Tel. 5378961. Considered a bargain for students, a bed here costs about $5 including two meals. Pleasant staff, clean rooms, lounge, TV, and a pretty garden, too.

**Hôtel International des Jeunes,** 21 rue du Congrès, Tel. 3184853. Fees run approximately $3 for a one-night stay, including breakfast. The hotel is about a ten-minute walk from central station. Not large, open only from March to November.

**Albergo,** 58 avenue de la Toison d'Or, Tel. 5382960. Large rooms but some beds sagged. Four people may be able to squeeze into a double room for about $25. Good location, super Italian restaurant.

#### Where to Eat

Brussels dining is expensive, so buy some of your food in grocery stores. Many small cafés, upstairs-type restaurants where lively people gather, are clustered along rue des Chapeliers, off Grand' Place.

**Trattoria,** located in the Albergo (see above). Good Italian cooking, moderate cost.

BRUSSELS

1. MANNEKEN-PIS
2. GRAND PLACE
3. MUSÉE DE L'ART ANCIEN

**Chez Georges,** 24 rue des Chapeliers, features mussels and other specialties. Specials of the day cost about $3.

**Le Breton,** rue des Drapiers 59. Young, lively crowd. Modest food in modest setting, about $4 for dinner.

## What to See, What to Do

**The Grand' Place,** an enormous square, is enchanting, reminiscent of another era. Seventeenth-century guild houses, a magnificent town hall with a 320-foot belfry—one of Europe's most celebrated Gothic structures—wide expanses of cobblestones intricately placed, and sidewalk cafés beckon you to linger awhile. But the rest of this brightly booming city, with its three full diplomatic corps, is bursting at the seams.

Just off the Grand' Place and on many of the small side streets, you will find shops selling handmade lace, a Belgian specialty. From tablecloths to mantillas and wedding veils, shops are filled with lace. Some lace is machine made, so be wary if you intend to buy. Belgians are proud of this age-old industry. We shopped at a place recommended by Temple Fielding—**Maria Loix,** rue d'Arenberg 52-54. The sales people were helpful, even though we bought modestly.

If you've never been to a European **flea market,** Brussels has one of the best, or so our flea-market specialists tell us. Many Americans who live in Europe make special monthly trips to Brussels to poke around. You will find old books, antique dolls, swords (probably not antiques no matter what the seller tells you), and some interesting wares. Incongruous as it may seem, in the midst of all the junk, classical music is piped rather loudly throughout the flea market. The market is held daily, every morning, but the best time to go is on Saturday and Sunday, in the Place du Jeu de Balle, not far from the Grand' Place. Antique and book sales are a specialty in the place du Sablon.

A well-known citizen of Brussels is the **Manneken-Pis,** a statue of a nude small boy urinating. Located at the corner of rue de Chene and rue de l'Etuve, the statue has been stolen many times. A new bronze was created from the original mold after the latest theft. He has also been sent many sets of clothing from people all over the world.

The **Musée de l'Art Ancien,** rue de la Régence 3, a principal museum of Brussels, displays Flemish art, particularly works by Brueghel, Van Dyck, and Rubens. Hours, 10 AM to 5 PM daily, closed Mondays. Free on Wednesday and Sunday, 5 fr. other days.

**Musée d'Art Moderne,** rue de la Régence 3, a small, modern-art exhibit. Free entry.

**Musée de Cinéma,** 9 rue Baron Horta, in Palais des Beaux Arts, a cinema museum, where classic movies play in their original language. If you're a flick fan, check here for a favorite oldie. Admission about seventy cents.

**Pol's Jazz Club,** 9 rue Marché au Charbon. Live jazz, silent movies. Entry fifty cents.

# ANTWERP

#### Where to Stay

As in Brussels, you won't find an abundance of low-cost hotels or rooms in private homes. But since Antwerp is not as big a tourist attraction, you probably won't have any trouble finding a place in a hostel.

HOSTELS

**Youth Hostel Opsinjoorke,** Eric Sasselaanstraat, Tel. 380273. Hostel is one hour from central station. Connect to bus 27. 100 fr. per night including breakfast.

**International Youth and Student Home,** Volkstraat 58, Tel. 384782. Take bus 23 from the central station. 120 fr. per night with breakfast.

#### What to See, What to Do

Most visitors come to Antwerp to see the magnificent paintings of Peter Paul Rubens that are displayed here. Museums are free; galleries charge small fees.

**Rubens House,** 9 Rubensstraat. Rubens' opulent dwelling, where he lived and worked for thirty years, now houses his personal effects and many paintings. Open daily from 10 AM to 5 PM.

**Royal Gallery of Fine Arts,** at Leopold de Waelplaats. Large well-hung collection of Flemish masters. Also has a modern-art collection. Open daily from 10 AM to 5 PM, closed Monday.

**Open Air Museum of Sculpture,** at Middelheim Park. Take bus 17, 26, or 27. Vast expanse of an estate with works by major sculptors, including Rodin and Henry Moore. Open from 10 AM to dusk.

**Centre Mondiale au Diamont,** Jezusstraat 28-30. Visit the center for an interesting diamond cutting and mining show. Open daily from 10 AM to 4 PM, Saturday and Sunday 10 AM to 6 PM. Free admission. Antwerp is the world's biggest diamond market and cutting center, and many large firms arrange group visits. Ask at the **Antwerp Tourist Office,** Suikerrui 19, or the information office in front of the train station for details.

# BRUGES

Bruges has been called Europe's purest medieval town. All of the city clusters together around the market, the town hall, and the canals. You can walk everywhere, from museums and cathedrals to castles and beneath bridges, and easily make believe you are passing through another time.

**Where to Stay**

The tourist office, not far from the main train station, in the heart of old Bruges, can locate a room for you. Or you might try one of these student places:

**Europa Jeugdherberg,** Baron Ruzettelaan 143, Assebroek, Tel. 336299. A youth hostel reached by taking bus 2 or 4 from central station to Steenbrugge; 100 fr. per night, including breakfast.

**Studentencentrum,** Hauwerstraat 27, Tel. 336226. Open in summer only; 155 fr. per night, including breakfast.

**What to See, What to do**

**Groeninge Museum** and the **Gruuthuse Museum,** next door to each other on Dyver, two excellent museums that should be on your itinerary. Both open daily from 9:30 AM to noon and from 2 PM to 6 PM. There is also a *son et lumière* (sound-and-light) pageant in the courtyard of the Gruuthuse in the summertime. Masterpieces by Van Eyck and Memling are found at the Groeninge.

**Basilica of the Holy Blood,** a stunningly beautiful chapel where one of Christianity's most famous relics is venerated.

**Town Hall,** built in 1376, is a Gothic site many shutterbugs seek out. You may have seen its facade and carved roof pictured on a calendar or post card.

**Centre de la Dentelle,** on Balstraat, is a workshop where young women learn the ancient art of lace making.

There are other museums and several other churches, St. Savior's Cathedral, St. John's, and the Church of Our Lady, in a town that casts a spell over visitors. Medieval turrets, stained-glass windows, clock towers, and shimmering canals that reflect the colorful flower markets are all part of beautifully preserved Bruges. Even the Holiday Inn blends into the medieval style.

# 9 FOCUS ON DENMARK

Population: 5,000,000          Language: Danish
Capital: Copenhagen          Currency: krone (kr.)

## THE LAND AND THE PEOPLE

Denmark has a special flair that many sea-dominated countries possess—an air of peaceful simplicity in spite of industry, yet surprising sophistication among its inhabitants.

Modern, wealthy, and highly taxed, the Danes are an innovative people. They are proud of their openness to new ideas concerning education and the environment. Most Danes speak a second language, often English, and they are well educated. A policeman is required to speak a second language fluently.

Denmark is totally Scandinavian, from its foods and cultural heritage to its social welfare system. Its countryside is pretty and pastoral, making it ideal for bicycle touring. The land is low and flat with the average elevation only ninety-eight feet above sea level. Denmark is also uncrowded, with cities clustered mostly along shorelines. Inland one can discover small villages and quiet, tree-lined roads.

## FOOD

Danish food is a good reason in itself for coming here. Pastries are abundant and not prohibitively expensive, although traveling in Denmark is costly. Smørrebrød, attractive open-faced sandwiches, dominate Danish lunches and snacks. With much eye appeal, cafeterias and restaurants display trays of these appetizing morsels to tempt you. They consist of small pieces of chicken, fish, ham, roast beef, egg, cheeses, and vegetables, or whatever the "smørrebrød maidens" choose. Danish beer is also popular, especially Tuborg and Carlsberg.

Fish dominates many menus, with plaice (type of flounder) common and fairly cheap. Herring in all shapes, from pickled to smoked, and *pølse,* a Danish-style sausage sold in street stands, are popular. If you try the *pølse,* also ask for bread, or you will get a hot dog only. *Hakkebøf* means hacked beef, or hamburger. *Biksemad* is chopped meat, potatoes, and onion—more or less like hash—fried with onion and topped with a fried egg.

## COPENHAGEN

Important Addresses

- **United States Embassy,** 24 Dag Hammerskjölds Allé., Tel. 123144.
- **American Express,** 12 Hans Christian Andersens Boulevard, Tel. 122301.
- **Police and other emergencies,** Tel. 000.
- **Tourist information,** Banegårdspladsen 2, in front of main station, Tel. 111415, open weekdays, 9 AM to 6 PM, closed Sunday.

An especially good city for walking, Copenhagen takes you back in time with centuries-old buildings, tiled roofs, quaint towers, and cobbled streets set alongside sparkling waterways. Yet it is an energetic city, which offers freewheeling night life and Tivoli Gardens, a delightful Old World amusement park fit for a fairy tale.

Stunning modernly designed shops and five pedestrian streets, along with an abundance of sunny days and smiling people, enhance the attractions of this capital city. If you come to Copenhagen by train, you will arrive at central station. **Kiosk P**, a helpful room-finding service for new arrivals, is located here. You cannot write ahead for a reservation, but they guarantee clean, comfortable lodgings at a fair price.

**Use It,** Copenhagen's youth-information center and traveler-welcoming service, will also find you a bed in a dorm or hostel and will provide you with maps, information on jazz clubs, places to eat, a weekly newspaper listing events, and any activities. Contact Use It at Magstraede 14, Tel. 156518. Open daily from 10 AM to 8 PM, it's only a fifteen-minute walk from central station.

Copenhagen's transportation system is excellent, with bus service covering a wide network. Tickets cost 2 kr.; books of tickets known as *pøletters* cost 12 kr. for eight tickets. Interrail passes and Eurailpass are valid on electric S trains, which make suburban runs, and you can easily head out into the countryside or beaches since they run every twenty minutes and continue until 2:30 AM, midnight on Sunday. Bicycling is fun here since drivers are used to cyclists. Rentals cost 15 kr. for a weekend, 7 kr. for one day, at **Københavns Cykelbørs,** 157 Gothersgade, Tel. 140717.

Where to Stay

Unless you have a hostel reservation, you should not arrive after midnight. Kiosk P is open between 9 AM and midnight and can help you locate a room, perhaps in a private home. Charge for this service is 7 kr. for a single room or dormitory. They will ask you to fill out a form stating your price range and preferences, from with or without

bath to type of accommodation. There's also a large electric board above the main window at Kiosk P that shows which hotels have vacancies, but they are the more expensive ones.

HOSTELS AND DORMITORIES

If you want to stay in a hostel but don't have an IYH membership card, you can buy a guest card at large youth hostels or at **Herbergs-Ringen,** Vesterbrogade 35 (Tel. 313612). They also have a list of hostels.

**Bellahøj Youth Hostel,** Herbergvejen 8, Tel. 289715, five kilometers from the city, international hostel membership required, 324 beds, 15 kr. per night, breakfast 10 kr. Check in before 10 AM or after 3 PM. Take bus 2 from Raadhuspladsen toward Bronshøj, and get off at Fuglsangs Allé.

**Vesterbro Ungdomsgaard,** Absolonsgade 8, Tel. 312070, open 5 May to 31 August, 160 beds, 34 kr. with breakfast, cafeteria. Take bus 6, 28, or 41 from Vesterbrogade, near central station, to Aalholm Plads and Rødovre.

**Copenhagen Hostel,** Avedøre Holme 33, Hvidovre, Tel. 491698, nine kilometers from the city, 500 beds, hostel membership card required, 15 kr. per night, reception open twenty-four hours. Take bus 10 from central station to Toftegards Plads, change to bus 132, and get off at Avedøre Holme. Or take the S train, direction Hundige to Frie.

**Thomas P. Hejle's Ungdomshus,** Nørre Voldgade 23, Tel. 156930, open 1 May to 1 September, no membership card required, 205 beds, 30 kr. per night with breakfast; good location, lockers, cafeteria. Dorms closed between 10 AM and 2 PM. Take the S train or bus 16 to Nørreport Station.

## Where to Eat

**Ristorante Italiano,** at Fiolstraede 2, in the center of the Latin Quarter near the university district. Good food for about 15 kr.

**Vista,** a self-service restaurant, at Vesterbrogade 40, where you can eat well for 15 kr., à la carte menu, open from 9 AM to 8 PM daily.

**Burger King,** Vesterbrogade, across from the main entrance of Tivoli Gardens, features the best buy in town, a Whopper for 10 kr., milkshakes, ham barbecue, French fries.

**Tivoli Gardens** has many restaurants. None of them are cheap but you can get open sandwiches for 10 kr. and strawberry crepes for 5.50 kr. Some garden restaurants serve roast beef shaved thin and piled on hard rolls.

## What to See, What to Do

**Tivoli Gardens,** open from May to mid-September, is in the center of town and has lots of action, music, concerts, toy-soldier marching bands, fireworks, illumination, fountains, gardens, and a small lake. Plus there are all the usual amusement-park features of roller coasters, fun houses, a tavern for dancing, and plenty of gambling games, in which your money can disappear quickly. Weekend entry is 5 kr., 4 kr. during the week. Check the concert schedule at Kiosk P, as many outstanding popular and symphonic concerts are held at Tivoli. Most are free; others are modest in price.

**Ny Carlsberg Glyptothek,** Copenhagen's beautiful gallery endowed by the Carlsberg family, is behind Tivoli Gardens. It houses fine Impressionist paintings as well as works by Gauguin and a sculpture display. For a break, relax by the fountain in the courtyard or stop by the snack bar, where you can get a bargain lunch.

**Louis Tussaud's Wax Museum,** on Hans Christian Andersens Boulevard, is overpriced, and some of the wax figures are not recognizable without their name plates. You will have trouble even making out those of John F.Kennedy and family. A good place to avoid, in our opinion.

**The Little Mermaid,** at Langelinie, is a target for most visitors to Copenhagen. You can see this graceful sculpture perched on a rock overlooking the harbor by taking the "mermaid bus" from Hans Christian Andersens Boulevard near the American Express, 2 kr. round trip. The sculpture was given to the city in 1913 and has been stolen several times, yet the mermaid has been recast from the original mold. There she sits and watches for her prince of the Andersen fairy tale.

**Canal and harbor tours** will also take you out to the Langelinie, Little Mermaid harbor. Here you get another view of the city and good vantage points for taking photos of old buildings, including the world's oldest stock exchange, castles, and towers and bridges. Trips leave every thirty minutes from the corner of Nybrogade and Raadhusstraede.

The **Carlsberg Brewery,** at Ny Carlsberg Vej 140, welcomes visitors and gives a fine tour, which begins with the entry through its unusual Elephant Gate. Tours start at 9 AM, 11 AM and 2:30 PM, with free brew at the end.

**Rådhuspladsen,** or Town Hall Square. The huge red-brick hall has a 350-foot tower, where you can look out over Copenhagen.

**Rosenborg Palace,** Gothersgade, with displays of the dazzling crown jewels, furniture, and other personal effects of Danish royalty, is near the heart of the city. Across from this museum are twenty-five acres of botanical gardens, and the **State Museum of Art,** with its first-rate collections of Matisse, Rembrandt, Rubens, the French Impressionists, and others.

**Thorvaldsen's Museum,** near Rådhuspladsen, and **Christiansborg Palace** both have sculpture exhibits.

One of the most interesting city tours we've ever seen offered is **Social Tour,** a three-hour daily tour from Raadhuspladsen departing at 9 AM (except Saturday and Sunday). You visit a day-care center, a nursing home for senior citizens, and a school, where you learn that social services and education in Denmark account for 55 percent of public expenditures and are financed by a high tax rate. You'll also get to see some of Copenhagen's beautiful gardens. Inquire at the tourist board or at the American Express for details. The tour costs 42 kr.

Also of note is the **Meet the Danes Program,** which allows you to spend an evening with a Danish family, free of charge. Contact the tourist board at least forty-eight hours in advance.

## Shopping

**The Walking Streets,** or pedestrian malls, are sometimes collectively called Strøget. Strøget, which is also the name of the main shopping street, has interesting shops, where you can buy some bargain-priced handmade and machine-woven Nordic sweaters, well-styled leathers, and other typically Danish-designed items.

**Den Permanente,** at Vesterport on Vesterbrogade, houses a permanent exhibition of handsome arts and crafts, unusual clothing, fabrics, weavings, furniture, housewares, and porcelains—designs of the finest quality with prices to match. Everything is handsomely displayed for browsing.

**Illums Bolighus,** at Amagertorv, on the Strøget pedestrian mall, also has outstanding Danish design ware. It is similar to what Den Permanente offers, but the prices are not as high.

**Royal Copenhagen,** and **Bing & Grondahl,** also found on Amagertorv, are renowned for lovely dinnerware, porcelain figures, vases, and bowls at prices considerably less than they are sold at in the States. Also upstairs and in the rear is a seconds, or irregulars, department, where you can find some treasures for a fraction of the cost of first-run pieces, especially if your taste runs to blue colors. Small mocha cups cost about $4, vases and bowls $4 to $10, depending on the size.

## Side Trips

Short trips outside Copenhagen include the one-hour train trip to **Elsinore** (Helsingör in Danish). There you can visit **Kronborg Castle,** where Prince Hamlet once lived. It's twenty-eight miles north of the capital. There's also a fine sandy beach close by, Julebaek, near the Kronborg, with icy waters but good people watching.

You can also take the hydrofoil and be in **Malmö, Sweden,** in about thirty-five minutes, time enough for lunch and shopping. There are numerous daily departures from Havnegade, near the Royal Theater, or phone 128088 for information reservations. Costs about $15 round trip, or 110 kr.

Another worthwhile trip is to the **Louisiana Museum,** where Danish modern art is on display in an unusual building, perched on a cliff overlooking the sea. There's a good restaurant here and also chamber-music concerts in summer. The entry charge is 4 kr. for students, open from 10 AM to 5 PM daily. The museum is located forty-five minutes by train toward Elsinore. Get off at Humlebaek, and walk ten minutes.

# 10 FOCUS ON ENGLAND

Population: 47,000,000
Capital: London

Language: English
Currency: pound sterling (£)

## THE LAND AND THE PEOPLE

There are two significant things to be said about England and the English. First, there's something charming about a people who attach magical qualities to a pot of tea! "Come now, luv, let's go and have a pot of tea," is the universal remedy for everything, one learns after two years of listening to the BBC. Second, you don't need unlimited funds to enjoy England.

In addition, the British are reserved and polite, yet they love to laugh at themselves, with their special dry sense of humor. Though a little run-down at the heels in the wake of their economic problems, the English remain in remarkably good cheer. Nevertheless, some group in London is always on strike, usually the transport workers. But Britain survives—and graciously. British theater and love for the queen is unchanged. British loyalty to their favorites, sporting or public, is legendary.

And perhaps one of the nicest things about traveling in England is that the language is the same, more or less. Talking with people and getting around is easier than it is in most of continental Europe. Schedules and newspapers, theater and commodities are all in your own language. This alone makes England a popular tourist country for Americans. Now, with Freddie Laker's trailblazing, low airfares from New York to London, England is even more of a bargain. The pound has hovered near a ten-year low for a long while, and the favorable rate of exchange makes shopping in Britain a pleasure.

If your family had its roots in the British Isles or Ireland, and you are interested in tracing your family history, write to:

British Tourist Authority
64 St. James Street
London SW 1 England

They will provide information on how and where to begin. This project can add another dimension to your travels here.

## TRANSPORTATION

Getting to the British Isles is not a problem. There are many daily direct flights from the United States as well as from the European continent. Student flights from Paris cost about $25. There's bus service from Heathrow Airport, which is considerably cheaper than a taxi. Buses queue up outside the terminal and cost £1 from Heathrow to Victoria Station. From Gatwick Airport you can also take the train to Victoria Station, for 95p, which runs every half hour.

There are numerous ferries linking the continent to Britain. BritRail and InterRail Passes are valid, or give you a discount, on some of them. See the map on page 67 for possible routes. They range widely in cost, as well as the length of time they take. Some ferries are overnighters. The Channel can be rough in winter, so consider the weather when you plan a crossing. There is adequate train service into London from ferry-arrival points.

You can also take a hovercraft across the Channel between Calais and Dover and Boulogne and Dover, or from Calais to Ramsgate, for about $7 student rate with your Student Railpass card. The trip takes forty minutes and can be bumpy depending on the weather. The hovercrafts hold 250 people and 30 cars.

An extensive network of diesel and electric trains operate throughout the country, and they are efficient, on time, and convenient. Bus service is also good. If you are going to travel in Europe as well, your best bet would be to buy an InterRail Pass, which includes the British Isles and Ireland, whereas the Eurailpass does not. If you are not using InterRail and plan to do a lot of traveling in Great Britain, consider the BritRail Pass, called Youth Pass, if you are under twenty-three. This one costs $55 for one week of unlimited second-class travel; $80 for fourteen days; $120 for a month. BritRail Passes must be bought in the United States. To obtain information, write to British Rail International, 270 Madison Avenue, New York, New York 10016. If you will be staying in one area for a week or more, you may save money by using regional passes called Railrovers. There are also Economy Returns, which specify that you must travel on Tuesday, Wednesday, or Thursday only, and day-return tickets for travelers who depart and return on the same day. If you plan to leave London for only one side trip, perhaps to the Lake District or to Edinburgh, you would do better using a fare-saver ticket rather than buying any of the passes. The passes are most useful if you are going to travel around a lot. The London Tourist Board at Victoria Station or in Selfridges Department Store on Oxford Street can supply you with all types of tourist information, including economy bus fares.

In London the fastest and the most inexpensive mode of transit is the London Underground, called the "tube." Get a map of the subway at any Underground station. The tube operates from 5:30 AM to about midnight, with a slightly earlier closing on Sunday. Fares depend on the distance traveled, with the cheapest at 5p. Weekly tickets and return tickets (round trip to the same station) are cheapest.

When you ride the Underground, hang onto your ticket as it will be collected when you leave the station. If you change trains, also keep your ticket and show it, to make it known that you are continuing on. You change trains by remaining within the same station, even though the route to get from one track to another may sometimes seem complicated. There are plenty of large wall maps, platform markings, and information booths where you can ask if you are in doubt. The red, fold-up map of the Underground and bus system is invaluable; so is the smaller, white Underground diagram, with all the lines and a station index. Both are free at Underground booths and tourist-information offices all over the city.

In the city, Rover bus passes cost 50p, and you can use them for unlimited travel on London city buses for one day after 9:30 AM. Red buses are city buses, Green Line Coaches serve London's suburbs and only stop for passengers at certain points in the heart of London. There's also a Go-As-You-Please Ticket, which gives four or seven consecutive days unlimited travel on London's red buses and Underground trains. Check on their cost in line with your transit needs.

London is a sprawling city, and you will need public transportation to get around. Taxis are fairly cheap, minimum fares 25p, with an extra charge after midnight or for luggage and extra passengers.

You can phone a twenty-four-hour **transit inquiry service** by calling 2221234. Consult the service if you have any travel problems.

## Bicycle Rental

**Kensington Bicycle Company,** Kensington Student Center, Kensington Church Street, London W 8, Tel. 9376089, open seven days, 8 AM to 7 PM, April to October; 10 AM to 6 PM October to March. Get off at High Street on the Kensington tube. Rent a bike, three to ten speed, for 85p per day or £4.50 per week.

**Bell Street Bikes,** 73 Bell Street, London NW 1, near Edgware Road tube station, twenty-four-hour service, Tel. 7240456, £1 per day, £5 per week, £3.50 each extra week.

## FOOD

Although the British can never compete with the French for culinary honors, you will find some surprisingly good food in both London and the villages. Fortunately, too, eating is relatively economical. Roast beef and Yorkshire pudding are specialties, as is steak-and-kidney pie. Local cheeses, from cheddar to Stilton, are very fine indeed. English cheddar is light in color—not orange, as we know it. The renowned fish and chips can be found all over; some are good, others heavy and greasy, but all are usually a good buy except in London's most touristy spots. Pastries and tarts, served with the cream jug handy, are "luverly." The British love their sweets, probably as much as the theater. Trifle and desserts are served on carts after lunch, at teatime, and all day long. Many a bed and breakfast, advertises "kettles in rooms"—a tidy electric teakettle—so you can have your earliest morning tea in your room. From early-morning tea to high tea or low tea—or tea for two—you will become addicted to it if you give it half a chance. Another drink popular with the British is beer, or stout, but it is served almost warm to the American palate.

A pub is a good place to find inexpensive food, and although you may not enter the bar of a pub if you are under eighteen, you can be served in the area where families eat. Don't hesitate to enter a pub if you are under age. Ask if you can be served lunch or dinner there. Lorry stops (truck stops) have been recommended by some young travelers and many English friends as good places to get a filling meal cheaply, for about 75p. In one pub not far from Oxford, England, two travelers ate loaves of French bread piled high with Yorkshire ham, slabs of English cheddar, and two glasses of wine for less than $3 for both!

Shepherd's pie is a pub specialty. It's filling and cheap and often comes with a side or two of vegetables and salad for about 75p. The Ploughman's Lunch, the daily special, is always a bargain, at less than a pound for a full meal.

## SHOP HOURS

Most shops do not close for lunch, except in small villages, and are open from 9 AM to 5:30 PM. In London, central shops remain open all day, six days a week, with late hours until 7:30 PM on Thursdays. Banks are open from 9:30 AM to 3:30 PM, Monday through Friday.

By all means, change your money at banks and *never* at the Underground station kiosks.

## LONDON

**Important Addresses**

- **United States Embassy,** 24 Grosvenor Square, W 1, Tel. 4999000.
- **American Express,** 6 Haymarket, SW 1, Tel. 9304411, Monday-

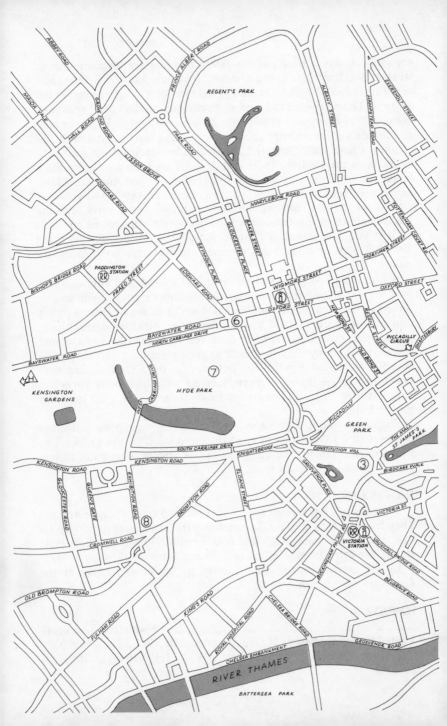

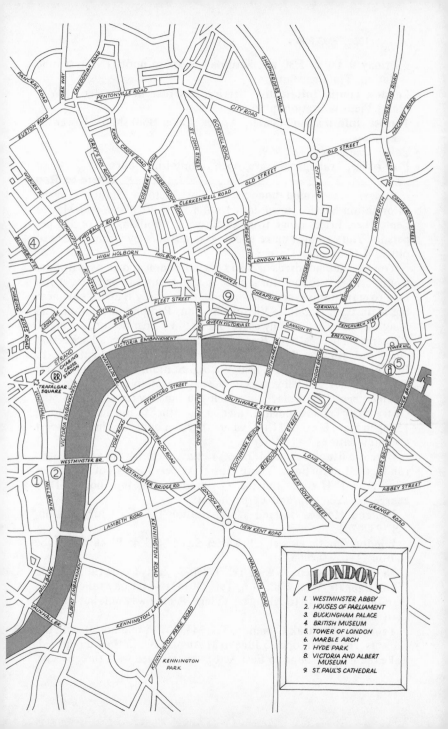

Friday 9 AM to 5:30 PM, Saturday, 9 AM to noon. (Nearest tube station, Trafalgar Square).
- **London Tourist Information Service,** 28 Grosvenor Gardens, SW 1, and Victoria Station, platform 15.
- **Tourist Information Center,** Water Lane Bookshop, Tower of London
- **Police emergency,** Tel. 999.
- **Post office,** Trafalgar Square, open twenty-four hours.

_____**Where to Stay**

**Budget Accommodation Service,** at Victoria Station Tourist Information Service, open daily from 8 AM to 10:30 PM, mid-May to September. Prices range from £2.50, with a booking fee of 35p per person. You can also make bookings in advance by writing the head office, 4 Grosvenor Gardens.

You can find hundreds of B and B's in London and all over Britain. Your best bet is to look for a place to stay around 10 or 11 AM, if you plan to stay in this type of accommodation. Many B and B's are near the main train stations—Victoria Station, Paddington Station, and King's Cross. They usually cost from £3 to £3.5 per person, per night. Rather than list scattered B and B's around the city, our advice is that you head for the **London Tourist Board Student Center,** 8-10 Buckingham Palace Road, near Victoria Station, open 9 AM to 10 PM daily, and they will tell you exactly what is available. They even have an emergency list of places at which you can stay for as little as 50p. Or try **NUS Travel Student Center,** at Victoria Station, near platform 15, open from 8 AM to 11 PM, where they can book you into low-cost accommodations.

Here is a list of reasonable places to stay. Included are a few hostels run by the International Youth Hostel Association. All of the hostels require an IYH card, and the maximum stay is four nights. They charge between 70p and £1 per night.

**Holland House,** Holland Walk, Notting Hill Gate tube station, Tel. 9370791.

**London Youth Hostel,** 36 Carter Lane, EC 4, Blackfriars tube station, Tel. 2364965.

**38 Bolton Gardens,** SW 5, Tel. 3737083, Earls Court tube station.

**84 Highgate West Hill,** N 6, Tel. 3401831, Archway tube station, then bus 271 or 210 to Highgate Village. A long way out, but cheaper than some.

**Tent City,** Old Oak Common, Tel. 7435708. A tent hostel, with hot showers, snack bar, open 5 June to 31 August. No IYH card required. Take the Underground to East Acton station, then walk three blocks.

**Kensington Student Center,** Kensington Church Street, W 8, Tel. 9375817, High Street station on the Kensington tube.

**International Students House,** 1-6 Park Crescent, W 1, Tel. 6369472, Great Portland tube station, enter Great Portland Street. Will take students on a longer term basis than hostels, one to three weeks or longer.

**Anglo-World Travel Ltd.,** Swiss Center, 10 Wardour Street, W 1, Tel. 7344651, 9 AM to 5:30 PM, Monday through Friday. Private homes in London, no booking fee to tourists. £2.50 per night, B and B.

**Aedis Accommodations,** 86 Balham Park Road, SW 12, Tel. 6727656. Call early morning or after 2 PM for on-the-spot bookings, some in private homes.

**Host and Guest Service Ltd.,** 592A Kings Road, SW 6, Tel. 7315340, 10 AM to 5 PM, Monday through Friday, specializes in family accommodations throughout England; also an *au-pair* agency.

**Universal Aunts Ltd.,** 36 Walpole Street, SW 3, Tel. 7309834, 10 AM to 4 PM, Monday through Friday. *Au-pair* positions, baby-sitting, listing of good landladies.

## Where to Eat

One of the best places to look for budget meals in England is in the pubs. There you'll find things like veal rolls, shepherd's pie, sandwiches, meat pies. The best hot meals are available around lunchtime. Expect to spend less than £1 for a generous meal.

Early-morning express trains out of London also serve a classic English breakfast—cereal, eggs and sausages, toast, and tea for around 75p, so consider this possibility if you leave early.

**Great American Disaster,** 335 Fulham Road, South Kensington tube station, is a favorite of travelers and Londoners alike, serving good hamburgers. Also at 9 Beauchamp Place, SW 3. ˙

**Stockpot,** 40 Panton Street, WC 2, Leicester Square tube station, has goulash and spaghetti at low prices.

There are dozens of Indian, Malaysian, and other Eastern restaurants all over London, and it's not worth your time to travel across town to find a specific one. There's bound to be one in your neighborhood. If you stick to the curries with rice, you'll find they are good and reasonable. Malaysian friends tell us authentic curries have meat and potatoes along with the rice.

**India Club,** 143 Strand, WC 2, (upstairs), Strand tube station, looks dingy, but features great curries and is popular with Indian students. Open until 11:30 PM.

**Loon Fung,** 37 Gerrard Street, W 1, Leicester Square tube station, in London's Chinatown, very good and inexpensive.

**Chelsea Kitchen,** of the Stockpot chain, 98 King's Road, SW 3, good and also cheap. Any of the Stockpots will give you good value.

**Casserole,** 338 Kings Road, SW 3, (upstairs) for inexpensive lunches and good Greek food.

**The Carvery,** located in the Cumberland Hotel, near Marble Arch, W 1, is recommended by friends for English prime rib or roast leg of lamb. Here you carve your own meat and select pastries from a cart. The price for dinner, about £3.50 is right, and you won't go away hungry.

The carvery idea is featured at many other hotel restaurants, but you should compare prices and check menus.

PUBS

**The Sherlock Holmes,** 10 Northumberland Street, off Charing Cross, is a well-known "theme" pub, and Holmes fans insist that he had lodgings here, as evidenced by his statement, "...a minute, Watson, while I slip across to the Yard." Scotland Yard was once opposite this address.

**Dirty Dick's,** 202 Bishopgate, EC 2, is an eccentric pub, covered with relics, but popular for its atmosphere.

**The Widow's Son,** on Devons Road, carries with it a touching story about a widow devoted to her sailor son who baked hot-cross buns on Good Friday, in 1822, and saved one for her son's arrival, only to learn that he had been drowned. Every year she saved a bun as a memorial to him. When the house became a pub, the custom was continued, and there's a long string of buns, stale and hard, hanging in a bag near the door.

**Ye Old Cheshire Cheese,** 145 Fleet Street, was the hangout of Doctor Samuel Johnson, the great English author. You can see 200-year-old playbills from theaters in Johnson's era and other memorabilia of his time.

Hilaire Belloc, French-born writer who thought highly of inns but not of the English, once wrote, "When you have lost your inns, drown your empty selves, for you will have lost the last of England."

## What to See, What to Do

There's a special telephone information service you can dial daily for a taped selection of London attractions and events: **Teletourist,** 2468041.

You could stay several weeks and still have more to see, for discovering London is always exciting. The city is like an old English garden. In spite of careful cultivation, there's still a bit of hodgepodge in its overall effect. In London's case, many villages have linked together through the years to form Greater London, and today the suburbs seem to stretch out to the seas.

For a general city survey, you might begin by taking **London Transport's tour** from Victoria Station for 65p. This tour will take you by several dozen of the city's famous sights, including **Marble Arch, Trafalgar Square, Hyde Park, Piccadilly Circus,** and **Westminster Abbey.** Depending on how much time you have in London, these tours can be useful as a quick orientation. Be sure to have a good city map handy, so you'll understand the layout. Piccadilly Circus is the Times Square of London, with neon lights and bronze statues and much traffic.

The **changing of the guard** is a high point on the London scene. This event happens daily from April to September at 11 AM, (10 AM on Sundays) at the gates of **Buckingham Palace.** Get there in advance for a vantage point close to the gates, or stand across the street. To reach the palace, take the tube to Victoria Station.

**Westminster Abbey,** at Parliament Square, SW 1, Westminster tube station, contains the Coronation Chair. In this Gothic church the kings and queens of England are crowned.

**St. Paul's Cathedral,** St. Paul's tube station, Christopher Wren's greatest work, built in 1675.

**Imperial War Museum,** Lambeth North tube station, has an impressive collection of weapons, relics, and models on all aspects of war since 1914.

**Victoria and Albert Museum,** Cromwell Road, SW 7, South Kensington tube station, and the **British Museum,** at Great Russell Street, WC 1, Russell Square tube stations, are probably London's best museums. The British Museum houses the Rosetta Stone and the Magna Carta. Hours at Victoria and Albert are from 10 AM to 6 PM daily, 2:30 PM to 6 PM Sunday. British Museum hours are from 10 AM to 5 PM weekdays, 2:30 PM to 6 PM Sundays.

**National Gallery,** Trafalgar Square, WC 2, Trafalgar Square tube station, has a large collection of Rembrandt and Rubens, among others. Open 10 AM to 6 PM daily, 2 PM to 6 PM Sunday.

**Tate Gallery,** Millbank, SW 1, Victoria or Westminster tube station, has twentieth-century art as well as works dating from the sixteenth century. Features paintings by Picasso, Chagall, and sculpture by Henry Moore and others. Open from 10 AM to 6 PM daily, 2 PM to 6 PM Sunday.

**Madame Tussaud's,** Marylebone Road, NW 1, Baker Street tube station, open daily from 10 AM to 6:30 PM, to 5:30 PM October to

March. Entrance 90p. In this famous wax museum, you will meet
Jack the Ripper and visit the Chamber of Horrors.

**Houses of Parliament,** St. Margaret Street, SW 1, Westminster
tube station, Monday through Thursday at 2:30 PM, 11 AM on Friday.
Join the queue at St. Stephen's Hall at least an hour before time. In
the free public gallery you can watch a session of the House of
Commons. This visit is an absolute must according to our best
researchers. You will witness a lot of political procedure and perhaps
even lively debate, especially if a hotly contended issue is under
discussion.

The **Tower of London** at Tower Hill, famous fortress and prison, is
well worth a visit in spite of the crowds and long queues. The line
moves quickly even on Sunday. Daily hours, 9:30 AM to 5 PM,
Sunday, 2 PM to 5 PM. Entry fee, 50p. Closed Sunday during the
winter. Not all the Beefeater Guards are friendly, but some will
happily pose for pictures. A thorough tour of the tower and environs
takes two or three hours, easily all afternoon, so don't plan much else
on that day.

**Hyde Park, Speakers' Corner,** is a lively spot on Sunday afternoon,
when passionate soapbox orators lecture on every subject from royal
allowances to health food. Obscenity is forbidden, but you may hear
earnest appeals for some religion or incendiary pleas for revolt. There
is horseback riding, a lake, the Serpentine, where you can swim, fish,
and row, or you can have tea in a café, as you watch the world go by
on a Sunday afternoon.

**London Zoo.** Take the Underground to Baker Street, then bus 74
or 74 b, or take bus 74 from Knightsbridge, Hyde Park Corner, or
Marble Arch. Open daily from 9 AM to 6 PM. This is one of the
world's best zoos, and here you can see Ching-Ching and Chia-Chia,
the giant pandas given to Britain by China. Animal feeding and
bathing times are posted, and there's an interesting Moonlight World
where you can observe nocturnal animals.

**Brass Rubbing Center** at Westminster Abbey and St. Margaret's
Church, open six days, from 9 AM to 6 PM, closed Sunday. Admission
is free, but a charge is made for rubbings that includes special paper
and instructions. Brasses were used between the thirteenth and
seventeenth centuries to commemorate people. A sheet of metal
set into the stone slab used to cover the grave in church floors,
or mounted on the wall or on a table tomb, brasses were often life-
size and engraved by an artist of the time. They give invaluable
contemporary illustrations of costume, armor, footwear, and hair
style. A dog or a favorite pet may be included. The process of making

a rubbing is something like placing a penny under a sheet of thin paper, then scribbling over the paper with a pencil until the surface image of the penny comes through. A handsome home decoration can be made in about an hour. There are numerous brass-rubbing centers throughout England, including one at Oxford.

PUBLICATIONS

*This Month in London,* a monthly that covers all events, published by the British Tourist Authority, is recommended.

*Time Out* comes out each Thursday, costs 20p, and is available in most bookstalls. It contains good entertainment information and reviews concert listings, both classical and rock.

*What's On in London,* also weekly, is similar to the above, but is full of ads for high-priced restaurants, often of poor quality. Skip this one.

SPORTS

See Wimbledon for 30p!

One of London's best known sporting events, the annual **Wimbledon Tennis Tournament,** is held for a fortnight from the last week in June through the first week in July. General admission tickets go on sale each day at noon, for £1. Play begins at 2 PM daily. The queues are long, but you can buy standing room easily enough if you get in line about 10 AM. You'll see some people in the queue who have camped there all night.

Once inside you can walk about anywhere. Center-court seats are sold out long in advance, but there is standing room at center court. Tennis play goes on from 2 PM until well past 8 in the evening. Around 4 PM, time for high tea, many people leave their seats and deposit their tickets in a recycle container. You can try then to get a center-court seat at the entrance for 30p. You may be surprised at how much great tennis you can see for very little money. In 1977, mixed-doubles, semifinals, and men's doubles were all played very late in the day. The money from recycled tickets goes to charity.

THEATER

**Ticket agents:**

**NUS Travel Student Center,** Victoria Station, SW 1, Tel. 8286272.

**Keith Prowse,** 155 Charing Cross Road, WC 2, Tel. 4341440.

**London Theater Bookings,** 96 Shaftesbury Avenue, W 1, Tel. 4393371.

**Selfridges Department Store,** Oxford Street, has a ticket agency and can book tickets for you.

London theater is excellent. The variety ranges from Shakespeare to Agatha Christie to avant-garde works, and it is always a bargain.

There are no performances on Sunday. For West End performances, London's equivalent of Broadway, you will pay £1 for the cheapest seats, and even front-row seats won't cost much over £3. Curtain time is 7:30 PM, and you should book in advance if possible. Write ahead to Keith Prowse or to London Theater Bookings. Enclose airmail international-reply coupons, and mail the request with sufficient international airmail postage on your envelope.

The **Royal Albert Hall**, at Kensington Gore, SW 7, is the scene of Promenade Concerts nightly during the summer (except Sunday) from mid-July to mid-September. These popular musical events are fantastic entertainment.

STREET MARKETS

**Camden Locks** street market, at the crossing of Chalk Farm Road and Regent's Canal Street, is a tightly packed, lively area of small stalls that sell junk, clothes, antiques, and crafts. Hours on Saturday and Sunday are from 8 AM to 6 PM. You may find tennis balls from Wimbledon signed by Bjorn Borg, or you can wander through Camden Locks crafts shops where everything sold is handmade and less expensive than in London shops. There are outdoor tables and evening jazz concerts. You can also take a pottery course from The Pottery, learn to sculpt at the Three Sculptors, or take a two-day course in photography and darkroom techniques at the Trace Studio. Write to any of the above in Camden Locks, London, NW 1. You will find the past and present mingling pleasantly here.

**Portobello Road,** W 11, off Westbourne Park Road. The nearest tube stations are Ladbroke Grove and Notting Hill Gate. Here you'll find scores of antique stalls, fruit and vegetable stands, junk stalls, and boutiques. Antiques tend to be high priced. There's always a crowd and also good pubs where you can enjoy people watching. Open Friday morning and all day Saturday.

**Petticoat Lane,** Middlesex Street, E 1, Aldgate East tube station, features busy stalls of secondhand clothing and popular junk, but the quality is cheap. It's fun to look, but be careful of what you buy.

**Shopping**

The section around Oxford Street, west of Oxford Circus tube station, is one of the best shopping areas. **Selfridges** has good buys. **Marks & Spencer,** with branches on Oxford Street and all over London, features excellent wool sweaters and low prices on their men's and women's wear, T-shirts, velvet suits, and pants. Kensington High Street is also reputedly good for values, offering Scottish woolens, fine cashmere, Harris tweed jackets at prices well below those at home. **Harrods,** on Brompton Road, in Knightsbridge, the most famous store in Britain, claims they can sell you anything. They have an elaborate food department with sumptuous gourmet items, as well as moderate-priced take-out dishes.

During the first two weeks of July everything goes on sale in London's good stores. Try Harrods, (normally rather expensive); Jaeger, 204 Regent Street; Aquascutum, 100 Regent Street; and Selfridges.

Generally, English cottons are inferior. They wash poorly, are limp, and you should avoid them. And unless you buy the best quality leather goods, shoes, coats, and handbags, pass them by as well.

**Foyle's Book Store,** 119-125 Charing Cross Road, WC 2, Tottenham Court Road tube station, is the world's largest bookstore, with some eleven floors of books and helpful clerks. Definitely worth a visit.

## TOURS

You could spend your entire holiday in London, but then you'd miss some of the best of Britain, such as Oxford, Cambridge, Stratford-upon-Avon, Stonehenge, the Cotswolds, and the English Lake District.

You can book a tour to any of these places through tour agents **Evan Evans,** with offices throughout London, with **Frames Tours,** or through the **British Transport Authority.** Each of the tours have departure points all around the city. Inquire by phone for details.

You can also explore on your own, with frequent train and bus service to all points listed.

## OXFORD

You can reach Oxford by train in one and a half hours, sixty-five miles from London's Paddington Station. Oxford is a university town of fine old college buildings, dating from 1249, located on the Thames. Visit some of the colleges, **St. Johns, All Souls,** and **Magdalen**—the latter with its beautiful gardens. There's a lovely chapel from the thirteenth century in **Merton College,** and the renowned **Bodleian Library,** where old and curious manuscripts can be seen. The **Ashmolean Museum,** the oldest in the country, on Beaumont Street, is open daily from 10 AM to 4 PM (Sundays from 2 PM to 4 PM), and has fine English art as well as Italian and German Renaissance. Cloisters, the ancient city wall, chapels with fourteenth-century stained glass, lovely quadrangles, and gardens—all add to the charm and clutter of old Oxford town, where one almost expects to see Cardinal Wolsey striding forth from **Christ Church.** Bicycle rentals are available, and there are good spots for buying picnic supplies.

## STRATFORD-UPON-AVON

Take the train from Paddington Station and change at Leamington Sap. The trip takes two hours, forty minutes. This picturesque old town, the birthplace of Shakespeare, has many half-timbered houses lining its streets. The house where the bard was born is on Henley Street. You can visit **Ann Hathaway's cottage, Holy Trinity Church,** where Shakespeare was christened and buried, and you can attend an evening performance at the **Shakespeare Memorial Theater,** built 100 years ago. One advantage of a tour package is that you can be assured of theater tickets, even in high season.

## CAMBRIDGE

Fifty-four miles from London, the trip to Cambridge takes about one hour by train from Liverpool Street or King's Cross Station. Very different from Oxford, Cambridge is a town set in a university. Broad expanses of lawn, handsome buildings, and wonderful English gardens in the center of town are its outstanding features. **King's College** with **College Chapel** is a fine example of ecclesiastical architecture and is the tallest building north of London. **Trinity College** and the **Great Court, St. Johns College,** the Benedictine abbey of **St. Radegund,** and **Christ's College,** with its particularly noteworthy gardens, are other high points.

You can **rent a rowboat** to row on the River Cam for an idyllic afternoon. Or you can rent a punt, a flat-bottomed boat that you propel with a pole, for about £1 per hour.

## STONEHENGE

This mysterious site is near Amesbury, Wiltshire. You reach it by rail from Waterloo Station to Salisbury, a journey of one hour thirty-seven minutes, then to Stonehenge by local bus. The vast slabs of stone that make up Stonehenge are considered to be the finest monument of the Bronze Age. Built in several stages, the first about 1800 B.C., the giant Sarsen stones were then dragged down in about 1500 B.C., from Marlborough Downs and erected as they are today. Stay overnight in Salisbury, and check with the Youth Hostel at Milford Hill House, Tel. 27572, or the Tourist Office at 10 Endless Street, where they can find you an available B and B. Read some of the available literature on its history, and you will appreciate Stonehenge even more.

## THE LAKE DISTRICT

Many travelers consider England's Lake District the most outstanding scenic region in the British Isles. Accessible by train to Windermere, the Lake District boasts an amazing share of natural beauty. Rich in history, this area has the largest lakes and the highest mountains in England—all of which inspired generations of writers and poets. William Wordsworth, born in this region in 1770, and Beatrix Potter, Peter Rabbit's creator, both knew the Lake District intimately.

The largest concentration of youth hostels in England is found in this region, twenty-two in all, so you can get off the beaten track and roam through charming villages and lovely greens. **Lake Windermere,** England's largest lake, could be a focus for your visit. Valleys radiate from this hub, making it possible to get from one vale to another rather easily, despite the nobly proportioned scenery. You can repeat the theme of mountain, dale, and lake in a one-day hike. There's excellent boating, sailing, fishing, swimming, and you'll find a photographer's delight in the pastoral settings here. You can wander out from Windermere toward villages like **Ullswater** and **Troutbeck.** At Troutbeck, Windermere, Tel. Windermere 3543, there is a fine hostel called **High Cross Castle.** You might also check with the **Lake District National Park Information Service,** District Bank House, High Street, Windermere, Tel. 2498 for maps and guides to the area. Ferry service on the lake connects you with other lakeside towns, and the region abounds with pubs and B and B's. So even though many students and tourists flock to the Lake District, you won't have trouble finding refreshment or accommodations.

## CHESTER

A town to the north that is well worth the visit is Chester, the last Saxon town to surrender to William the Conqueror. Founded in A.D. 70, Chester is encircled by medieval stone walls, and you will be quickly reminded of the Middle Ages when you walk the streets lined with two-story timbered shops and houses. Chester is fifteen miles south of Liverpool and can be reached by train from London in about six hours.

# 11 FOCUS ON FRANCE

Population: 51,000,000          Language: French
Capital: Paris                 Currency: franc (fr.)

## THE LAND AND THE PEOPLE

Throughout France you will hear nonstop, animated discussions—opinions expressed about everything, often self-mocking, often critical. When you think of France, you may automatically picture a Parisian scene, yet to learn about this complex country you must visit its many regions, for France's soul is in the country, in the provincial villages and small towns. The people in each region are proud of their heritage and secure in their belief that their province is more important than the neighboring ones; they have better food, greater wine, and are more vital and more a part of history than their neighbors. There is always a political and intellectual ferment in progress.

When you think of Paris you may think first of art. Paris is considered by many to be the art capital of the world, and art remains among the ten top industries of France. You can see paintings by the finest masters the world has ever known, as well as those of contemporary, young artists. Their works are shown in galleries all over Paris, as they seek recognition, hoping to be singled out from the more than 60,000 artists in the city.

From the windswept Atlantic shores and the Normandy beaches to the sparkling waters of the Riviera, France is endowed with abundant natural wonders. Its mountains extend from the Alps to the Pyrenees, and the valleys include the Loire and the Rhône. From Alpine winters to Mediterranean summers, the climate beckons the sports lover. The scenery is not untouched by human beings, but embraced by gentle hands coaxing the best from it.

## FOOD

The French are as passionate about their food as they are about their politics. To them, preparing and consuming food is an art, a science, and an entertainment. The terms *gourmet* and *gourmand* are rightfully French words, for France is unrivaled for gastronomic marvels as well as for everyday good eating.

French food includes an enormous variety, with specialties from region to region. Emphasis is always on using *fresh* products, and no

French cook would dream of buying bread today for tomorrow's meal. In fact, a great furor resulted when bakers wanted to take Sunday off. So you will see French people everywhere carrying long loaves, unwrapped, tucked under their arm, and boys on bicycles delivering *croissants* to hotels early in the morning.

Breakfast consists of coffee, tea, or chocolate, and *croissants* and crusty, fresh French bread with jam. Bread is called *pain*. In hotels and small pensions this meal is usually included in your room rate.

Midday meals can be ordered between noon and about 2 PM. Many restaurants will not serve you beyond that time. Dinner is served from about 6 PM or 7 PM. Generally European dinner hours are much later than those in the United States, and in the average restaurant meals are served in a leisurely way.

Many traveling teen-agers buy their picnic lunch at a grocery store and in the open-air marketplace. French bread, pâté, sliced meats and cheeses, yogurt, a liter of apple juice or *limonade* (a carbonated drink similar to 7-Up), along with a splurge of pastries, can be bought for less than $2. Finding a spot to spread out a picnic opens doors to conversations with other young travelers or local inhabitants.

An *épicerie* or a *charcuterie* are French-style delicatessens, jammed with delectable goodies. A *boulangerie* sells bread; a *pâtisserie* sells pastries and candy. Cheeses are superb, and you should try some of the specialties. Brie, Camembert, Boursin, and Rambol are soft cheeses we recommend. Also try chocolate mousse and smooth custards, which you can buy for about 2 fr. in grocery stores.

French onion soup with its high-hat Gruyère cheese topping is only one of the renowned soups you will find in France. There's also the *soupe de poisson,* or fish soup, especially popular in Normandy, or the bouillabaisse, a thicker fish chowder, in which even the shells are part of the stew. Beef, veal, lamb, and chicken are popular meats. Beef may be called by any of these names: *Chateaubriand, entrecôte,* or *tournedos.* They are all top-quality cuts. *Steak tartare* is raw, seasoned hamburger, very lean. *Boeuf* means beef. *Poulet* is chicken. For eating experiences, try *boeuf bourguignon* (beef in burgundy) and *coq au vin* (chicken in wine). If you've never tasted escargots (snails), why not try them in Paris? *Quiche Lorraine,* often served as a first course, is something like a French version of pizza, except the filling is thicker and made with eggs, cream, onion, and bacon. Other types of quiches are also popular in take-out shops. They may be eaten cold or reheated.

Also recommended: *crème de marrons,* a chestnut purée made with rich chocolate and finely ground chestnuts.

Many Parisian restaurants offer a fixed-price dinner for a modest sum. It usually includes three courses, so check menus for this bargain.

France is the world's leading wine producer, and its vineyards are an important part of the country's agriculture. The wet season in vine-growing regions produces juicier grapes, yet their sugar content is lower, so quality and quantity have an inverse relationship. It is quite common for households in France to serve wine to children. Drinking water never appears with meals.

Some of the best wines come from Burgundy, Bordeaux, and the Rhône Valley. A popular and inexpensive red wine you might try with red meats and cheeses is Beaujolais; a white wine commonly served is Chablis, which is good with chicken, seafood, and veal. Red wines are served close to room temperature; white ones are usually chilled.

**Important.** A 15 percent service charge is usually added to the food prices in most restaurants. However, some menus may state at the bottom, in small print, "a 15 percent service charge will be added." If so, the price listed after the food does not include the charge.

## SHOP HOURS

9:30 AM to 6 PM in large cities; grocery stores in villages may close for lunch.

## PARIS

_____ **Important Addresses**

- **United States Embassy,** 2 avenue Gabriel, Tel. 2657460 (Métro: Concorde).
- **American Express,** 11 rue Scribe, Tel. 7427500 (Métro: Opéra).
- **Police headquarters,** 9 boulevard du Palais, Tel. 3264420. Police emergency, Tel. 17.
- **CIEE,** 49 rue Pierre Charron, Tel. 3592369 (Métro: Saint Georges).
- **National Office for Tourist Information,** 127 avenue des Champs-Élysées, Tel. 7237211, 9 AM to midnight daily.
- **Office du Tourisme Universitaire,** 137 boulevard St.-Michel, Tel. 3266097.

Paris is exciting, full of vitality, and crowded. The City of Light has charisma and a passion for life that few other cities can equal. Hemingway wrote, "If you are lucky enough to live in Paris as a young man, then wherever you go for the rest of your life, it stays with you, for Paris is a moveable feast."

One of the things you will be most grateful for is Paris's marvelous

Métro, one of the world's finest subway systems. It is fast, efficient, and cheap. Every train station is also a Métro stop, and you can get a pocket-size map of the system at any of them. Save money on Métro fare by buying a book of ten tickets, a *carnet,* which costs 9 fr. If you plan to stay for several days or a week, you can buy tourist tickets that give you unlimited bus travel and as many first-class Métro rides as you like. Four-day tickets cost 30 fr., and seven-day tickets are 50 fr. You can also use Métro tickets on buses, but bus rides use up more tickets for the same distance. The last Métro run is at 12:45 AM, so keep time in mind if your lodgings are on the outskirts of the city.

If you arrive in Paris by train without reservations, head first for the National Office for Tourist Information near the Georges V Métro stop. They can find you a room within almost any price range, but you cannot write ahead for reservations. If you arrive past midnight (but before 1 AM), take the Métro or the bus to boulevard St.-Germain or boulevard St.-Michel, and you will find twenty or more small hotels within a two-block radius of each station, all modestly priced.

---

### Where to Stay

The French expression for youth hostel is *auberge de jeunesse,* and youth hostels are your best bet, although none are in the heart of town.

**Auberge de Jeunesse,** 7 rue Philippe de Girard, Tel. 2034381, near avenue Jean-Jaurès. Helpful people. 7 fr. a night. Hostel closes at 11:30 PM.

**Auberge de Jeunesse,** avenue de Villeneuve-St.-Georges (Choisy-le-Roi), Tel. 8909230. Limited spaces for individuals, more for groups. Near Orly Airport, about eleven minutes from St.-Lazare Railroad Station or St.-Michel Métro to Choisy-le-Roi.

**Auberge de Jeunesse,** 4 rue des Marguerites, Rueil-Malmaison, Tel. 9678868. From St.-Lazare Station, fifteen minutes to Suresnes.

There are nine more hostels in outlying towns near Paris. Write to the French hostel association, **Fédération Unie des Auberges de Jeunesse,** 56 rue Mesnil, Paris, Tel. 5531695. You must buy a federation membership to use the facilities.

**Cité International Universitaire,** Services des Admissions, 19 boulevard Jourdan, 75690 Paris CEDEX 14, Tel. 5896852. You can write ahead to this office, enclosing a $5 deposit with your room request. Rooms are available during the entire year, but more vacancies are available in summer. Location is good for students. Take the Métro to the Cité Universitaire stop. Rooms cost about 18 fr.

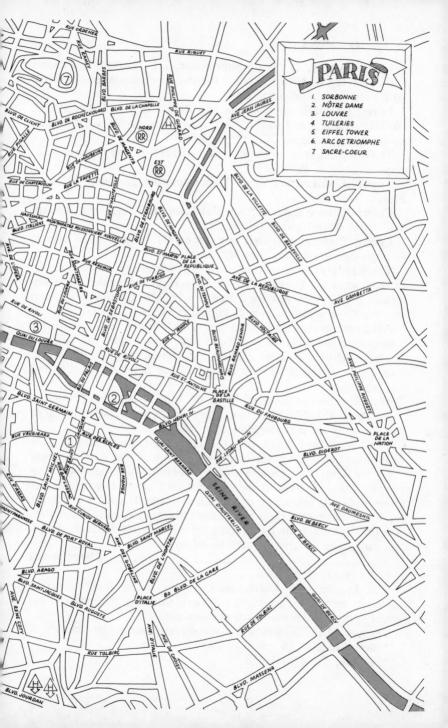

**Le Fauconnier,** 11 rue du Fauconnier, Tel. 2129912. Has rooms and can recommend many other student accommodations in Paris. 20 fr. for room and breakfast.

**Foyer International d'Accueil de Paris,** 30 rue Cabanis, Tel. 1072569. Large, and staff is knowledgeable about what else is available for students. Nice atmosphere.

The following three organizations can also help you find a place to stay or study in Paris:

**Centre d'Information et de Documentation Jeunesse,** 101 quai Branly, Tel. 5664820.

**Centre Parisien d'Accueil aux Boursiers du Gouvernement Francais,** 6 rue Jean-Calvin, Tel. 7072622.

**Centre Parisien d'Accueil aux Étudiants Étrangers,** 38 avenue Georges-Bernanon, Tel. 3260749.

There are also more than 100 camping sites around Paris. For a list of them write to: **Touring Club de France,** 65 avenue de la Grande-Armée, 75782 Paris. Ask for a map showing sites close to the city and one for those within a twenty kilometer range.

Accommodations are often in short supply, so make your reservations in advance, especially for Easter and the summer holidays. (Note: I have deliberately chosen not to list small, inexpensive hotels since they change all too rapidly in quality and availability.)

**Welcome Service Bureau,** Hotel de Ville, 4 place de l'Hotel de Ville, Paris, Tel. 2771540. They can reserve a hotel room for you or provide a list of accommodations.

Good areas for students to stay include the Latin Quarter and the Sorbonne. Left-Bank hotels compared to those on the Right Bank (of the Seine River) are generally cheaper and more to the taste of young people. The Left Bank is the southern area of the city, where lifestyles and costs tend to be more student oriented, whereas the Right Bank, or northern area, is more expensive, sedate, and fashionable. Ask the tourist bureau to give you a list of hotels in these areas should you strike out on student accommodations.

## Where to Eat

STUDENT RESTAURANTS

**Cité International Universitaire,** 19 boulevard Jourdan, has a cafeteria, and if you are staying there, it will serve the purpose, but better spots can be found for evening meals.

Try any of the following for a good and inexpensive meal:

**Albert Chatelet,** 10 rue Jean-Calvin

**Mabillon,** 3 rue Mabillon

**Grand Palais,** cours la Reine
**Censier,** 3 rue Censier
**Maison de l'Étudiant,** 26 rue du Faubourg St.-Jacques
**Alliance Française,** 101 boulevard Raspail
OTHER RESTAURANTS

**Mother Earth's,** 66 rue des Lombards (Métro: Chatelet). Students say this one is worth seeking out and feels like home. Meals run about 14 fr.

**La Coupole,** 102 boulevard Montparnasse. Everyone, from the hip to the elegant, comes here.

**Le Volcan,** 10 rue Thouin, (Métro: Cardinal Lemoine). Typical Parisian food, say some Paris residents, not expensive, about 17 fr.

**La Petite Hostellerie,** rue de la Harpe, pleasant enough and the food is good, about 18 fr.

**Pub St.-Germain-des-Près,** 7 cour du Commer-St.-André, has house specialties from 12 to 18 fr.; roast chicken with fries, 10 fr. If you choose carefully, you can eat well for a modest sum.

**Chez Lipp,** 151 boulevard St.-Germain (Tel. 5485391). Excellent and typical; very popular with Parisians. Dinners about 20 fr. without wine. Can be crowded, so go early or reserve if they accept reservations.

**Au Beaujolais,** 19 quai de la Tournelle, (Métro: Maubert-Mutualité). Modest surroundings, salamis and smoked meats hanging from the ceiling; not expensive, but tantalizing. Quite special, we think. Also favored by Parisians.

**Crêperie de la Mouff,** 9 rue Mouffetard. Recommended by students for excellent crêpe choices.

With 8000 restaurants in Paris you will find some special ones on your own, including the Armenian, Vietnamese, Greek, Malaysian, and others that are popular, should you seek something beside the Gallic fare. Sample the sidewalk cafés and the vendors selling crêpes—be adventuresome in your dining!

_____**What to See, What to Do**

While we can offer the tourist sights everyone seeks in Paris, nearly all of us have a special memory of a special place we found on our own, a small shop or outdoor market, a rather unknown plaza and fountain we sat by to drink in the heady sounds and sights of Paris.

You will definitely want to see the **Eiffel Tower** and visit the **Louvre** and the **Sorbonne.** Unless you plan to spend a week or so at the Louvre, choose the sections you favor most or you will begin to think that everything looks the same. Of particular interest to you might be *Mona Lisa, Winged Victory, Venus de Milo,* and *Whistler's*

*Mother*. Hours are 9:45 AM to 5:15 PM, closed on Tuesday, free on Sunday. 5-fr. admission, half with student-ID card.

Plan a sightseeing route to include **Nôtre Dame,** the **Arc de Triomphe, Napoleon's Tomb,** and **Place de la Concorde,** which is crammed with cars and flags near the spot where Queen Marie Antoinette was guillotined. In Montmartre walk the 300 or so steps up the steep hill to **Sacré-Coeur,** a white, domed church fashioned after the Taj Mahal, for a fantastic view of the city on a clear day.

For a different type of escape, you might want to visit the famous **sewers** of Paris. Go to the place de la Résistance at the quai d'Orsay on the Left Bank, where tours of the sewers are open between 2 PM and 5 PM Monday and Wednesday.

You can also tour the **catacombs** at 2 place Denfert-Rochereau, on Saturdays at 2 PM, for 1 fr., where artistically piled bones and skulls may intrigue you. They were used as a hideout during World War II and are a present-day offbeat attraction.

While theater and night life in Paris are expensive, there are some **student cafés** and **discos.** You'll find them in small streets near boulevard St.-Michel and around rue Descartes and rue Mouffetard, near the rue de la Contrescarpe. Along the boulevard Montparnasse and the boulevard Raspail you can sit at cafés for a late snack.

There are, of course, famous nightclubs in Paris, but they are terribly expensive and usually not worth the money. They include the **Lido,** at 78 avenue Champs-Élysees; the **Moulin Rouge,** 82 boulevard de Clichy; and the **Folies Bergères,** 32 rue Richer. All have extravaganzas of bare and leggy girls. Tickets are very expensive, but you might pick up a cheaper one for a midweek performance.

A not outrageously expensive theater recommended to us by Americans who lived for four years in Paris is the **Bobino,** 2 rue de la Gaîté, for consistently good shows featuring pantomime artists, such as Marcel Marceau.

Visit the **Jeu de Paume** (Métro: Concorde), where you can see Impressionist collections of Gauguin, Cézanne, Dégas, Monet, Renoir. It is a small museum, not so overwhelming as the Louvre. 9:45 AM to 5 PM daily, closed Tuesday. 5-fr. entry, half with student-ID card.

The **Musée Rodin,** 77 rue de Varenne (Métro: Varenne). Rodin's *The Thinker* graces the small garden in front of the entrance. Open 10 AM to 2 PM daily, 2 PM to 6 PM Sunday. Closed Tuesday. 5-fr. entry, half with student-ID card.

**Musée National d'Art Moderne,** Centre National d'Art et de Culture Georges-Pompidou, "Beaubourg," 43 rue Beaubourg (Métro: Rambuteau), has a fine collection of Picassos and Braques, with other changing exhibits. 10 AM to 10 PM daily. 10-fr. entry for entire center, 5-fr. entry for museum only.

**Musée de l'Orangerie,** place de la Concorde (Métro: Concorde). One of Monet's famous *Water Lilies* is here, and there are important temporary exhibitions also. 10 AM to 12:15 PM, 2 PM to 5 PM daily. Closed Tuesday. 8-fr. entry, half with student-ID card.

THE MARKETS

An interesting phenomenon, the markets of Paris are many. The once famous Les Halles is no more, but there are others worth visiting. The **Bird Market** is held every Sunday at place Louis Lépine, and the **Flower Market** is open daily except Sunday at place Louis Lépine. There's also a **Flea Market** at the end of the la Porte de Clignancourt at the end of the Métro line. Here all kinds of things can be found, in amusing and incongruous display, on Saturday, Sunday, and Monday. There's an open-air **Stamp Market** at the corner of avenues Gabriel and Marigny, on Sunday, public holidays, and Thursday afternoons. Along **rue Mouffetard** you'll see colorful sidewalk food stands on Wednesday, Friday, and Sunday, with students, artists, and merchants shouting and selling. There are about eighty other food markets, and they are usually open daily from 7 AM to 1 PM. A secondhand market is held at **Marché du Temple**, Carreau du Temple, daily except Sunday and Monday, with shops and stalls in the open air.

At the **Gare d'Orsay** you can see one of a few legally authorized auction houses for private sales in Paris. While the big sales take place on Monday, Wednesday, and Friday, on Tuesday and Thursday—slow days—household and other goods are sold. You'll find the best bargains on these slow days, from packets of old drawings to oil lamps and secondhand books.

PARKS AND GARDENS

When you need to get away from people for a while, Paris gives ample opportunity to do so in its many lovely parks and gardens. The most impressive of all are the **Tuileries**, which are also magnificent at night when they are illuminated. In the gardens of the **Palais Royal** or in the sprawling **Bois de Boulogne** you can take respite from the sounds of human voices. But there's more than greenery in the Bois. There are two lakes, a children's zoo, camping, tennis and polo, and horserace tracks. Also worth a visit is the **Jardin du Luxembourg**, a spacious park with lakes on which to sail small boats and lots of open space where you can throw a Frisbee or watch elderly men play lawn-bowling games.

_____**Side Trips**

A short trip out of Paris puts you at **Versailles**, the palace of Louis XIV, impressive even with crowds of tourists. To get to Versailles, take the train from Gare Montparnasse. The palace is open daily from 10 AM to 5:30 PM and costs 2.5 fr. with a student-ID card. Take a picnic to enjoy in the pleasant parks surrounding Versailles; admission is free to the grounds.

You could see the highlights of Paris in a week, or you could stay for years and never tire of the cultural and dining pleasures. But other parts of France to consider include the French Riviera and Monaco, Chartres, Normandy's beaches, Rouen, Strasbourg and environs, ski areas, such as Chamonix, and the Bordeaux wine country.

## NORMANDY

One student described **Rouen** as "the perfect size for touring, enough sights to catch the eye, yet spare the feet." Sights include a Norman town with an impressive **cathedral** in the Gothic style, another church called the **Church of St.-Ouen**, and a fourteenth-century clock tower and gatehouse called the **Grosse Horloge**. The place where Joan of Arc met her fate in 1431 is called the **Place du Vieux Marché**, and you can also see the tower where she was imprisoned. In the **Musée des Beaux Arts** and the **Musée des Antiquités** you will find masterpieces by Impressionists as well as works from the Renaissance. The public **swimming pool** at Rouen waves a hearty welcome after a hot summer day on the train. The **youth hostel** near town is at 17 rue Diderot, Rouen Rive Gauche (76100 Seine-Maritime), Tel. (35) 720645. If the hostel is filled, go to the **Syndicat d'Initiative** (tourist office) near the cathedral, not far from the train station, and they will find you a room.

As if the countryside in springtime were not reason enough to visit the Normandy coast, you can find a number of other enticements as well. The country in May and June is an incredibly rich panorama of wild orange poppies and white Queen Anne's lace, all strewn about above the rocky cliffs and breaking surf, an Impressionist painting in itself. Although **Dieppe** has been called simply a port town, it has much to offer in its peaceful seaside setting, including food worthy of the famous Dieppe Cooking School, to which many visitors come to learn the art.

All along the coast are the World War II blockhouses that hold memories of Normandy's bloody history. A golf course, three kilometers south of Dieppe, is dotted with bunkers, and one tee is atop a squatty bunker you can climb down into. Also south of Dieppe are the **World War II beachheads, Omaha, Utah,** and others, with war memorials to the thousands of soldiers who lost their lives here.

On the way to Mont-St.-Michel, stop off at **Bayeux** to see the Gothic **cathedral** and the **museum** that houses the world famous Bayeux Tapestry. The tapestry tells the story of William the Conqueror's fight with Harold of England. You can see it from 9 AM to noon, 1:30 PM to 7 PM, from mid-March to mid-October; shorter hours in winter, closing at 5 PM.

One student who first heard of **Mont-St.-Michel** in a high-school French class was determined to see the handsome **abbey**, which rises like a crown out of the sea on the Normandy coast. A daily train from Paris (Montparnasse station) brings crowds of tourists to the abbey in summer, and they flock all over the place like seagulls looking for a perch. To avoid the mob scene as these students did, enter with a tour group (the only way you can get in with your ticket, which costs about 5 fr.), then find a way to see the abbey's beauty on your own. Do be sure to go inside, as simply walking around the outside is not enough to appreciate the Romanesque church. Tides rush in about twenty-four miles per hour, so don't walk on the beaches surrounding the abbey when a high tide is expected, twice a month for several days. At these times the abbey is almost completely cut off from the mainland, accessible only by a small strip of roadway. Don't bother to visit the museum at the monastery.

There's also a famous omelet kitchen near Mont-St.-Michel, **La Crêperie St. Michel.** Indulge yourself with one of these omelet delicacies cooked in pure butter over an open fire.

On the mainland there's a **hostel** not far from Mont-St.-Michel, in the town of Genêts, Ancienne Gare, place des Halles.

## THE RIVIERA

In spite of the cost, the French Riviera is a razzle-dazzle must-see, particularly Monaco, a tiny, glittering principality surrounded on three sides by France that seems to be wall-to-wall Rolls-Royces. Generally, the Riviera is a sun-drenched shoreline of craggy cliffs and sheer drops that plunge onto lava rock beaches, where many coves and inlets shelter small sand beaches. There are also some long stretches of coarse sand beaches where sun worshippers do their thing.

The French Riviera is easily accessible by train from Paris. It's a seven-hour trip by day or a twelve-hour overnighter. From

Marseilles, you can be in Nice in six and a half hours. There are also daily flights from London and Paris or bus service from Marseilles.

Major resort towns along the Riviera include Nice, Cannes, and Monte Carlo, which is in Monaco. Although they share a common bond of sunny shores and sparkling sea, each has a character of its own. Cannes has the best beaches, Monaco the most unique atmosphere (and most expensive), while Nice is the most relaxed with the most youthful atmosphere, according to young travelers. You can find affordable pizza parlors, grocery stores, and cafés that won't break the bank. Nice is fifteen minutes by train west of Monaco, while Cannes is nearly thirty minutes west of Nice. There is excellent train service.

Youth hostels and campgrounds are plentiful all along the Riviera, but they're outnumbered by the many expensive hotels. Restaurants are expensive too. Students stretch their budgets by buying as much as possible in grocery stores or eating in hostels.

Recently, the highlight of a summer for several student travelers was their time on the French Riviera where they stayed for $3 a night. The atmosphere from start to finish was as unreal as if they were in a fairy tale. Beach scenery was remarkable, with tan bodies and the world's teeniest bikinis. At their **hostel** in the town of Cap d'Ail, boulevard de la Mer, Tel. 068110, diminutive French ladies served delicious meals for 14 fr. (about $2.80) that included soup, salad, bread, choice of chicken, veal, or beef, fresh vegetables, and French cheeses for dessert. Wine was cheap. This hostel was perched on a cliff a few hundred meters above the beach and is about ten minutes outside of Mer, on the way to Monaco.

### Monaco

Approaching the French border from Italy through Menton, the excellent train seems like a guided tour in itself, as you wind in and out of cliffs and tunnels and view gorgeous beaches and crystal blue waters. If you arrive early in the morning, you may be treated to a special rosy glow that shines on this already naturally favored landscape. Monaco is dazzling. Sleek, elegant women, sleek, elegant cars, lights shining on the marina, fabulous yachts, white mansions, warm breezes, lush vegetation, and sensuous pink flowers. "The place has class, yet it all seems unreal," is how one student described his impressions of Monaco. If you are a car buff, you can see everything from a hot-pink Rolls to a custom one-man opera-coupe Cadillac, all lined up at glittering casinos.

Two students tried to stroll nonchalantly into a casino. They got six feet beyond the door. You can't get in if you are under twenty-one, although you may be able to play the slots in the lobby of the Loew's Hotel Casino. In any case, do tour the **Loew's Hotel**, if only to see the decor. Take the elevator to the roof-top pool for a great view of the yacht harbor.

Besides soaking up the atmosphere of Monaco, don't miss the **Jacques Cousteau Oceanographic Museum and Aquarium**. Entry fee is about 6 fr. Cousteau films run constantly, and intriguing jars of preserved sea creatures are on display. Exhibits include one crablike creature, with legs the size of a man's, and a small yellow submarine.

Walk up to the **Casino** even if you can't get in. Along the way, don't be surprised to see an elephant clomping along or a giraffe munching on a branch. The first time one student realized what he was seeing from a distance, he could scarcely believe his eyes. He did not realize the zoo has this intriguing natural setting, hammered into the side of the Rock of Monaco.

## Nice

Nice is within striking distance of Monaco, and you could stay here while touring both. The train station has a long tourist desk filled with pamphlets and information, and the Syndicat d'Initiative is just outside the station. Nice is more Italian in feeling than other French Riviera resorts; in the **Old City** you will find winding streets, tiny cafés, sidewalk tables, open-air markets, seafood carts, relatively inexpensive food, and a most informal atmosphere. The Old City is inland a few blocks from the hotels that line the harbor. Student travelers like it here, even though the beach is not the best. The **beach at Cap Ferrat**, about ten kilometers (six miles) away, is better.

In Nice a sailing school, water skiing, and skin diving are available at **Service Jeunesse et Sports**, 117 rue de France, 06 Nice, Tel. 375432. The crystal-blue waters of the Mediterranean are excellent for diving and undersea exploration.

_____**Where to Stay**

**Relais International de la Jeunesse**, boulevard de la Mer, Cap d'Ail, is the private hostel mentioned above. Good meals, pleasant attendants. Easy to find through a small tunnel from train station and less than half a mile up the road to the right.

**Cap Ferrat, par Arcachon,** 33970 Gironde, Tel. 606462. A standard hostel with seventy-two beds. Located between Monaco and Nice, almost in Nice.

**Auberge de la Jeunesse**, route Forestière du Mont Alban, Nice, Tel. 892364.

**Cités Universitaires**, 18 avenue des Fleurs, Nice, Tel. 87100.

**Relais International de la Jeunesse**, "Clairvallon," avenue Scudéri, Nice, Tel. 812763.

**Foyer Hotel Sonocotra**, Quartier Chateau à St.-André de Nice, Tel. 548570.

**Foyer Soleil Nice Sant-Roch**, résidence Roquebillière, tour 4, boulevard Pierre-Sèmand, Nice, Tel. 554740.

## Cannes

Cannes has the Riviera's best beach, although it is crowded and has grainy sand. This resort town is sportive rather than opulent in character, with smaller boats instead of fantastic jet-set yachts. From carts near the beach and harbor, you can buy clams and seafood heaped on huge mounds of ice, or you can buy steaming bouillabaisse, a seafood chowder. Prices are not low, but not outrageous either. Interesting shops sell everything from knives to firecrackers. Seasoned student travelers find Cannes an altogether pleasing place, very nice in the evening.

The **Syndicat d'Initiative** at the train station can give you a list of restaurants, cabarets, and beaches, as well as suggest accommodations.

_____**Where to Stay**

**Frejus**, Domaine de Bellevue, route de Cannes, Tel. 402185. Excellent hostel with cooking facilities, just over one kilometer from train station.

**Auber Hotel**, 27 avenue Auber. A few blocks from train station toward the sea. 15 fr., plus 2 for showers.

**Campground, Pont de Siagne**, La Siagne Robinson, par R.N. 559, Tel. 389912. Shaded, near the beach, and offers a good grocery facility and restaurant. 500 campsites.

**Caravaning Bellevue**, avenue Maurice-Chevalier, La Bocca, Tel. 472897. Over 600 sites near the sea, and provides a restaurant, too.

Here are several other places to stay along the Riviera that students recommend.

**Hôtel de Cogolin**, near St. Tropez, 83 Cogolin-Plage, Tel. 438444. Rents a three-person bungalow for $5 a night.

**Relais International de la Jeunesse**, boulevard de la Garoupe, Cap d'Antibes, Tel. 343440.

**Campground at Plateau St.-Michel,** Menton, Tel. 358123. 275 sites in view of the sea.

**Youth hostel, Plateau St.-Michel,** Menton, Tel. 359114, three kilometers from Menton train station. A good hostel with cooking facilities.

## CHAMONIX

On the slopes of Mont Blanc perches Chamonix, one of Europe's popular ski resorts—enchanting in winter and inviting in its summer Alpine garb. There are accommodations in all price ranges and skiing for all ability levels, from snow bunny to hot-dogger.

Several small towns cluster around Chamonix. Les Bossons, Les Pélerins, Les Bois, and Les Praz are all within two and a half miles. The village of Chamonix has small shops, sporting-goods stores, bakeries, and a supermarket or two for picnic-lunch supplies.

Take the cable car, called the *téléphérique*. The **Aiguille du Midi** (expensive at 25 fr. with a hostel coupon) is the highest cable car in the world and goes up 11,526 feet. An alternative is the **téléphérique du Brévant** (with student-ID discount the round trip runs about 21 fr.). Don't try to save money by walking down, as our travelers report this could be extremely treacherous and not worth the risk to save a few francs. Take a warm jacket with you, and don't forget your passport. Believe it or not Italian border guards will check your papers—even at these heights! The views of Swiss, French, and Italian Alps are fantastic. Chamonix, known for its craggy peaks, glacial lakes, and small animals, such as marmots, scurrying around, offers endless hiking possibilities. Also, there is **Mont Blanc** itself, towering at 4807 meters (14,420 feet). Ski runs include the spectacular Aiguille du Midi, a nine-mile trail, beginning at almost 4000 meters. You can buy one ticket for the entire valley and use it on eight cable cars, five gondolas, five chairs, fourteen T bars, one poma lift, and there are 120 instructors to show you the way.

There's a **youth hostel** at Les Pélerins, just a short hike across the river and up a hill from the Les Pélerins station. Hot showers and rooms go for 14 fr. per night.

You might also try the **Refuge des Amis de la Montagne**, route de la Cascade. Tel. 531783. Dormitories cost 15 fr. per night. It's near the Mer de Glace train station.

Or write the **Office du Tourisme**, place de l'Eglise, Chamonix, Tel. 530024, and ask for a list of accommodations in your price range.

The valley also has several cinemas, cabarets, a casino, a Centre Nautique, with swimming and sauna, several tennis halls, and omnisports halls, where you can try basketball, tennis, handball, dance, and judo.

## CHARTRES

One of the most visited towns in France—and for good reasons— Chartres offers a **cathedral** that is a noble masterpiece of Europe. It is thought to be one of humanity's crowning architectural glories, and the spires of this Gothic and Romanesque blending are visible from ten miles away. The cathedral's stained-glass windows tell complex biblical stories in colors that are near miracles and are unequalled today. The lacelike details of the choir screen, with its magnificent design, are noteworthy.

Henry IV became a Catholic and was crowned king here, the only coronation ceremony ever held in this cathedral.

In the **Vieux Quartier** of the village you can walk among the old houses now restored in medieval style. In summer the **Syndicat d'Initiative** near the cathedral can inform you about what's happening in Chartres, from music fests to art exhibits.

**Auberge de Jeunesse** is located at 23 avenue Neigre, Tel. 212764.

## STRASBOURG

Strasbourg weaves an unusual spell, combining a medieval appearance with urban activity and village charm. Old timbered *Fachwerk* houses and arched bridges across the Ill river, along with the beautiful cathedral and other churches, will add to your pleasure

*Strasbourg Cathedral*

here. Though close to Germany, Strasbourg is very French and rightly proud of its regional cuisine, especially the *pâté de fois gras* (goose-liver pâté) and special quiches.

The **Syndicat d'Initiative** at place de la Gare, Tel. 325149, can find you a room for a few francs fee, or try **Auberge de Jeunesse**, 9 rue de l'Auberge de Jeunesse, Tel. 302646. Take bus 3, 13, or 23 from city center for the two-kilometer trip.

Strasbourg hosts an international **music festival** in June and also tends to be crowded at Easter time, when swarms of Germans drive over the border to try the Michelin-starred restaurants in the area and sample French wines.

# 12  FOCUS ON WEST GERMANY

Population: over 17,000,000      Language: German
Capital: Bonn                   Currency: deutsch mark (DM)

## THE LAND AND THE PEOPLE

The German word *Wirtschaftswunder* (economic wonder), which is used all over the world, aptly describes Germany today. There is, though, a growing malaise in this highly industrial, hard-working country, whose currency is one of the strongest in the world. Young people chafe at government-imposed restrictions like the loyalty oath you must take before you can be a Government employee. Yet the youth of Germany are an extremely privileged lot. Few have part-time jobs during their school years, even in summer, unless they are not college-bound. Students have been segregated at the age of ten into those who will train for college and those who will work at trades. The two groups are educated differently, with the privileged ones attending *Gymnasium*, which is somewhat like our high school, until they complete thirteen years of education. Afterward, they take a final series of examinations, the *Abitur,* which may well determine their career. Once admitted to university, young people can make a career out of being a student. Parents are obliged by law to continue support for a student until he or she is thirty-two years old.

Land use in Germany is carefully controlled, as is most everything. The townspeople huddle together in tight quarters, and farmlands are also regulated as to what may be used for nonagricultural purposes and what is needed to grow food for the population. Germans have carefully preserved their prized forests, which they love. In Germany you are never far from a *Wald,* complete with mapped-out walking and cycling routes. In fact, you may find a traffic jam in the forest on a Sunday afternoon—foot traffic, that is! Germans are determined walkers and physical-fitness addicts. If you don't carry a tennis racket or wear a jogging suit, you are not in style in Germany today.

Germans love their coffee and *Kuchen* (cake) and their sweet wines. In late afternoon, you will see matrons downing two five-inch-high pastries covered with whipped cream in the many sidewalk cafés.

Though very private people, Germans are often extremely hospitable and kind to visitors. They will go to great lengths to explain their customs, special holiday events, and their traditions to you. They are very culture-exchange minded, with pen friendships begun

134

in childhood and likely to last into old age. A formal people and much bound in tradition, Germans prize their old cities and buildings and cherish history, except for the Nazi interlude, which is generally avoided as a topic of discussion. They are affluent and aware of their economic capability and influence in the world. Men and women like to be well-dressed, and handsome, tall women are especially fashionable.

You will find a wide variety of things to enjoy in Germany, from pleasant farms to bustling modern cities, Bavarian villages with *Lederhosen*-clad children, mountains to climb, rivers to cross, castles to explore, and great symphonies to hear. You will rarely have a poor meal in a German restaurant. Tables are well-set with linens and flowers, even in small guesthouses. Hotels and pensions are scrubbed and shining, complete with smothering down quilts and enormous pillows. It could be called a tourist's paradise except for one small drawback: Germany is expensive.

## TRANSPORTATION

Germany has an excellent train system, state-owned and operated. Trains are efficient, frequent, and you can use InterRail or Eurailpass. Large cities have the U-Bahn (Untergrundbahn), a city-operated subway system that takes the same tickets as city buses. The S-Bahn (Schnellbahn), the high-speed railway, is run by the Bundesbahn (federal railroad system), and you can use your pass. The U-Bahn runs almost entirely on an honor system. You buy your ticket at an automat and then punch it when you enter the car. City transit systems are efficient and fast. In the automats you will see many types of tickets, including those for students. Buy the five-ride student ticket (for about 2.50 DM), since it is cheaper than buying singles. If you are caught not punching your ticket, you will be fined 10 DM to 20 DM ($5-$10). Inspectors hop on and off cars intermittently, and although you may get by one time by pleading you don't understand the system, don't count on it. On all U-Bahns you must have a ticket, *Fahrkarte,* before you enter, but on some buses you can buy a ticket from the driver. You may transfer from one bus to another without buying a new ticket, provided it is within the same travel zone. Zone maps are shown on the automats.

German trains generally stop for one minute at each station *(Bahnhof)*. Know ahead of time when yours is coming, and hoist your luggage out in the aisle or on the platform near a door. The same goes for boarding the train from station platforms. Be ready and alert. There's usually a conductor or official on the platform to make certain passengers have boarded before he waves the train on, but don't expect the train to delay if you are not on board.

Arrivals are always given in the local time of the destination. For example, last summer two boys expected to arrive in Venice at 0800 German time. They paid no attention to the time change between borders, and they slept through their stop! Find out what the local time will be at your destination. If you have paid for a sleeper, or *Schlafwagen,* the conductor will alert you at least twenty minutes before you arrive.

Meals on German trains are quite expensive, although you can buy food from carts that come through the cars. Even from the cart, however, it's not cheap. Coke, orange juice, chocolate, or coffee cost 2.50 DM, more than $1. Your best bet is to buy a two-liter plastic bottle of *Apfelsaft* (apple juice), or any other beverage, and bring it along. You can buy a one-liter size in most grocery stores for 1 DM, but the two-liter size is best for a long trip.

Buy bread and meats and any other food items in a grocery store. The chain stores Hertie and Kaufhof are department stores that have supermarkets on the ground floor. They have wide varieties and reasonable prices. A popular neighborhood chain store is Edeka Market, but nearly all of them close at noon and reopen at 2:30 PM.

The *Bundesbahn* has over 200 stations all over the country, where you can pick up a bicycle for 4 DM to 8 DM if you have a train ticket. You can then ride to the next bicycle station. Get a map at main stations showing bicycle routes and pick-up and drop-off points.

## FOOD

Think of Germany, and *Würste,* or sausages, in every shape and flavor, from *Bratwurst* to *Weisswurst,* come to mind. *Schwein Kotelette,* sauerkraut, and chewy dark breads are some of the bountiful foods served here. Serving sizes are phenomenal. You will never leave a German table hungry. Food is sometimes heavy, with potatoes, dumplings, and *spaetzle,* a gnarly, poached noodle, in gargantuan portions.

*Spargel,* white asparagus, is a springtime delicacy, and restaurants proudly advertise the advent of a new crop.

Beer and wine are cheaper than coffee and soft drinks. Cokes cost about $1. Drinking water is not available on the streets or in public places. White wines are a speciality and may be ordered until 10 PM in restaurants by anyone over fourteen.

Food is nicely served on pretty dinnerware, for the Germans love their porcelain and glassware. Glasses are carefully marked, such as .21 liter, so you are served the exact portion for which you pay. The procedure is meticulous, like so many things German.

Other culinary specialties are game, from venison to pheasant, which are delicious with a berry sauce. Trout from Alpine lakes and smoked salmon are other delicacies.

Menus in the average restaurant have a decidedly similar content: veal, pork, rumpsteak (well-done beef, cooked with onions like a pot roast), chicken, and ham (either *gekocht* or *geräucherte,* boiled or smoked). There are no finger foods in Germany. Sandwiches are served open faced with meat atop heavily buttered rye bread and are fork-and-knife affairs. Pizza is also served plate size and is not to be eaten with fingers.

German soups are excellent, particularly the *Gulaschsuppe,* which is hearty, well-seasoned, and inexpensive. Note: *Gulasch* and *Gulaschsuppe* are two different foods. *Gulasch* is beef chunks prepared in thick paprika gravy, served over noodles. *Gulaschsuppe* is a thick soup, very filling and cheap. Large portions for under $1, served with a slice of bread. *Gulasch* is a main dish, an entree, and costs about $4. Nearly all German soups have the word *suppe* attached as part of the description. Examples: *Zwiebelsuppe* (onion), *Tomatensuppe, Bohnensuppe* (bean), etc.

Meal hours are rigid. Breakfast is the usual continental fare of rolls and a beverage. The main meal is at noon and is served until 2 PM. Between 2 PM and 4 PM some restaurants lower the shades, and you won't even know they exist. Around 4 PM you can order *Kuchen,* cakes and pastries, coffee or wine, but no food until 7 PM. A typical fixed-price menu for the main meal would include soup, salad, meat, and potatoes. Wine, coffee, or any other beverage is extra. The evening meal, *Abendessen,* is simple, with sliced cold meats, cheese, and potato salad. Note: Any baskets of rolls or bread on the table are not considered part of the meal cost. You will be charged .50 DM, about thirty cents, for each one you munch.

Tax *(Mehrwertsteuer)* and service *(Bedienung)* are included in your total bill *(Rechnung)* as part of the listed price of the food. Hotels and inns serve simpler meals than restaurants and are less expensive. A *Weinstube,* tavern, serves mainly wines, soups, sausages, and cheese with bread. Be prepared to spend a while at a German meal, for there is no such thing as quick service at a sit-down restaurant. It takes forever to get your check, and many restaurants have magazines and newspapers for patrons to read. They assume you intend to stay awhile. Your only hope for a quick meal is the *Schnell Imbiss,* a refreshment counter along the streets where you can buy wurst popped into a large roll.

When you enter a restaurant, don't sit at the *Stammtisch,* which is a table reserved for regular customers. You should also know that it is common to share a table in most of Europe, and if there are no empty tables, other customers will automatically sit at yours if there are empty chairs. Do the same. You may ask, *"Ist dieser Platz frei?"* ("Is this place vacant?")

Since Cokes are expensive, and water is unheard of except for *Mineralwasser* (carbonated, and not cheap either), we suggest that you buy a liter of beverage in the grocery store. Young travelers recommend buying picnic-lunch needs and your daily liter of beverage, or taking along a large plastic canteen to fill in the hostel. Buy what you need early in the day, since grocery stores close for the noon break. German women normally buy their cold cuts daily in amounts as low as 100 grams. So don't be embarrassed to buy only a few slices of meat or cheese. Remember neither rolls nor meats keep well. In the marketplace you will find beautiful fresh fruits. They are not cheap, and you must not touch, or you'll find a sturdy *Frau* slapping your hand. But tell her (you can point to them) which apples or peaches you want, or you may get a bruised one from the back of the pile.

## SHOP HOURS

Department stores stay open daily from 8:30 AM or 9 AM until 6 PM, while smaller shops close at noon until 2:30 PM or 3 PM. On the first Saturday of the month shops are open all day, until 6 PM, but on other Saturdays they close at 2 PM.

Banks: 8:30 AM to 12:30 PM, 2 PM to 4 PM, Monday through Friday.

## SHOPPING

Clothing is expensive in Germany, so save your dollars for another place unless you want specialty items, such as *Lederhosen,* hiking boots in Bavaria, or loden coats and capes (waterproof, sturdy, usually forest green or bright red). German stainless steel is well known; the Solingen knives are made in the town of the same name. The beautifully intricate, carved-wood Christmas ornaments are delightful, but also expensive. You can spend $20 and still have only a few, perhaps six or seven miniature cuckoo clocks, tiny doll cradles, and little chimney sweeps. (They really do knock at your door, by the way, all dressed in black complete with top hat, to sweep your chimney. The custom is an anachronism required as part of your lease.)

German stores hold sales in July and February, when clothing is marked down drastically, sometimes at a 50-percent savings. These sales are a good time to buy ski and hiking wear.

German cities are concentrated, very clean, geared for walkers and park-bench sitters, and are conscious of their past. You should try to see Berlin and also Munich, each with a different appeal, and perhaps the Bonn-Cologne-Rhineland region if time allows. From Munich you can explore Bavaria, Garmisch, and Germany's highest peak, the Zugspitze, or travel into the countryside to see some of mad King Ludwig's fantasies transformed to stone—Schloss Herrenschiemsee, near Prien, and Schloss Neuschwanstein, close to Füssen. From Bonn you might attend a wine fest, take a river cruise along the Rhine or Mosel, or a bicycle trip down the Rhine through Remagen to Koblenz.

Germany has cool weather year round with much rain and only occasional hot, sticky summers. When it is clear, the climate can be very pleasant for touring.

Germans observe many holidays, both Catholic and national. There are always two days for both Christmas and Easter, plus many, many holidays in May and June. Schools are in session until mid-July (early July in some northern cities now). At vacation time the *Autobahns* and train stations are jammed, as they are at Easter and Christmas when school children have three weeks holiday. From mid-July through August many restaurants close up, or have a "holiday menu" with only a few choices. In summer many German families take a four-week vacation to the North Sea, to Spain, to Africa—or to the *Kur,* cure resort, for the rejuvenating hot baths and daily walks.

The tourist office is called the **Verkehrsamt** or **Verkehrsverein,** and it is often located in or near the train station. It can provide you with maps and brochures listing tourist attractions in the area, local shops hours, and so on. Hotels are the highest-priced accommodations; pensions and *Gasthäuser* are next. *Fremdenzimmer,* or *Zimmer Frei,* spare rooms for rent in a private home, are usually the cheapest lodgings. Breakfast is included in the room price. There are many German hostels, and most are well kept. Hotel prices vary from city to village, but expect to pay about $7 per person in the lowest range of hotel, about $16 per person in a better place. Hostels cost $2 with hostel card and student ID.

## BERLIN

- **United States Consulate,** Clayallee 170, Tel. 819745.
- **American Express,** Kurfürstendamm 11, Tel. 8814333.
- **Post office,** Main, or Hauptpostamt, Möckernstrasse 138.
- **Visitors' bureau,** Fasanenstrasse 7-8, Tel. 240111.
- **Police,** Tempelhofer Damm 1, Tel. 6991.

Whoever thinks of Berlin without thinking of the Wall? Whatever else you may see in West Berlin, it will never etch itself into your memory in quite the same way as the utterly grim symbol of the Cold War seen here. The trip into East Berlin is well worth the time, and you should go with a group. Bus tours leave twice a day from Kurfürstendamm and Uhlandstrasse or Meinekestrasse and Kurfürstendamm. They cost 17 DM plus 6 DM extra for the Pergamon Museum. Any foreign citizen with a valid passport may enter East Berlin with a tour. You must see the Wall to believe it.

Most visitors come to Berlin by train, and there are connections from major German cities. Get off at the main station in the West section, the Bahnhof Zoo (Zoological Garden). Rail passes are not valid in the East sector, and the next stop would put you into East Berlin. There are also student flights into Berlin and bus service from the airport into town.

**Jugendherberge Ernst Reuter,** Hermsdorfer Damm 48-50, Tel. 4041610. Take U-Bahn to Leopoldplatz, switch to U-Bahn line 6 to Tegel, then bus 15 toward Frohrau. 8.50 DM with breakfast.

**Jugendherberge,** Bayernalle 36, Tel. 3053055. A short distance from the Neu Westend station. 8.50 DM including breakfast.

**Jugendgästehaus,** Kluckstrasse 3, Tel. 2611097. Bus 24, 29, or 48 to the Tiergarten district, where the Philharmonic and many diplomatic residences are located. 11 DM.

If hostels are full, go directly to the **tourist bureau** at Hardenbergstrasse, Tel. 310171, where you can get a list of student hotels and pensions. These accommodations cost from 5 DM per night; some require a minimum stay of three nights. The tourist bureau will also find you a room at a low-cost pension if you have no reservation. They charge 1 DM for the service, and you could easily spend that amount on phone calls or bus fares on your own, so it's worth going there right off. Hotels and pensions are often filled, so write in advance if possible. The tourist bureau will also make reservations for groups. Pensions in Berlin cost from 14 DM, but very few are priced in that range. Most cost 20 to 25 DM, or about $8 to $10 per

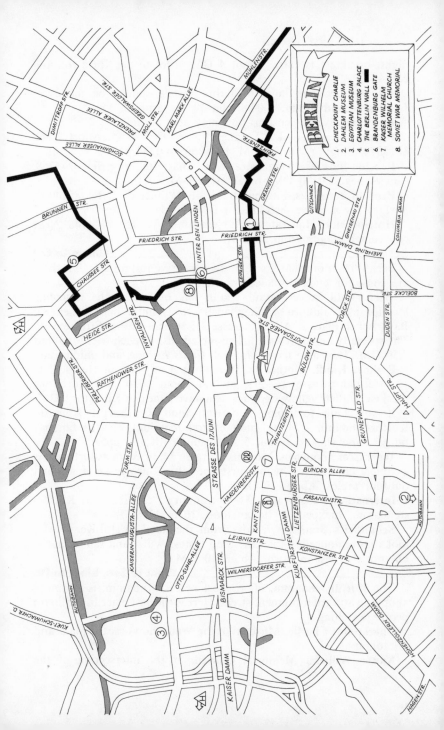

night; breakfast is extra, about 4 DM, a lot to pay for a roll and coffee.

All advance bookings to Berlin hostels should be made to: **Landesverband Berlin,** 1000 Berlin 19, Bayernallee 35.

Here are several pensions you may also consider:

**Pension Fasaneneck,** Fasanenstrasse 61, Wilmersdorf, Tel. 8815874. Single room 20 DM, breakfast 4 DM.

**Pension Sina,** Giesebrechstrasse 20, Charlottenburg, Tel. 3244768. Singles begin at 20 DM, breakfast 4 DM.

**Pension Terminus,** Fasanenstrasse 48, Wilmersdorf, Tel. 8814909. 30 DM for a single, breakfast 4 DM.

**Hotelpension Hanseat,** Kurfürstendamm 35, Tel. 8814746. Near city center, singles from 18 DM.

_____ **Where to Eat**

Berlin has more than its share of expensive restaurants, but there are some for budget-minded travelers too.

**Wienerwald,** a restaurant chain, has outlets at the following locations: Schildhorn 4; Stephanstrasse 1; unter den Eichen 85; Bayerischer Platz 2; Akazienstrasse 31; Martin-Luther Strasse 6-10. The specialty here is roast chicken served with French fries for about 7.50 DM. They also serve schnitzel, *Gulaschsuppe,* and onion soup.

**Berliner Kindl,** another chain, is located at Theodor Heuss Platz 12, Hermannstrasse 217-219, and at about eight other locations marked by their yellow sign. You can have a meal at Kindl for 8 DM.

If you long for some American food, try **Burger King** on Kurfürstendamm 224, (a good central location) with its familiar burgers and shakes. About 5 DM should fill you up.

**Tegernseer Tonnchen,** Mommsenstrasse 34, in Wilmersdorf area, is a touch of Bavaria, with wurst specialties, hearty servings, and outdoor tables. About 10 DM.

**International Ristorante,** 51 Lietzenburger Strasse, near Kurfürstendamm. Inexpensive Italian food, 10 to 12 DM.

**Schultheiss Brauhaus,** across from the hotel Bristol-Kempinski, looks more appealing than the food tastes. Wurst and sauerkraut— but not the best in town. About 10 DM.

_____ **What to See, What to Do**

The **Kurfürstendamm,** often shortened to Kudamm, is a famous shopping and entertainment street. Here is the best place in Berlin for people watching.

**Checkpoint Charlie, Museum of the Wall,** shows escape plans and photographs.

**Kaiser Wilhelm Memorial Church,** at the intersection of the

Kudamm and Tantzienstrasse, is the gutted remains of the original edifice, built in 1891-95, around which an impressive new polygonal church has been built. Free concerts are held, and the schedule is posted on the board outside.

The **Berlin Zoo** is Europe's largest, with 3000 mammals and 8000 reptiles. Adjoining the Zoo is the **Aquarium,** which houses the world's most comprehensive collection of fish. A combined aquarium-and-zoo ticket costs 2.50 DM with your student ID.

The **Strasse des 17 Juni** commemorates the date of a rebellion in East Berlin in 1953, and this street leads to the **Brandenburg Gate,** Berlin's most famous landmark. Formerly the gateway to city center, since 1961 the gate has stood just behind the Wall in the Soviet sector.

The **Soviet War Memorial,** guarded by Soviet sentries armed with submachine guns, is quite close to the Brandenburg Gate. Berliners call this memorial "The Last Plunderer." It honors the Russian Army's entry into Berlin at the end of World War II. Near the Wall there are observation platforms where you can climb up and watch people on the other side watching you.

Lest you think Berlin is all grimness and war memories, there are also many lovely palaces, concert halls, and museums.

The **Egyptian Museum,** Schloss-strasse 70, is the place to see the over 3000-year-old bust of Queen Nefertiti and one of the most important collections of ancient Egyptian art treasures in the world. Some artifacts date from 5000 B.C. Free entry. Closed Friday.

Across the street from the Egyptian Museum, the **Antiquarium,** or antique department of the Berlin Museum, has jewelry from 2000 B.C. to the sixth century A.D. and vases and other artifacts from the Homeric era through the Roman period. Also free.

**Charlottenburg Palace,** at Luisenplatz, is in the same neighborhood as the above two museums. It has the largest seventeenth-century rococo room in the world. It was built in 1695 by Frederick Wilhelm I as the summer residence for the electress and later first queen of Prussia, Sophie Charlotte.

**Schöneberg City Hall** is Berlin's city government seat, and here the Liberty Bell, a copy of the Philadelphia bell and a gift from the American people, sounds daily from the tower at noon, for three minutes.

Facing the John-Foster-Dulles-Allee, **Congress Hall** was the American contribution to the International Architectural Exhibition in 1957 and is now a convention center.

The **Dahlem Museum,** at Arnimallee 23-27, was the only West Berlin museum left undamaged by World War II. In addition to a

fabulous collection of prints, paintings, drawings, and sculpture by European masters, it houses rare illustrated books and medieval manuscripts. If you like Rembrandt, he is represented by more than twenty works. You can spend a few hours or a lifetime here. Free admission.

From theater to concerts, Berlin's cultural life is extensive, but reserve well in advance for these events. During July and August, there are fewer activities, so check with *Berlin Programm* for details. There are student discounts for most concerts. Contact the **Theater-kasse** (student-ticket office) at the Technical University on Harden-bergstrasse and Ernst-Reuter-Platz. The **Deutsche Oper,** Berlin's great opera house, is only a short walk away on Bismarckstrasse.

Berlin has an astounding number of parks, lakes, and beaches. **Grunewald** (green forest) is a large woodland with three nature preserves and a string of blue lakes. By the **Grunewaldsee,** one of the lakes, is a centuries-old hunting lodge that is now an art museum. In summer, concerts are held in the courtyard. If you haven't brought picnic supplies, you can stop at one of several restaurants in the wood. **Wannsee,** a bay of the **Havel River** on the western border of the Grunewald, is Europe's largest bathing beach and a good spot to cool off in midsummer—usually wall-to-wall bodies, but good people watching nonetheless.

## MUNICH

_____ **Important Addresses**

- **United States Consulate,** Königstrasse 5, Tel. 23011.
- **American Express,** Promenadeplatz 3, Tel. 228166, open 9 AM to 6 PM daily, Saturday, 9 AM to noon.
- **Police headquarters,** Ettstrasse 2, Tel. 2141; emergencies, Tel. 110.
- **Post office,** Bahnhofplatz 1, near the main train station.
- **Tourist bureau,** at the main train station, Tel. 2391256, open daily 8 AM to 11 PM.
- **Youth Information Center,** Paul-Heyse-Strasse, Tel. 531655, open daily 11 AM to 7 PM.

_____ **Where to Stay**

The tourist bureau in the main train station may be your best source for finding a room if you arrive without reservations. Expect to pay a minimum of 12 DM per night for a *Zimmer Frei* in Munich. There's also an information center at the Arrival Hall of the airport, which is open Monday through Saturday, 8:30 AM to 10:30 PM.

Here are a few inexpensive student accommodations:

**Newman-Haus,** Kaulbachstrasse 29, Tel. 1414300, has inexpensive single and double rooms. Breakfast is extra.

**Jugendherberge,** Wendl-Dietrichstrasse 20, Tel. 131156. Take Tram 21 to Rotkreuz Platz to this large hostel with 585 beds. 4.50 DM per night.

**Jugendherberge,** Burg Schwaneck, out in Pullach, Tel. 7932381. Take S-Bahn line 10 toward Wolfratshausen to Pullach. This old castle makes for an interesting hostel. 145 beds, 4 DM.

**Jugendgästehaus,** Miesingstrasse 4, Tel. 7236560. Large and some distance out of town. Take tram 8 or 29 to Boschetsriederstrasse or S-Bahn 10 or 22. 10 DM per bed.

**Haus International,** 40 Elisabethstrasse 87, Tel. 185081. Take tram 7 and get off at the stop Hohenzollernstrasse.

**Campground: München-Thalkirchen,** Tel. 7231707, is two and a half miles from city center, along the Isar River. Take the tram to Hellabrunn Zoo. A well-equipped campground, it is open 1 March through 31 October, costs 2.75 DM per night. You can rent a tent for 2 DM.

_____**Where to Eat**

There are at least ten **Wienerwalds** scattered around the city, where you can enjoy roast chicken for 8 DM. But be careful of the basket of goodies on the table. You pay for whatever you eat, and the sausage sticks, _Brötchen,_ and crackers will tempt you.

**Der Weinstandtl,** Burgstrasse 5, is the oldest city tavern in Munich, about five centuries old. It has a main floor plus a cellar and good food at modest prices (12 DM for steak).

**Gastätte Weinbauer,** Fend-Strasse 5, is in the Schwabing district where things are pretty lively all night long. Good low-priced food— less than 10 DM.

**McDonald's,** of American fame, grills burgers at Martin-Luther-Strasse 26, at prices only slightly higher than Stateside ones.

**Gastätte Leopold,** Leopoldstrasse 50, also in Schwabing, features dinners of typically German proportions for about 12 DM.

**The Hofbrauhaus,** at Platzl 9, is right near the famous Glockenspiel. It is the most famous Munich beer hall, where suds and tourists bubble in equal amounts. But it's popular with students too.

**Bei Milan,** Weingasse 7, is also near the Glockenspiel. Go for Balkan specialties; it's very fine, a bit high in price, costs about 15 to 20 DM for dinner.

Check the menus posted outside most restaurants, and if the food appeals and the price is right, don't bother to wander all over town

for some specific spot. There is simply not that much variation in quality in the average German restaurant.

_____ **What to See, What to Do**

With a tour starting at the main station, you can enjoy the heart of Munich in a few hours. From here go straight to Karlsplatz, locally called Stachus. Go through the old city gate, or **Karlstor,** into the pedestrian zone, Neuhauserstrasse and Kaufingerstrasse. On the left is the **Burgersaal Chapel,** and 200 meters farther on is the Renaissance facade of **Michaelskirche.** Beside it is the **Richard Strauss fountain.** The twentieth-century composer of *Der Rosenkavalier* and many other operatic and symphonic works is one of Munich's favorite sons. Continue on to **Frauenkirche** (Church of Our Lady), a massive Gothic cathedral built in 1488, until you arrive at the historical heart of the city, **Marienplatz.**

**Peterskirche,** the city's oldest church, of baroque architecture, the **Altes Rathaus,** and the **Neues Rathaus** (old and new city halls) are found here. The new *Rathaus* has a famous **Glockenspiel,** where each day at 11 AM and at 5 PM, enameled figures play the carillon.

There's lots of street life here at Marienplatz—outdoor tables, cafés, flower vendors—and it is a delightful place to spend a Saturday afternoon.

From here you can continue to the left of the Altes Rathaus on Burgstrasse, and you will run into **Alter Hof,** the earliest royal residence. Then go on to Max-Joseph Platz. The **National Theater,** the **Bavarian Opera,** and the **Residenzmuseum** at Max-Joseph Platz 3 are here. The treasure room of the palace is open from 10 AM to 4:30 PM daily, 10 AM to 1 PM Sunday. Students pay an entry fee of 50 pfennigs. Here you can see glittering masterpieces by lapidarists and jewelers from the Middle Ages on. The Residenzmuseum, a collection of opulently furnished rooms, which are replicas of the kinds of chambers where Bavarian dukes and electors slept, is open 9 AM to 12:30 PM, 1:30 PM to 4:30 PM.

The **Alte Pinakothek,** at Barerstrasse 27, has a vast collection of old masters, from Rubens to Dürer. It's open 9 AM to 4:30 PM, Tuesday and Thursday evenings 7 PM to 9 PM. Student entry fee is 1.50 DM, free on Sunday.

**Haus der Kunst,** Prinzregentenstrasse 1, picks up where the Alte Pinakothek leaves off, with important works by Monet, Cézanne, and Van Gogh, including one of Van Gogh's famous "Sunflowers" paintings. Hours are from 9 AM to 4:30 PM, also Tuesday and Thursday evenings 7 PM to 9 PM, closed Monday. Free on Sunday, 1 DM admission other days.

**Deutches Museum,** near Ludwigsbrücke, an island in the Isar, is an outstanding technological museum with enough fascination to hold you all day. One jaded student traveler who thought he had seen them all rated this museum, "fantastic, the best I've ever seen. Plan to stay awhile." This museum demonstrates the idea that most learning can be accomplished through actually doing rather than just reading about what might seem farfetched. "You can tinker with all kinds of things, planetary gears, grandfather clocks, and walk through models of coal mines. I hated to leave at five," he said.

**Nymphenburg Palace** is a minor Versailles, the country place of Bavarian rulers, far out in the northwest part of the city. Ludwig I planned a Gallery of Beauties, with portraits of twenty-four ladies who took the king's eye, including the notorious Lola Montez. There are beautiful grounds and concerts in summer. Hours 9 AM to 6 PM, 2 DM entry.

**Olympic Park,** site of the 1972 Olympics, has fine sporting facilities, and you can swim in one of the pools for 3 DM. Take the U-Bahn 3 to Olympiazentrum. Entry to the stadium is .50 DM. Tennis courts are also available.

**Schwabing,** the student and artist area, about nineteen blocks north of the main train station, has ample night life, and you can find plenty of beer halls, singing, conversation, discos, and places for hanging out by going to this section. Take the U-Bahn to Biselastrasse or to Münchener Freiheit.

_____**Side Trips**

**Dachau,** about ten miles northwest, is the infamous German concentration camp, where more than 206,000 prisoners suffered between 1933 and 1945, and at least 32,000 people were murdered. This grim reminder of a reign of terror is open daily, including the museum and chapel, from 9 AM to 5 PM. Take the S-Bahn line 2, then transfer to a bus at Petershausen station.

**Garmisch-Partenkirchen,** high in the Bavarian Alps south of Munich, offers a winter paradise on the Zugspitze, as well as beautiful scenery year round. Good hiking and a sensational cable-car trip.

**Berchtesgaden,** where the salt mines and Hitler's Eagle's Nest retreat are the main tourist attractions, also sits in the midst of Alpine splendor. You can ride the cable railway to the summit of the 4500-foot-high Jenner, hike along the 175 miles of mountain trails in the region, or tour the **Salzbergwerk,** the salt mines that were the source of Berchtesgaden's wealth when it was an independent principality. To protect yourself from the chilly temperatures and dampness on this underground trip, you don a white coverall and hood. The tour includes gliding across a subterranean lake in a rowboat.

**Neuschwanstein,** the fairy-tale castle perched on a mountain peak, is a creation of mad King Ludwig II of Bavaria and must be seen to be believed. Disneyland's castle was patterned after this monument designed by an incurably insane builder. A fantastic setting for a summer Wagner concert, Neuschwanstein is accessible by train to Füssen.

**Linderhof,** a tiny, romantic, and elegant palace with exquisite gardens and grottos, another of King Ludwig's creations, is near Oberammergau and Garmisch, accessible by bus from either town.

Leaving Munich, head north through some of the towns on the road to Nuremburg, stopping off in villages where the winds of time have left scant impression. Here too you'll find towns such as **Rothenburg,** where tourism touches everyone. Rothenburg, with its timbered *Fachwerk* houses, is medieval yet very active, and it is on the **Romantic Road,** a touristic route.

## BONN AND BAD GODESBERG

These two cities in another region of Germany are definitely worth a brief stopover. While nearly everything in this area is expensive, the hostels are modest, and some good inexpensive restaurants make it possible to enjoy this region on a budget.

**Bonn,** the West German capital, is a thriving city on the banks of the Rhine. There is a **university, Münster Platz, Beethoven House, Kunstmuseum, Rathaus** (city hall) in pink and gold rococco, and many forests and parks. It is an ideal base for exploring the Rhineland, either by train or bicycle.

**Bad Godesberg,** at Bonn's door, is where most government buildings and foreign embassies are found. There's a large American community, including the American Embassy Club, the Bonn American School on the Rhine, an American theater, commissary and PX, all located on Martin-Luther-King-Strasse in the vicinity of Kennedy Allee.

_____**Where to Stay**

Youth hostels are located at:

**Haager Weg 42,** Bonn, Tel. 281200, in the Venusberg section of Bonn. This one is adjacent to a forest with many footpaths and bike trails. You can easily walk into town from here. Take bus 20 or 21 from the bus station next to the train station. 285 beds with breakfast go for 7 DM per night.

**Horionstrasse 60,** Bonn, Tel. 363991. Take bus 15 and ask the driver to let you off near the Jugendherberge. It's high on a hill, near fine residential districts. 4 DM a night, 100 beds, meals available, helpful hostel staff.

## Where to Eat

**La Crêperie,** in the shadow of Bonn's rococco Rathaus, is a popular watch-the-world-go-by spot for local people. Not really cheap, good large crêpes go for about 6 to 8 DM. Outdoor service and indoor tables.

**Alten Post,** in Bad Godesberg, has good family meals and is popular with residents. The specialty is *Schlammerschnitzel,* rye bread topped with ham, scrambled egg, and pork filet, for 6.50 DM, and salads.

**Im Bären,** Acherstrasse in Bonn, is in a walking area popular with students. House specialties cost 10 DM or less.

**Sebastianusklaus,** on Sebastiansweg, Bad Godesberg, is a short walk down the hill from the Horionstrasse hostel. They serve excellent pepper steak for 10 DM, which is the most expensive thing on the menu, also *Gulaschsuppe* for 2.50 DM. Other meals are about 8 DM. Well-kept, flowers on the table, popular neighborhood

*a sidewalk café in Bonn*

restaurant. Lunch, noon to 2 PM, dinner, 6 PM to 10 PM. Closed Monday.

**Das Bild,** a popular disco on Hohestrasse in Bad Godesberg, draws American students as well as Germans. Loud and lively.

All along the Rhine and Mosel in late summer you will find **wine festivals** where you can taste the new wines, mingle with the crowds, buy wurst and *Brötchen,* sing and dance, or hear a jazz or rock concert while the illumination of the Rhine castles takes place. These fests begin in August and have nightly lightings of famous castles— the Lorelei and dozens of others—that punctuate the Rhineland.

# 13  FOCUS ON GREECE

Population: 8,795,000
Capital: Athens

Language: Greek
Currency: drachma (dr.)

## THE LAND AND THE PEOPLE

A Greek tour guide remarked that his ancestors defined their heritage by saying, "Everyone who is not Greek is a barbarian." A visit to Athens and the monuments of classical Greece may help you understand the source of this age-old pride. In the splendor of ancient Greece, philosophers, poets, and writers had leisure to reflect and to question ideas that would later influence Western civilization.

Greece has far more than the ruins of Athens and Delphi to entice travelers to come and stay awhile, however. Southern Greece boasts 300 sunny days a year, golden beaches, Zorba-the-Greek-type islands, where time is gauged by different standards. Pink-and-white houses hug rocky shores, windmills reminiscent of Don Quixote abound, a surprising sophistication exists in some resorts and shops, and the cultural life rivals that of Europe's great cities. And there's a bonus: Greece is cheap.

Hotel and meal prices are comparatively low. It's easy to find an interesting *taverna* where you can spend the evening for $3, including dinner. Greece is not a wealthy country. About 40 percent of the people raise olives, figs, tobacco, and livestock. Woven textiles, fluffy wool rugs, and goat's-milk cheese are vital to the economy. Tourism is another important industry.

## TRANSPORTATION

Direct air flights to Athens are your best bet, and there are many student flights from cities all over Europe. Traveling to Greece by train is time consuming and not efficient. You can also take the ferry overnight from Brindisi, Italy to Pátrai, Greece, for $34 one way ($51 round trip), then a four-hour bus trip into Athens. The ferry leaves at 3 PM and arrives at 8:30 AM. One-way air fare from Rome to Athens is about $55.

## FOOD

A few Greek specialties you should try are: *dolmades,* stuffed vine leaves filled with seasoned chopped meat, served hot with egg-and-lemon sauce, rice, and onions; *moussaka,* a meat-and-eggplant combination, layered and topped with a white cheese; and *souvlaki*, a kind of shishkebab, sold in restaurants and along the streets. It costs about thirty cents for a small skewer on the street, and three would do nicely for lunch. Try *kalamaraki*, hot fried squid that tastes like chicken, or marinated octopus, a popular first course. A superb casserole is *yuvetsi*, lamb with noodles. *Pastitsio*, layers of meat and macaroni with cheese sauces, is a Greek triumph. Tiny meatballs served with lemon sauce, *yovarlakia*, are also excellent. Fried cheese pies, *tyropitta*, are also recommended. *Barbouni*, something like mullet, is a regional fish that's very tasty. Roast lamb, *arni*, stuffed with feta cheese, will pull you in off the street with its pungent aroma.

Skip the beef in Greece; stay instead with lamb and chicken or fish, large fresh salads, and fruit. Salads consist of tomatoes, cucumber, and feta cheese, seasoned with olive oil and oregano.

*Baklava* is a flaky honey strudel, filled with ground nuts. A similar pastry is *kataifi*, made of ground nuts, cinnamon, and thin threads of dough.

Coffee is Turkish style, super strong and syrupy sweet, served in small cups. *Ouzo*, a licorice-flavored liqueur, is the national favorite, both as an apertif and after-dinner drink. It's deadly. Coca-Cola and other soft drinks are available, and house wines of modest quality are served in small pitchers. A common Greek wine is retsina, which is flavored with resin. While it may not suit your palate, it is unusual. Ask for *aretsinato* if you want wine without the resin.

## SHOP HOURS

Recently Athens merchants tried to abandon the midday closing of about two hours. Store clerks protested and picketed, so at last report Athens had returned to their traditional shop hours: 8:30 AM to 2:30 PM on Monday, Wednesday, and Saturday; 8:30 AM to 1:30 PM and 5 PM to 8 PM on Tuesday, Thursday, and Friday. Flea-market hours are flexible. Usually they are open until 8 PM on weekdays, 5 PM on Saturday.

## SHOPPING

The Athens **flea market** in the Plaka around Aristoyiton Street and Monastiraki is a good place to do some browsing and fruitful haggling, too. You'll find cotton peasant blouses of all descriptions that, although cheap and not of good quality, are suitable to wear with jeans or as a beach coverup. Look them over carefully, as seams tend to be uneven, and remember they will shrink or stretch when washed.

Fisherman-knit sweaters can be found for under $10 but should also be checked over carefully. They are a good buy, nonetheless.

Woven shoulder bags make great lightweight souvenirs to send or take home. They're very inexpensive, about $2 each, and come in all imaginable colors and weaves. Macramé bags and vests are also good buys at $6. Copper pans, sold as "genuine" antiques, are abundant and excellent buys; a large casserole with cover costs about $20.

Necklaces and bracelets called "slave jewelry" are popular. They are made of brightly colored beads strung on leather thongs, or they come with gold or silver trim. If you buy several from the same seller, you should pay no more than $3 each. The same ones at home cost from $10 to $15.

Silver filigree earrings and gold earrings are also good buys as are worry beads, which come in all price ranges and materials. A Greek lawyer tells us that worry beads originated when prisoners counted off the days of their sentences with them. Thirty-three is the proper number. You will see men, old and young, fingering the funny little beads, called *kombouloi,* in parks and on buses, in restaurants and sidewalk cafes, just about everywhere in Greece.

## ATHENS

**Important Addresses**

- **United States Embassy,** 91 Vasilissis Sofias, Tel. 712951.
- **American Express,** Syntagma Square (Constitution Square), Tel. 3234781.
- **Police and emergencies,** Tel. 100.
- **Post office,** 100 Eolou Street, 7 AM to midnight. Another post office is at Syntagma Square, near American Express.
- **International Student and Youth Travel Service,** 11 Nikis (upstairs), just off Syntagma, hours 9 AM to 7 PM, Tel. 3233767.
- **National Tourist Organization of Greece,** main office, 2 Amerikis Street, Tel. 3223111.

More than 400 years before the birth of Christ, the Acropolis, or Upper City, became the center of life for Athens. Temples, altars, and public buildings were built on this great flat-topped rock that marks the city, which Pindar described as "glistening Athens, violet-crowned." The lively, sprawling city of Athens today enjoys its most profitable ruin, The Parthenon, as well as other remaining buildings on the Acropolis. These ancient monuments, plus the Byzantine churches and nineteenth-century houses, make a curious blend with the outcroppings of tall, modern buildings. The old quarter of the city, the Plaka, at the foot of the Acropolis, is the restaurant and nightlife district for both tourists and Athenians. A labyrinth of narrow streets, ruins around every corner, and a lively flea market near Monastriaki Square characterize the area.

The touring center of the city is not large, and you can orient yourself quickly by finding **Syntagma Square** (Constitution Square), where the most expensive hotels and restaurants are concentrated, as well as the most traffic. The post office, American Express, and banks are also found in this area, in addition to the tourist bureaus, agencies that book side trips, and student-travel offices.

## Where to Stay

Early spring is delightful in Athens, but by June the city becomes extremely crowded with tourists in spite of very hot summers. There are many campgrounds, hostels, and room-finding services to choose from, however. For advance bookings in hostels write: **Organosis Xenonon Neotitos Eklados,** 4 Odos Dragatsaniou, Plateia Klafthmonos, Athens.

**57 Kypselis Street,** Tel. 8225860. Take trolley 2 from Syntagma. 200 beds, 50 dr. per night.

**20 Kallipoleos Street,** Viron, (Odos Akademia) Tel. 7664889. 100 beds, 50 dr. Take bus 103.

**Student Hotels,** 32 and 46 Nikis, both cost about 70 dr. ($2). They are across from International Student and Youth Travel Service.

**Lotus Travel Office,** at 7 Filellinon Street, just off Syntagma, Tel. 3221680, is a student-travel center where you can find a room and get information on low-cost island tours and bus tours to Delphi and Corinth.

**Viking Tours,** at 3 Filellinon, also has a room-finding service and tours. Tel. 229383.

If you have packed a knapsack and sleeping bag, try **Campsite Voula,** Tel. 8952712, southeast of Athens on the Apollo Coast, located on fifteen acres along the road from Athens to Cape Sounion. Has a supermarket, kitchen, laundry, showers. Open year round.

## Where to Eat

Menus are posted outside restaurants, so you can easily check out prices before entering. Pick one menu item as a basis for comparison—*souvlaki* is a good choice since it's served in most places.

The **Plaka** is the best restaurant district, but little happens here before 7 PM. It is known for its *tavernas,* which are simple little restaurants that serve authentic Greek food and the Greek wine retsina, often directly from barrels. Most offer guitar music; many

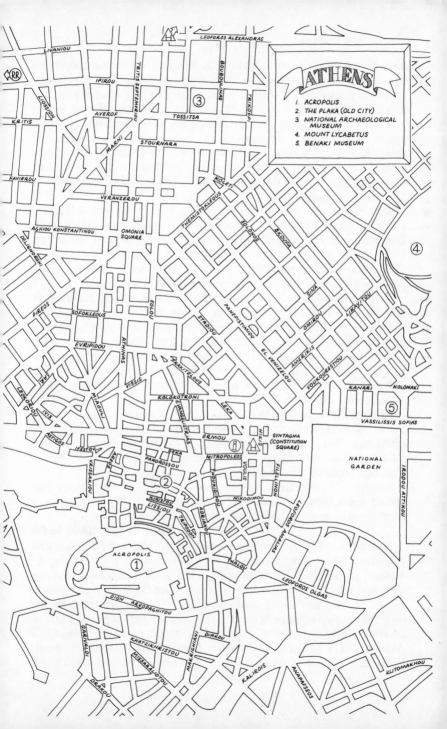

have Greek dancers and bouzouki (a stringed instrument something like a mandolin) entertainment. Dancing may go on for hours, although guests are not always welcome to join in. Colorfully dressed hawkers outside *tavernas* will try to entice you inside, "Come see my kitchen." Do so. You will probably see scrubbed, stainless-steel kettles, immaculate refrigeration units, and all sorts of interesting things bubbling on the stove. Pick out your own hunk of fish; have it weighed if you like. Point to the savory stews you'd like to try. Checking out the food doesn't obligate you to stay. Move on if you're not ready or not impressed.

**O Fantis,** a *taverna* at 12 Lissiou Street. Tour the sparkling kitchen, and sniff what's cooking. Beef on a skewer for 106 dr., salad for 30 dr. Local college-age folk dancers, not costumed, danced for hours. Patrons are not encouraged to join the dancing.

**Dionysos,** 7 Lissiou Street, also in the Plaka, features popular costumed dancers and a great view, so prices are higher.

**Taverna Attalos,** at Erechtheos 16, promises a lively atmosphere and the food is good. Prices are modest for kebabs of meat and fish.

**Delphi,** at 13 Nikis Street, a few steps from Syntagma Square, is unpretentious and very cheap, but not bad. Chicken breast, vine leaves, bread, and salad won't break your budget for 100 dr., less than $3. Try *cappucino* if the strong Greek coffee is not to your taste.

**Keller Taverna** in the Plaka, near Lissiou Street, a downstairs place that's cheap and typically Greek.

**Minion Grill,** in the Minion Department Store at 13 Patission Street, is a self-service restaurant where a lot of males gather in the afternoon. Not great food, but prices are modest, and you can find a pastry or two for a snack or grilled chicken during store hours. Chicken costs 40 dr., and they have *ice water*!!

Try the **Atlantic Grill,** on Patission Street, for sandwiches and grilled specialties, for about 66 dr., or almost $2. Poor service but conveniently near the National Archeological Museum.

_____ **What to See, What to Do**

Nearly everyone heads for the **Acropolis** to see the **Parthenon,** and you should too. It's about a fifteen-minute walk from Syntagma Square, or take bus 16. Walk around the Acropolis with a guide or with a good guide book, which will point out the optical illusions in the Parthenon and the chariot tracks in the time-worn rock. By the way, the rocks and steps hewn into the rock are very slippery, so tread carefully. You can prowl around the Parthenon, the **Temple of Athena Nike,** and the **Erechtheum** from about 9 AM until sunset. Entry is 5 dr. for students, free on Thursday and Sunday. There's much scaffolding around the Parthenon and the Caryatids on the Erechtheum, so you may have trouble getting good photo angles. You can also enter the **Acropolis Museum** for the same admission. At the base of the Acropolis is the **Theater of Dionysus**, dating from 400 B.C. to A.D. 326 and the **Odeon of Herodes Atticus,** which was carved into the rock in A.D. 161 as a memorial to the wife of Herodes Atticus, who was a second-century Greek scholar and the teacher of Marcus Aurelius. Summer concerts are held in this unforgettable setting.

The Acropolis is stunning by night, especially under a full moon, so try to see it then as well. It's open on full-moon nights from 9 PM to 11:45 PM. From 1 May to 30 September, except on nights of a full moon, there's a sound-and-light show on **Pnyx Hill** opposite the Acropolis. Check with the student tourist office for information, but avoid the package deals that include folk dancing and a drink at a *taverna* near the Acropolis. The show is impressive, but the prices at the *tavernas* are not.

The **National Archeological Museum,** 44 Patission Street, is open daily 8 AM to 7 PM, except Monday, Sunday 10 AM to 2 PM, admission 5 dr. for students. The museum features an enormous collection of Greek artifacts with one entire floor devoted to vases and pottery. Jewelry and the numismatic collection are also displayed here. Take bus 2 from Syntagma Square (costs about twenty-four cents) and get off at the third stop. You can also see a model that shows how archeological sites are excavated and studied.

**Benaki Museum** has more of the same, plus Greek costumes and weapons. It's at Koubari Street, near the National Garden, and costs 5 dr. for students; free on Sunday and Thursday.

The **Agora** along with the restored **Stoa of Attalos** and **Temple of Hephaestos** are other outstanding ruins. The Agora was a combined marketplace and civic center, and reconstruction was funded by the American School of Classical Studies in Athens through the Rockefeller Foundation.

**Mount Lycabetus,** a high point from which you can view the city, is worth a visit. Ride the cable railway from Plutarchou and Aristippou Streets to the top for 8 dr. The snack bar and restaurant on the summit will welcome your trade.

## Side Trips

The **Temple of Poseidon** at **Cape Sounion,** an hour's bus trip down the coast from Athens, is a romantic, beautiful setting for watching the sunset. The drive to the seacoast is unforgettable. The road to Cape Sounion, at the southernmost tip of Greece, takes you through the vineyards and olive groves on the Mesoghia Plain. Built in fifth-century B.C., the Temple of Poseidon stands on a cliff high above the sea.

From the temple's vantage point the rest of the world seems to stand still. City buses from Athens run on the hour from Mavromateou Street and cost 40 dr. one way. One problem: The last buses returning to Athens leave Cape Sounion by 9 PM in the spring and a bit later in the summer. Check the schedule so you won't be stranded. Student tours on charter buses through Student Travel Service cost 200 dr. round trip.

**Delphi** is in a spectacular natural setting on the lower slope of Mount Parnassus. From the sixth century B.C. until the third century A.D., Delphi was the site of the most important temple of Apollo. According to legend, Zeus himself had designated Delphi as the center of the world. In this sacred place, the oracle of Apollo imparted advice to supplicants from all over the known world. Delphi is worth a day trip, even though the bus takes four hours one way. It's only 180 kilometers from Athens, but roads snake through the valleys to this mountain-slope setting. Daily buses go from 260 Liossion Street, Athens. Check with travel offices for student discount rates, recently quoted at 440 dr. round trip. Better still, stay the night at the **Youth Hostel** near Delphi, Odos Appolonos, Tel. 82268. Delphi also has campsites and several small hotels.

## CRETE

Beautiful Mediterranean landscape coupled with the fascinating remains of a great civilization lure visitors to Crete. The stunning Palace of Knossos and other great Minoan fortresses combine with rugged mountains, tortuous valleys and gorges, and hauntingly lovely olive and citrus groves to weave an ancient spell over this sunny isle. A visitor will find much to explore, particularly archeological finds that tell us most of what we know of Europe's first civilization, which began in Crete about 3000 B.C., and reached extremely advanced stages. Unlike most ancient cultures, Cretans considered women equal with men. Perhaps that's why they were so peaceful!

You can get to Crete by taking an overnight boat trip or by daily forty-five-minute flights from Athens to Heraklion (often called Iraklion).

_____ **Where to Stay**

**Youth Hostel,** Odos Handakos, Heraklion. Tel. 081286281. 20 to 30 dr. a night.

**Youth Hostel,** Mallia, thirty-seven miles by bus from Heraklion, Tel. 089731355. 20 to 30 dr.

**Hotel El Greco,** number 4, 1821 Street, Rethymnon. Moderate cost.

**The Knossos,** number 43, 25th of August Street, Heraklion. Moderate and centrally located.

_____ **What to See, What to Do**

**Knossos,** the most famous Minoan palace, is a few miles outside Heraklion. According to legend, Knossos is where the Minotaur was kept captive. Archaeologists have restored many corridors, chambers, and storerooms of the palace. In town, go to the **Minoan Museum,** where many discoveries from Knossos excavations are on view. The **Palace of Phaistos,** thirty-six miles away, on the southern coast, can be reached by bus. Other sites include the ruins at **Mallia** and **Aghia Triada.**

The island is dotted by charming fishing villages, windmills, and verdant fertile valleys where mountain goats wander and blazing wild flowers awaken the senses. Although much of Crete's appeal comes from another era, it is very much alive today. You can find sandy beaches—usually small, secluded coves—and happy people. Less than fifty miles from Heraklion, **Rethymnon** and the surrounding small towns are well known for their medieval character, outstanding seafood *tavernas,* and lovely beaches. The architecture in Rethymnon tells the history of Crete. Mosques and fountains remain from the Turkish occupation in the seventeenth and eighteenth centuries. Before the Turks, Venetians held the island for over 400 years, leaving behind a fortress and many houses in this once-important port.

The **Crete Travel Bureau,** 25th of August Street, Heraklion, can give you tourist information and suggest or find you a hotel room. Tours to Crete can be booked for one, two, or three days through the **International Student Travel Service** in Athens or any of the other private agencies centered around Syntagma Square. Private agencies provide student discounts. The International Student Travel Service arranges boat trips to all the Greek islands, and their rate to Heraklion is listed at 299 dr.; flight to Crete via Olympic Airways is quoted at 785 dr.

## ISLAND CRUISES

Experienced travelers say you haven't seen Greece until you cruise to a Greek island on the turquoise waters. There are many ways to go. You can take the bus into **Piraeus,** the seaport near Athens. There's a **Youth Hostel** there at 127 Odos Voulgari. Sixty beds are available, and the charge is 50 dr. per night. From here, you can find a boat going to the island you want to see. You can also book a cruise with a variety of agencies, including those specializing in student travel where you'll get a discount.

An island trip offered year round and suggested if you have only a few days to spare is a one-day cruise to Aegina, Hydra, and Poros, with an hour or two on each island. One student agency offers this for 500 dr., about $5, including lunch. But I would recommend you skip this one and instead take a boat only to **Hydra,** for about 99 dr., as Aegina and Poros haven't much to offer except the same tourist junk you've seen everywhere, but in nicer shops. Hydra is a do-as-you-please little island, where artists and poets congregate and wealthy shipping magnates once lived. There is a remembrance of times past in the eighteenth-century homes and the quayside town hall and church, both once part of a monastery. In the church hangs a ship model from a chandelier. A sparkling white-and-blue village has shops, restaurants, and a pleasant feeling. The beaches and water are excellent. You can easily climb the rambling pathways from the harbor to higher points for a view above the city.

You can take a boat to **Mykonos** for 210 dr., and although tourists have found this island long ago, it still has appeal. Whitewashed houses snuggle against the shore, artists and poets do their thing, couples stroll hand in hand, old priests in black robes walk by blinding-white churches.

Or from the port in Piraeus you could take a small fishing boat for 17 dr. to **Selinia,** where a domed Byzantine church guards the shore and a few empty sailboats dot the beach. Walk for hours, and no one will disturb you. You may see a fisherman dive for lobster.

# 14 FOCUS ON IRELAND

Population: 2,966,000          Language: English
Capital: Dublin          Currency: pound sterling (£)

## THE LAND AND THE PEOPLE

In this green land of *Cead mile failte,* "100,000 welcomes," you will
wonder what makes the Irish so strong. On the surface they are a
simple people. Yet underneath they are tough as nails, quick to chew
over the latest elections about which everyone has strong opinions,
wanting something more from their land, wanting the young to stay,
and wondering why they leave for jobs in London. There is strong
feeling in Ireland—a strong feeling for change. The beautiful, wistful
spirit of the land is there and may for a time lull you into thinking life
is slower, gentler. Along the Ring of Kerry you will see the donkey
carts jostling along, hauling milk cans to dairy each morning. You
will see the wild, haunting beauty of the Dingle Peninsula, where
*Ryan's Daughter* was filmed. To the north in County Galway you will
wonder how anyone could possibly sustain a livelihood in this
incredibly rocky land.

The countryside and the people are an enigma. They seem at once
content and yet restless, finding solace in their pubs, lyric poetry,
literature, theater, and the church. They yearn for improved
productivity and industry and still want things to stay the same.

Go to Ireland, and your memories of it will never leave you.

## TRANSPORTATION

Shannon International, Cork, and Dublin airports are the major
arteries into Ireland, with direct flights from New York and most
large European cities. You can also come by ferry from Swansea to
Cork, from Liverpool to Dublin, from Holyhead to Dun Laoghaire, or
from Le Havre to Rosslare. Ferries from England cost about £5. Some
take six and a half hours; some are overnighters. Student flights from
London are a bargain at £12 through student-travel services.

Ireland is a nation of hitchhikers. Our Irish friends assure us that
it's perfectly safe to hitch a ride; in fact, hitching is the accepted mode
of transport in parts of the country. Trains connect the main cities,
though rail service is infrequent to the western shores. Buses are few
and far between, and if you are fortunate enough to have a car, be
sure to offer walkers a ride to market.

Not incidentally, bicycle rental is a popular means of seeing Ireland. You can rent a three-speed for about £1 per day at any of the following Dublin establishments:

**Charley's**, 35 Ballybough Street, Tel. 744090.

**R. W. Stevens, Ltd.**, Bachelor's Walk, Tel. 743826, or at Pearse Street, Tel. 778009.

**Eltoy, Ltd.**, 38 Mary Street, Tel. 740556.

They say the English drive to the left, the Americans on the right, and the Irish down the middle. 'Tis so, I'm afraid. Be wary. Some roads are winding and narrow, especially in the popular Ring of Kerry countryside, and though the distances are not great, allow a generous amount of time to cover fifty miles. Stop awhile, too, for tea and the warmth of the turf fire and the talk. The Irish love to talk, although you will find they may not always tell the truth. One pretty lass who hitched a ride with us contradicted herself three times in thirty miles. But take time for the stories and the welcome of the Irish.

Another recently popular method of seeing Ireland is by horse-drawn caravan for a slow-motion trek, covering about fifteen miles a day. The caravans are seen all over the western coast, sleep four to six, and there are special farms where you can stop for the night with other caravanners. Costs are from £55 to £82 per week, but split that sum four or five ways and it's only $20 per person. Caravans are covered wagons equipped with bed linens and cooking utensils, and you are in charge of feeding the horse at overnight centers. Stop awhile to fish, to hike, to find a tennis court or golf course along the way. Golf courses will welcome you; they're about $3 a round. Club rental is available. Any tourist office can give you information on caravans. You can begin your trek around Shannon Airport, in Cork, or in County Galway.

### SPECIAL TOURS

In conjunction with Aer Lingus and British Airways, the Irish Tourist Board offers "Guaranteed Holidays, No Surcharges." This package includes round-trip flight from London to Cork or Dublin or Shannon and a horse-drawn caravan for one week for £57. This rate applies up to 1 July and is slightly higher in midsummer. Or you can choose a package that includes auto rental and seven nights accommodations at Irish cottages for £77 in June and September, £83 in July and August. They also offer a budget, weekend-getaway holiday, London to Dublin, for £48, which includes hotel and breakfast for two nights. You may extend your stay for £3 per day. The Irish Tourist Board publishes a brochure called *Caravan and*

*Camping Parks,* which is available at tourist boards for 10p. This brochure includes places where you can rent tents and equipment.

For each of the above you must travel with an adult or be eighteen years old. Inquire at your nearest British Airways or Aer Lingus office or at a travel agent. Or write to: **Cara Ireland Tours Ltd.,** 52 Poland Street, London WI. Ask for the Flyaway Ireland brochure.

## ACCOMMODATIONS

All over Ireland you will find signs announcing B and B's, so you won't have any problem finding a place to stay. The Irish Tourist Board does an excellent job of listing accommodations in two booklets: *Irish Homes Accommodation,* which contains approved farmhouses and town-and-country homes, 15p. at the tourist board office; and *Hotels and Guesthouses,* also 15p., which includes a rating system from A to D for hotels, A to C for guesthouses. All have been inspected and Government approved. The booklets indicate services offered, seasonal rates, and what facilities you can expect. The standard rate at a B and B is £2 to £3 including breakfast. Hotels vary depending on quality, area, etc. In each region I will list a few B and B's or hotels, but you need not worry about going off without reservations even in high season.

Ireland also has an extensive youth-hostel system, which is cheaper than most B and B's. Some young travelers complained about strict hours or of having to help with some of the housekeeping chores, such as scouring a sink, but that's part of the game at many hostels anywhere. It is usually necessary to be up and have beds made by 9 AM. Lights go out at 11:30 PM.

## FOOD

Ireland is still cheap compared to countries on the Continent. A bed and breakfast, with its hearty Irish starter of oatmeal, eggs, sausage and bacon, fresh slabs of soda bread, juice, and a pot of tea, costs only £3 a night. A pot of tea served with hot scones and homemade jam and butter is fifty cents. Avoid the large new hotels and chain hotels. They are tourist oriented and will charge accordingly. On the other hand, an old hotel may serve surprisingly cheap food. Restaurant prices include a standard tip of 12 percent, but guesthouse prices usually do not.

Food is substantial but not fancy. Standards like roast beef can be outstanding, and so is fresh salmon and trout. Pubs and lorry stops are good places to find cheap hearty fare. As in England, pubs serve a large noonday meal called the Ploughman's Lunch, which in former times was just that. It's substantial, with things like shepherd's pie, huge mounds of mashed potatoes, vegetables, and fresh bread, and it will cost under £1.

The Irish love their cream, and a stout jug is placed on nearly every table. Slosh it over your apple pie, fresh berries, the richest pastry, or ruin your tea with it.

You can find solace in the Irish pubs as long as you do not intrude on local territory without being invited. Women are not welcome, although two females could enter a pub in Dublin without astonishing anyone. Guinness stout, strong ale served warm, is the national brew. A singing pub, whether in Dublin or in the country, will warm your heart even on the worst of days.

## SHOP HOURS

Shops and stores are open from 9 AM to 1 PM, 4:30 PM to 8 PM; banks, 8:30 AM to 1:30 PM.

## DUBLIN

### Important Addresses

- **United States Embassy,** 42 Elgin Road, Ballsbridge, Tel. 64061.
- **American Express,** 116 Grafton Street, Dublin, Tel. 72874.
- **Dublin Regional Tourism,** 51 Dawson Street, Tel. 47733, closed on weekends; also located at 14 Upper O'Connell Street.
- **Post Office,** center of O'Connell Street.
- **Irish Student Travel Association (USIT),** 7 Anglesea Street, Tel. 770535.

### Where to Stay

**Morehampton House,** 78 Morehampton Road, Donnybrook, Tel. 680325. Open all year. Ten minutes by bus from city center, £1.50 per night.

**Youth Hostel,** 39 Mountjoy Square, South Dublin 1, Tel. 745734, April through September, £1.50.

The Dublin **tourist information office,** at Dawson Street, will make reservations for you in any part of the country, with a charge of 30p. to 60p. Office hours are 10 AM to 5:30 PM daily, but may vary to suit local circumstances.

There are low-priced hotels near the Connolly Station along both Upper and Lower Gardiner Streets. You can find a single here for £3 to £5.

Other choices in the city include:

**Mount Herbert,** 7 Herbert Road, Tel. 684321, eighty-eight rooms, singles £4.25 with full breakfast, and the staff is very pleasant.

**Clarence Hotel,** 6-8 Wellington Quay, Tel. 7761178, is an old hotel, with seventy rooms along the River Liffey. £7 per night, not including breakfast.

**Mont Clare,** Clare Street 2, Tel. 762896, is about £5 with breakfast.

**Powers Royal,** Kildare Street 2, Tel. 765243, £7 with full breakfast.

Since most of the smaller guesthouses have only a few rooms, it does not seem practical to list them. You can walk along and find dozens of them within a block of each other, all with similar rates.

Or you could head out of the city toward Clontarf on bus 30 or 44, and you will find plenty of B and B's along Dublin Bay on Clontarf Road and on Kincora Road. This is on the way to Howth, a pleasant seaside fishing village you may want to visit.

In nearly any direction on the edges of Dublin, you will find neatly maintained, red-brick guesthouses with names like St. Anne's, St. Jude's, St. Mary's Guesthouse, Mrs. O'Neill's, and Mrs. Ryan's. Except during the Dublin Horse Show in August, you will have no trouble finding a room. During the horse show, reservations are necessary only in Dublin.

## Where to Eat

**Trinity College Cafeteria** at College Green is a good bet for student fare at modest prices. Also, near the intersection of O'Connell and Abbey Streets are **Burgerland, Old Kentucky Chicken,** and **Pizzaland,** all within a few steps of each other. **McDonald's** at 11 Grafton Street might appeal too.

For ice cream, **Daville's 32 Flavors** is on 13 Westmoreland Street and St. Stephen's Green North, at 22p. per scoop. Not bad for the money.

While none of the above have any Irish flair or atmosphere, you can eat cheaply at them. The **Farm Inn Deli and Bakery** on Merrion Row has a nice assortment of take-out picnic makings, and it is not far from St. Stephen's Green, which is a perfect picnic spot. **The Hole in the Wall** on Templebar has sandwiches and chicken pieces for 65p.

Try **Kilkenny Kitchen,** above Kilkenny Design Shop, overlooking the cricket field of Trinity College. Good for lunch, snacks, and afternoon tea. Lovely pastries cost 25p., and tea is only 10p. Soups, wine, and home-baked breads are also served.

**Bruxelles Pub,** on Harry Street, a short street just off Grafton, is a two-story restaurant. Downstairs salad-and-sandwich specials are served daily for 85p. Try the apple pie, 30p., upstairs in the Victorian Bar. It's lively with Dubliners around 6 PM.

Other pubs to try where sandwiches and light suppers are served: **Bewley's** on George's Street and on Grafton; **O'Donaghue's** at 15 Merrion Row near St. Stephen's Green, is lively and jammed with singing Irish and would-be Irish.

The **Clarence Hotel Grill Room,** on Wellington Quay, is crowded and serves a superb, enormous prime rib for about £3.50. For rare, say "underdone."

_____ **What to See, What to Do**

A good starting point would be to head straight for **Trinity College,** 10 AM to 5 PM daily, Saturday 10 AM to 1 PM, and poke around the cobbled walkways and buildings on your way to the **Library** where the famous *Book of Kells* can be seen. This eighth-century manuscript is thought to be one of the world's most beautiful books, with pages illustrated in intricate detail. Also on display are ancient science books and other early books. You might find little gems of wisdom, like the following taken from the oldest book in the world, *Ebers Papyrus,* 1550 B.C.:

> Remedy to Stop Crying of a Child:
> Pods of the poppy plant
> Fly-dirt which is on the wall.
> Make into one, strain and take for four days.
> It acts at once.

You can also find ingenious remedies to "drive away wrinkles from the face."

The Library is open from 10 AM to 5 PM, Monday to Friday, and from 10 AM to 1 PM on Saturday.

The **Trinity College Bookstore** is a good place to buy works of Irish writers and poets or to buy reproductions from the Book of Kells, about £2 each, with mailing tube.

**Christ Church Cathedral** (daily 9 AM to 5:30 PM) and **St. Patrick's Cathedral** (daily 9 AM to 6 PM, Saturday 9 AM to 4:30 PM), where Jonathan Swift is buried, are worth a stop, and both are free. Georgian Dublin, with many public buildings built in the seventeenth and eighteenth centuries, includes **Merrion Square**. The **Bank of Ireland** in College Green (tours during normal banking hours) was the home of the Irish Parliament. The **Custom House** and **Leinster House** at Kildare Street, the present meeting place of the legislature, are other fine public buildings that are examples of Irish classical architecture. The **Four Courts** on the northern quays is the home of the Irish Law Courts. The structure was designed by James Gandon in 1785 and rebuilt in 1922 after a fire.

The **National Gallery of Ireland,** at Merrion Square West, is open daily 10 AM to 6 PM and until 9 PM on Thursday. Free admission, with guided tours on Saturday at 3 PM. The restaurant is open during gallery hours.

The **National Museum,** at Kildare Street, has Irish antiquities dating from the Bronze Age. Open 10 AM to 5 PM weekdays. Free admission, closed Monday.

**St. Stephen's Green,** at the top of Grafton Street, is a pleasant respite in the midst of a busy city. In summer, free daily concerts given with dancers and balladeers from 1 PM to 2 PM show you a bit of the Irish. A nice picnic spot too.

**Phoenix Park,** with 1760 acres in Dublin's northwestern corner, contains the **Zoological Gardens,** with an especially good collection of large cats. The American ambassador's home and the president of Ireland's home are also here. Another just-out-of-the-city place to visit is **Martello Tower,** which contains the **James Joyce Museum.** Take bus 7 or 8 to Sandycove. Open from 11 AM to 4 PM.

The **Guinness Brewery,** at St. James's Gate on the banks of the Liffey, welcomes visitors Monday through Friday 10 AM to 3 PM. Entry is free, and you can sample the legendary dark brew after you see how it's made.

Tennis, golf, greyhound and horse racing, and soccer games are popular tourist attractions. Soccer matches cost £1.50 admission. There are more than eighteen golf courses in the Dublin area, and you can rent clubs. Tennis clubs and public courts have attractively low fees—3p. for those under eighteen, for one hour, but no rental racquets are available. Public courts are at Herbert Park, Ballsbridge, Bushy Park, Ellenfield Park, St. Anne's Estage, and Johnstown Park, among others. Check with the tourist bureau if you need details.

BRASS RUBBING

Commemorative brasses are one of the special features in old churches. (See page 110.) Making a brass rubbing is much like placing a penny under a sheet of paper, then rubbing a pencil or crayon across it to get the image of the penny to appear. To make a rubbing at a church, here are some guidelines:

• Always obtain the vicar's permission. You may be asked to pay a small fee.

• Take the following supplies, unless you go to a known brass-rubbing center where they'll have all you need: paper, parchment or art paper, masking tape, scissors, brass-rubbing wax, soft brush or rag. Buy the paper and wax at an art-supply shop.

• Brush away any dirt or grit from the surface of the brass. Place paper over the brass, and fasten firmly in place with masking tape. Be careful of protruding rivets, which may tear your paper.

• Feel the outline of the brass with your finger, and rub evenly up and down the figure.

• Be quiet and respectful in the church. Always leave it in the condition in which you found it.

The **Edin Brass Rubbing Center** at St. John's Church, Prince Street, is open daily 10 AM to 6 PM, Sunday 1 PM to 5 PM. They'll sell you, for a modest fee, all the supplies you need to make a handsome rubbing, and they'll show you how it's done.

AT NIGHT

The Irish love their theater, and you can check in the *What's On in Dublin* guide (15p. on the streets or at the visitor's bureau) for current plays. Theaters include the famous **Abbey Theater,** the **Peacock Theater, Gate Theater,** and the **Project Arts Theater** as well as other smaller ones. Ticket prices are moderate.

Dublin has a number of singing pubs, some better than others. For good Gaelic ballads, take bus 31 to Howth, nine miles northeast of Dublin, to the **Abbey Tavern,** highly recommended by Irish friends as one of the best. **Slattery's,** at several locations, including Capel Street, gets a good crowd of young people and charges about £1 entry. Go early, as they close up shop before midnight.

You may also be lucky enough to catch the popular folk-singing group Wolf Tomes at the Gresham Hotel on O'Connell Street or elsewhere about town.

## OTHER TOURING

For a complete tour of Ireland, head south from Dublin down to Cork, then west to pick up the Ring of Kerry, a special route that makes a ring around some gorgeous country. Then go north to Galway and Connemara, where the silver sea pounds the rocky shores and where the Gaelic is the language heard in pubs. It's lovely to listen to, even when you barely catch a word.

Some highlights in this tour include **Kinsale,** a County Cork fishing village with some fine beaches nearby. There's a fine **hostel** at nearby Summer Cove, Tel. Kinsale 72309. You can hire sailing boats or fishing gear in Kinsale. Irish friends also recommend Clonakilty, a pretty village just down the pike on Clonakilty Bay.

In the city of **Cork,** visit **St. Finbarr's Cathedral** and **Shandon Steeple,** where you can see the tower and famous 200-year-old bells, which you may play for 20p. **Blarney Castle** is not far away. Cork is a lively town, and you should check at the **tourist office,** 42 Monument

Building, Grand Parade Street, to see what's happening at the moment. A film festival is held in September, a music festival in May, Irish theater in summer.

There are lots of B and B's in and around Cork that cost under £2, as well as several hostels. The in-town **hostel** is at 1-2 Redclyffe, Western Road, Tel. 432891. Take bus 8 or 5 to University College.

The 109-mile road route, the **Ring of Kerry,** and the **Lakes of Killarney** are increasingly popular with tourists. You will see many caravans poking along the winding, often steep terrain. This is not a good area in which to bicycle; the coast of the Dingle Peninsula would be better.

Killarney is a favorite of many returning Irish who have left the homeland, but it is also full of American tourists and the music lovers who come for the Bach Festival in July. Sir Walter Scott called Killarney "the grandest sight I have ever seen." While here and there in rural County Kerry you will see signs of our times, you will more than likely see old thatched cottages too. The pace of the motor age does not come naturally to this part of Ireland.

As you head north toward Limerick and Shannon, you can take in a medieval banquet at restored **Bunratty Castle** in County Clare. Although expensive at £7.90 for the evening, the dinner includes four "removes" (courses), wines (ancient mead, we're told), and entertainment. The castle is furnished as it would have been five centuries ago, with a good deal of history behind each handsomely carved piece. Dark-eyed colleens in medieval velvet costumes will tell you about the castle, serve you a fine dinner from *braume brose* to *syllabub* (no silverware, only a dagger), and entertain you with haunting Gaelic songs.

Adjacent to Bunratty Castle is a **reconstructed Irish folk village** that's also interesting. You can see crafts being made, from Irish baskets woven out of River Shannon reeds to fisherman-knit sweaters and shawls. Also just beside the castle is a lively spot called Dirty Nelly's, with lots of action and the ever-present lilting Irish voices singing their hearts out.

## GALWAY AND CONNEMARA

From Galway, on the west coast, you can take a boat to the **Aran Islands,** where much of the Irish knitwear is made. You can go for a day trip, which only allows five hours to visit, or you can find rooms in one of the guesthouses there and return the next day. The fare is £5.75.

In Galway there's a special summer theater that has traditional music and song and can be heard three nights a week. It is called **Taibhdnearc na Galliumh.** Inquire at the visitors' bureau.

**Galway Crystal Factory** invites visitors to their showrooms, with prices about half the Stateside tags. Shipping is available. Like all of Ireland, Galway is a bargain for shopping, with sweaters and knitwear selling for less than half their price in the States.

West of Galway, you find a decidedly noncommercial Ireland. You can take a bus from Galway to Clifden, on the western shore, and there's a youth hostel called the **Twelve Bens Hostel** at Recess, County Galway (Tel. Ballinafad 18). If the bus passes through Ballinahinch (some days it does, and some days not), it goes right by the hostel entrance. The Twelve Bens are a group of mountains that dominate the Connemara landscape. Good **hiking and fishing** for brown trout and salmon will add to your pleasures here. The hostel is thirty-eight miles from Galway, seven miles from Clifden. Other towns along the way include Oughterard, Cashel, Leenane. There are pubs and B and B's scattered near villages, and there's always the talk. **Ballyconneeley Golf Course** and some safe and sandy beaches at **Carna** and **Roundstone** may also entice you. You can find an inviting cove and be astonished that hardly another soul is in sight. If you venture off into the countryside, a copy of *Irish Home Accommodations* will help you find a place to stay.

In **Clifden,** a happy fishing village, there are some hotels, shops, and pubs as well as a smattering of antique dealers. **Millar's Woolen Mills** in Clifden, wholesalers to many American shops, sells handsome tweed caps and hats. They also have long woolen skirts, capes, and Irish "rugs" (lap throws or blankets) in exquisite mohairs and soft plaids at low prices.

A rocky seascape of whitewashed cottages, winding walls of stone that stretch to meet a silver sea, and the sweet scent of turf fires, Connemara is a lovely place to visit. Here and wherever you go in Ireland, you will find laughter and tears curiously mixed with song, and if you are lucky, you'll find someone who says the best thing possible, "You are one of our own."

# 15 FOCUS ON ITALY

Population: 53,000,000          Language: Italian
Capital: Rome                  Currency: lira (L)

## THE LAND AND THE PEOPLE

The Italian way of life—somehow robust yet gentle—offers a superb invitation for visitors. No one ever says Italy is quaint or quiet or bland. Like an artist's palette, Italy has a variety of colors as suits a civilization that boasts much of the finest art the world has ever known.

"Sunny Italy" describes the climate pretty well. In summer temperatures are high—Rome, Florence, and the south especially are hot. If you are touring these areas then, plan to spend some time away from the cities, on the beaches or mountains. In winter the weather varies considerably even over short distances. It is mild in the Riviera and the lakeland near Lake Maggiore and Lake Garda and very cold in the Alps and the Dolomites. Italy shares some of the Alps' finest mountain peaks with her neighbors—Mont Blanc (15,782 feet) with France; the Matterhorn (14,782 feet) and Monte Rosa (15,217 feet) with Switzerland.

Less renowned than Italy's art, churches, and museums are the beaches and magnificent mountains in this land that seems like an overflowing cornucopia, something for every taste. The people are lively, the city traffic incredible. In sharp contrast to northern Europe, Italy is flamboyant. There is a happy feeling in the street life, the sidewalk cafés, or the few tiny tables clustered outside every food-serving place. Buses are crowded, streets somewhat littered, and life swings along at a merry clip.

## TRANSPORTATION

Major cities, like Rome, Milan, Florence, Venice, and Naples are connected by a network of trains of the best kind—fast, frequent, and inexpensive. Eurailpass and InterRail passes are valid in Italy, and the Italian State Railway sells its own special two-week rail-travel pass for about $50. Regular second-class fares are cheap, even without a pass.

If you plan to visit smaller cities, you should know that several types of trains exist. Ironically, the *Accelerato* is a local. The *Diretto* is not as slow, and the *Direttissimo* is a long-distance fast train. The

*Rapido* carries only first-class passengers and is a quality express service.

Hitchhiking in Italy is not a good idea.

In cities, bus transportation is about the cheapest way to go. You can ride buses nearly anywhere for six to fifteen cents. Buses run frequently, yet they are crowded, particularly at peak hours. Try to travel after 10 AM and before 1 PM when the shops close and people rush home for noon meals and siestas. Again around 4 PM buses are crowded, as stores reopen at 4:30 PM. Taxis are moderate in cost, but can still eat up a budget in a hurry if you overindulge. Ask about the fare before you get in.

## FOOD

The cost of eating in Italy is cheap to moderate.

One visitor said he began to see spaghetti in his sleep, especially after he first sampled spaghetti ice cream. You can eat spaghetti at least a hundred different ways and for every course, from soup to dessert, but after a week or so in Italy you'll want to discover other culinary delights. Pasta of all sorts and shapes is the national specialty. It comes as green noodles made with spinach, which is delectable in a buttery cream sauce. It comes under names like *fettucine, cannelloni* (stuffed with finely ground veal or chicken), *ravioli,* and *tortellini.* Pasta is usually served as a second course before meat and vegetables, and the sauce does not have the meatiness that many Americans may be accustomed to. You can, though, have a filling meal if you order a pasta that's served with enough meat and cheese. *Sauce bolognese* is made with meat and tomatoes, while *sauce alla gorgonzola* is a cheese sauce, creamy and wonderful.

Italian restaurants are hard to resist. They are called *hostaria,* in the most expensive category; *ristorante* are also expensive and, of late, can be as expensive as the *hostaria; trattoria* are cheaper; *tavola calda* are the cheapest. A *rosticceria* or *alimentaria* is a take-out place. You will seldom find a bad meal in Italy, even though fewer restaurants now display tourist menus than in years past. *Osso buco* (veal stew) is an Italian specialty you might like to try.

Most menus are à la carte, so check out the prices. Tax and service are added onto the price listed.

You will find fresh fruits the likes of which you may never taste again anywhere in the world. Peaches and lemons in summer have fantastic flavor. On a hot day you can buy a large slice of icy watermelon for about 50 L, which is a lot cheaper than a Coke. Street vendors hawk ice cream that varies tremendously in quality and in cost. The closer the stand is to a tourist attraction, the higher the price will be. You may pay seventy-five cents for a few tiny scoops. Our best find was a stand near Vatican City on a small street near the bus stop, where thirty cents bought generous scoops of top-quality ice cream.

## SHOP HOURS

Usual hours in Rome and most of Italy are 9 AM to 1 PM and 4:30 PM to 8 PM, Monday through Saturday. In Rome, shops close Saturday afternoon through July and August.

## SPECIAL NOTICES

**Coin Shortage.** When you arrive in Italy and change your money into lira, get a good supply of small coins. They are hard to come by

when you want to make a phone call or to pay for an ice-cream cone. You may be given change in funny-looking paper bills that are valid only in that city, in postage stamps, or in candy kisses. One student said with a laugh, "I thought for sure some clerk would soon twist the button off her blouse and give it to me for change, we had received so many different kinds and shapes of coin—some only good for phone calls, others were bus tokens."

**How to Use Telephones.** Telephones in Italy work with a special token called a *gettone*. It costs 50 L, and you can buy it at any bar, tobacco shop, or exchange booth that displays a round, yellow sign with a black phone. Drop the *gettone* in the slot on top of the phone, then dial.

The European long-distance number is 184. For long-distance calls to the United States and for directory information dial 170.

**Females Beware.** When in Italy, female travelers should be especially careful not to wear tight clothing, halter tops, shorts, and so on. You can expect to be ogled by men even if you *don't* look sexy. A young Italian told two American male teen-agers, "If we see a woman in shorts, we just think she is a prostitute. She is looking for trouble." Another experienced traveler commented that her female friends got into serious trouble with police over men who accosted them. Take care, and don't go out walking alone at night.

**Public Holidays.** There are more public holidays in Italy than in any European country. While most galleries and museums are open on holidays for a half day, banks, shops, and offices are closed.

## ROME

_____ **Important Addresses**

- **United States Embassy,** via Vittorio Veneto 119a. Tel. 4674.
- **American Express,** piazza di Spagna 38, Tel. 68875.
- **Police,** via S. Vitale 15, Tel. 113.
- **Main post office,** piazza San Silvestro.
- **Laundromat,** via Montebello 11.
- **SOFA (student tourist office),** 77 piazzale del Verano.

_____ **Where to Stay**

**Relazione Universitarie,** via Palestro 11, Tel. 4755265. They will find you a room for around $4 per night and are open daily 9 AM to 1 PM, 2 PM to 6 PM. Closed weekends. Ask about student discounts for sightseeing or for other help.

**International Youth Hostel** (Ostello del Foro Italico), viale delle Olimpiadi 61, Tel. 383213. Not in midcity, but friendly and clean. 2000 L includes breakfast.

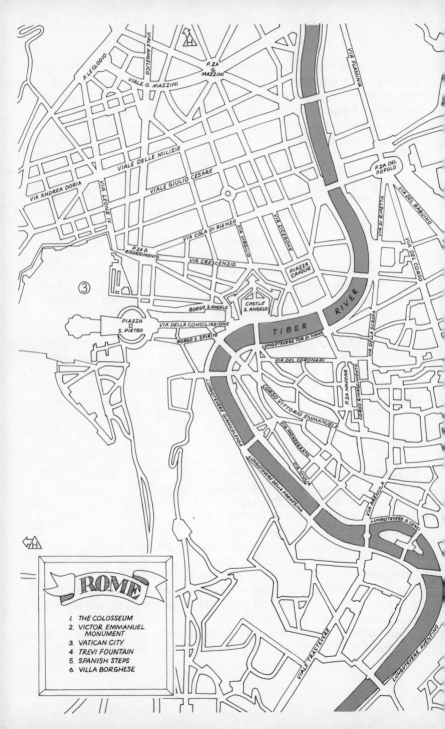

**Campground: Seven Hills** is about eight kilometers outside the city on via Aurelia. Take bus 64 outside the central station to plaza Vittorio, change to bus 46 to largo Bocca, where you change to bus 246, which takes you to the via Aurelia campground, visible from the highway.

**Student Hotel,** via dei Bichi 17. Take bus 98 from the Vittorio Emmanuele Monument, a half-hour bus ride. Dorm space for less than 1000 L, singles slightly higher.

**Foresteria del Pellegrino,** piazza della Trinita dei Pellegrini 36, centrally located in town, about 1200 L.

**Casa del Conservatoria,** via del Conservatoria 62, Tel. 659612, is also in town; clean, with showers, 3000 L.

The following *pensioni* are near the main station:

**Pensione Vittoriana,** via S. Martino della Battaglia 4, Tel. 478330. 300 L per person in double room, breakfast included. Neat, clean, and old-fashioned.

**Pensione Cervia,** via Palestro 55, Tel. 491057. Singles for 2600 L, multiple-occupancy rooms for up to four persons, 1800 L. Showers 300 L extra.

**Pensione Manita,** via Montebello 114, 200 L for a double.

**Pensione Katty,** via Palestro 35, Tel. 4751385. You can stay in a shared room for 1800 L.

A large area surrounding the main station has cheap pensions, where rooms are in the 2000-lire-per-bed range. When you leave the station, head for via Montebello, via Magenta, or via Palestro, which are all lined with such places.

At the station the **Ente Provincial per il Turismo**, the local tourist bureau, will find you a room, give you maps and information. The bureau's hours are from 8 AM to 8 PM. Another tourist-office branch is located at via Parigi 11, near piazza del la Republica. Open daily, 8 AM to 1:30 PM, 4:30 PM to 7 PM. The office has listings for 300 beds, dormitory-style, 2000 L each. You cannot write ahead to the tourist bureau for a room reservation, but they assured us that they can find you a room when you arrive. They can also direct you to student hostels.

## Where to Eat

Turn right when you leave the main train station, and you will find some of the best low-cost restaurants around Rome. **Pizza Rusticas** serve huge trays of assorted pizzas and other snacks for 300 L. Don't be put off by these already-cooked cold pizzas. They taste quite good reheated, and two or three make a decent lunch or light supper. You will often see a menu with two columns of prices for the same item, one nearly double the other. The low price is charged if you eat at the counter, the higher if you sit at a table. Be careful of this system at street-side eating spots. You can just as easily take your pizza or salami roll to a nearby bench and save money, unless you want to enjoy the table atmosphere.

Our travelers tell us that touring the city is a good time to carry a day pack, in which you can carry a liter of beverage. The example given: a six-ounce orange drink near a tourist monument cost about fifty cents; a liter at the grocery store cost the same. They much preferred to pack a lunch and buy fresh cold fruits and eat in the plazas as most young travelers do. It's good for socializing, they say.

Because Rome has so many small restaurants, don't trek across town to find some special one. Here are a few near the center of town we have tried. Fixed-price tourist menus cost from 2500 L to 4000 L and include soup, pasta, salad, main course, dessert (often fruit), and a glass of wine, Coke, or mineral water.

**Taverna Pretoranna,** via Palestro 48, tourist menu 1800 L; roast veal 200 L; half a chicken 950 L; spaghetti 400 L; simple pizza 700 L; soups 300-400 L.

**Piccadilly,** piazzi Barberini, near the train station, is a large cafeteria and restaurant. It draws a young crowd, and the food is not bad if you stay away from the American fare.

**Rosy's Snack Bar,** via Montebello 61. Great fruit milk shakes, reports our best researcher—very thick, delicious, and made with fresh fruits. He sampled every flavor: 400 L each.

**Il Giardino,** via Zucchelli 29, near the Spanish steps. Very good food, pleasant atmosphere, reasonable.

**Giovanni,** via Salandra 1. Typical local food, but order carefully.

**Giovanni,** via Marche 19. Like the other Giovanni, keep this one for a change of pace when you want something special. Fine food for about $7.

**Giardinaccio,** via Aurelia, two blocks from Vatican City, offers veal steak for 2500 L, pasta for 700 L. A *coperto* (cover charge) of 350 L includes the abundant Italian bread. Not bad, but service not great.

### What to See, What to Do

First off, don't wear shorts if you expect to enter Rome's churches. You will be refused entry ten times out of ten, say our experienced travelers. The same for halters. Women should carry a head covering.

To chart your course for a Roman holiday, here's a brief rundown on some significant places:

The **Colosseum** is impressive by night and at sunset, but go in the daytime, too, when you can walk around inside this magnificent stadium and look down into the pits that housed hungry lions. You can almost see gladiators and Roman chariots. Team up with a few other tourists for a guided, thirty-minute tour led by one of the unofficial guides wandering the premises. Prices are definitely adjustable. Expect to pay about 1000 L, or better still trail along closely behind an English-speaking group. Daily hours are from 9 AM to 12 PM, 2 PM to 5 PM, but check them out with the visitors' bureau. Much renovation is under way in the Colosseum so some areas are partially closed and hours tend to change. Outside the Colosseum you will pass under the **Arch of Constantine**, erected in A.D. 315.

The **Baths of Caracalla** are considered the grandest of Rome's ruined public baths and are near the Colosseum. In summer, operas are performed here.

The Roman **Forum** is one of Rome's greatest archeological treasures as is **Trajan's Column.** At both sites ancient Romans met to discuss politics, worship, and sell their wares.

**Piazza del Campidoglio**, on **Capitoline Hill**, is the site of Rome's city hall, a powerful example of Michelangelo's genius. The center building is the **Palazzo Senatorio**, erected on the site where the Roman senate met. Flanking the piazza are two superb Renaissance buildings, the **Capitoline Museum** and the **Palazzo dei Conservatorio**. The Capitoline's collection of Roman sculpture includes the famous statue, *The Dying Gaul*. In the Conservatorio you'll recognize the well-known sculpture, *Boy Extracting a Thorn from His Foot*. An equestrian bronze of Emperor Marcus Aurelius is in the center of the square.

**Piazza San Pietro**, in front of St. Peter's, and **Piazza Navona** are also great squares worth exploring, as is the quite different **Piazza di Santa Maria**, full of Americans and bohemian types mingling with sharp-eyed, yet friendly, Romans. Bernini and Borromini were the chief architects. Piazza Navona boasts three fountains, making it a stunning setting for outdoor nightlife. The central fountain is the work of Bernini.

The **Spanish Steps**, at piazza di Spagna, are graced with another lovely Bernini fountain. Near American Express, they are a favorite gathering place for young travelers.

The **Borghese Museum and Gallery**, in 245-acre Villa Borghese Gardens, was once the dwelling of a cardinal. In addition to a sumptuous collection of works by Carravaggio, Titian, Tintoretto, and many other artists, you can see the renowned sculpture by

Canova, his reclining nude of Pauline Borghese, Napoleon's sister. Bernini's masterwork, the statue of Apollo and Daphne, is here.

The **Victor Emmanuel Monument**, which has been described as "spectacular" or "in horrible taste," is an impressive conglomeration of gleaming white marble honoring the first king of unified Italy. The Unknown Soldier is also buried here.

To appreciate the beauty of Rome's baroque-era churches, attend mass in the centrally located **Santa Maria della Vittoria**, where you can also view *St. Theresa in Ecstasy* by Bernini, or any of the basilicas and dozens of neighborhood churches. The experience may heighten your impressions of the Eternal City.

The **Catacombs** were underground places of refuge and burial places of early Christians. Although some people call them "creepy," most visitors find them fascinating and worth the half-hour trip out of the city. Take bus 27 from the train station toward the Colosseum. Change to bus 118 at the first stop, and ask the conductor to let you off at the Catacombs. Fare is 200 L with a student-ID card.

Built in 27 B.C., the **Pantheon** is an open-domed basilica and one of the attractions you can visit on an early-evening stroll.

The **Trevi Fountain**, of *Three-Coins-in-the-Fountain* fame, is outstanding. According to custom, toss in a coin to assure your return to Rome.

**Vatican City.** To get to Vatican City take bus 64 from the central railroad station. You can enter the **Basilica of St. Peter** between 7 AM and 7 PM, 1 April to 30 September. From October to March it closes at 5:30 PM. You will probably find a mass being offered at several of the small altars. If one is in progress at the main altar, you may be barred from entering.

The largest church in the world, St. Peter's is on one of the world's most beautiful squares, Piazza San Pietro. The square took sculptor-artist Bernini ten years to build. When the Pope is in residence, as many as 400,000 people jam into this square every Sunday for the papal blessing. In the church itself, art treasures are found everywhere, including Michelangelo's *Pieta* in the first chapel, now protected by a bulletproof shield.

Beside St. Peter's, the **Sistine Chapel**, with its shadowy frescoes by Michelangelo, and the **Vatican Museum** are outstanding. If you are getting saturated with art, tackle only a fraction of the museum. We especially liked the modern-art section, a refreshing change of pace. The chapel and museum close at 2 PM daily, but you are usually not admitted after 1:15 PM, so plan accordingly. There is an entry charge of 800 L.

It's not difficult to attend a **papal audience**, held every Wednesday at 11 AM in the new audience hall. But you must get tickets a day in advance, and personnel in the information office to the left of the entrance to St. Peter's will direct you to the proper office. Standing room is so far away that you have to watch the television screen to see the goings on. If you can get only standing-room tickets, find a tour group on the way in for seats and tag right along. We did. At each checkpoint where the colorfully clad guards in their Michelangelo-designed garb check the tickets, all held by the tour guide, it was nearly impossible for him to count off exactly how many people were in the group. Blend in with the crowd, and you should get a seat.

Tour St. Peter's, but skip the Gardens, at least on an organized-tour ticket. They take too much time for what you see.

ROMAN NIGHTLIFE

Our best suggestion is simply enjoy the street life, sidewalk cafés, fountains, and plazas. Walk along the **Via Veneto** if you like, although better places exist for young people. Enjoy the magnificent squares and well-lit monuments by night. On the small side streets you will feel part of the Roman scene instead of a spectator looking on. Via Veneto and **Via Condotti** are lined with fashionable shops that beckon tourists with fat wallets. *Cappucino* here costs about $1, half that elsewhere.

Get a copy of *You in Rome* for a weekly schedule of events, art shows, and concerts. There are English-language movies and fine concerts. The **Academia Nationale de St. Cecilia** has a full concert schedule, and tickets are cheap. You can buy them several days ahead at the box office, 9 AM to 1 PM daily, or on the day of the concert. Tickets cost 1000 to 2000 L for a first-class concert. The **Pio Auditorium**, a short walk from piazza San Pietro, also has inexpensive concerts and fine symphonies in a luxurious hall.

## PISA

Here's a short trip you may consider while staying in Rome or en route. It's a four-hour train trip to Pisa from Rome, and the main attraction, of course, is the legendary **Leaning Tower** of Pisa. You can walk up into the tower for the full effect of the incredible shift the tower has taken. There's a worldwide contest under way for some means to prop up the tower, and maybe you'll think of something new! One suggestion under serious consideration is that a giant concrete hand be used to support it. For information on Leaning Tower suggestions, write to **Ente Provinciale per il Turismo**, Pisa. Pisa is full of tourists so avoid buying from the sidewalk junk sellers.

## FLORENCE

- **United States Consulate**, lungarno Vespucci 38, Tel. 298276.
- **American Express**, via Tornabuoni 12r, Tel. 262651.
- **Police**, Tel. 483201. Emergency number, 113.
- **Tourist Office**, piazza Ruccellai, Tel. 298906.

A favorite city, Florence is a mecca for art lovers, history buffs, and for the young. Street life is lively in this city of red-tiled roofs (city law allows no other kind), where the Arno River went wild in 1967, as it has throughout the centuries. The whole city seems to be one enormous gallery, with a famous monument or church around each corner.

**International Youth Hostel**, viale Augusto Righi 2-4, Tel. 601451. Recommended as one of the best; fifteen minutes by bus from the train station. Take bus 17B, red route, to the end of the line. 1500 L, 11 PM curfew.

**Centro di Ospitalità Santa Monaca**, via Santa Monaca 6, Tel. 296704. The cost is also 1500 L at this private hostel. Midnight curfew.

**Casa Famiglia Santissima Annunziata**, piazza SS. Annunziata 8, Tel. 298616 and 268338. Low-cost, dorm-style arrangement. Open 31 July to 20 September.

**Hotel Universo**, piazza Santa Maria Novella 20, Tel. 272184. Near the station.

**Campground, viale Michelangelo 80**. Take bus 13 from the train station to this spectacular campsite overlooking the city. You'll spend about 1200 L per person per night. Large youth population, disco, grocery store, restaurant. Students say they dined well here on large bowls of spaghetti, roast chicken, beef, or veal, salad, and wine for about 3000 L, including service.

Near the station and the university are many districts with small pensions and hundreds of rooms at 2000 to 4000 L, usually double rooms, with breakfast included. Try **via Faenza** and **via Nazionale.** *Pensioni* include **Pensione Picadilly**, via XXVII Aprile, Tel. 483238, or **Soggiorno Caterina**, via Barbano 8, Tel. 482705.

**Pensione Silla,** at lungarno Serristori 5, Tel. 284810, is a step up in cost. Friendly family atmosphere and helpful hostess, Sra. Silla Avellino. Located on the other side of the Arno, it's an easy walk to Ponte Vecchio. Terrace with view of river and Uffizi Gallery. A winner at $15 for two, including breakfast and private bath. Cheaper rooms without bath are also available.

FLORENCE

1. UFFIZI GALLERY
2. DUOMO
3. PONTE VECCHIO
4. PIAZZALE MICHELANGELO
5. BOBOLI GARDENS
6. PITTI PALACE

_____ **Where to Eat**

Florentine food is something to write home about; you won't be disappointed in many of the small *trattoria*, dinners 3000 to 4000 L.

**Ristorante Jolly**, 13 Canto de' Nelli. Self-service, around the corner from piazza San Lorenzo. Reasonable, modest food.

**Olympia**, via dei Servi 66, serves low-cost student specials, very popular.

**Trattoria Roberto**, via de Castellani 4, near the Uffizi Gallery.

**Sostanza**, on via del Porcellana, a street you probably would not go on if not recommended, is not a *trattoria* that appeals from outside. But it has excellent food—heavenly cannelloni, huge steaks, great desserts. Long tables so expect to share one with other diners. Dinner costs about $6.

**Paoli**, via Tavolini 12, Tel. 216215, is more expensive, but sparkling and perfect for a special evening when you want candlelight and flowers. About $9 per person.

**La Loggia**, piazzale Michelangelo 6. In a romantic setting above the city, this restaurant is also for a special occasion. Alfresco dining among portico columns with tall, icy drinks. Not cheap, about $10.

I have deliberately listed some finer eating establishments in each city, so you won't become tired of doing your traveling on the cheap. Splurge once in a while. Break up the salami-and-cheese routine.

_____ **What to See, What to Do**

**Uffizi Gallery** (daily hours 8:30 AM to 4 PM) is one of Europe's outstanding galleries and houses works by Botticelli, Michelangelo, da Vinci, and Rembrandt.

The **Duomo,** or cathedral, is officially Santa Maria del Fiore. At piazza del Duomo, it has a massive interior with murals of *The Last Judgment* and a *Pieta* by Michelangelo. The cathedral was begun in the late thirteenth century by Arnolfo di Cambio. After he died Giotto and then Brunelleschi added their talents.

**Ponte Vecchio**, or old bridge, was built in 1345 at the narrowest point of the Arno. The bridge is lined with little shops, and since the sixteenth century most of them have been goldsmiths and jewelers.

**Piazzale Michelangelo** is the nineteenth-century square, where you get a fantastic sweeping view of the city. In the center is a bronze copy of Michelangelo's *David*. (The original is in Florence's **Accademia**.)

**Boboli Gardens**, adjoining the Pitti Palace, are especially attractive with numerous ponds, an amphitheater, and a pleasant summer coffeehouse.

The **Baptistry of St. John** at piazza San Giovanni is a Romanesque building from the eleventh century. The gilded bronze doors known

as the *Doors of Paradise* are noteworthy. Inside are beautiful mosaics and Donatello's wooden statue of Mary Magdalene. Open daily 9 AM to 12:30 PM, 2:30 PM to 6 PM.

AT NIGHT

**Space Electronic Disco**, via Paluzzuolo 37, is a recommended disco with dancing to live music by top American and English rock bands and a multimedia light-and-sound show. Medium priced.

**Piazza San Marco** is a popular gathering spot for students, as is piazzale Michelangelo, where sidewalk vendors—from artists sketching profiles to sellers of cheap jewelry and leatherware—never seem to roll up their wares.

SPECIAL FESTIVAL

On 24 June, San Giovanni's Day, there's an annual festival in Florence with a huge parade and over 500 people dressed in Michelangelo-designed costumes for a ceremony called Calcio in Costume. Four teams play an ancient brand of football in an elimination tournament. Decked in medieval pagentry, twenty-seven-man teams rough it up on sand-covered squares, each team representing a region of Florence. Fair maidens in flowing dresses cheer the teams on, and you can watch from inside the square for about $5—or you can find a free vantage spot easily enough. "An outrageous festival, in tune with the natural pace of the city," according to one student. "It makes American football look like a tea party."

### Shopping

Most shops open 9:30 or 10 AM in the morning, then close around noon for siesta, and reopen at 2:30 or 3 PM until 7 PM.

Florence offers outstanding shopping for good leather, gold chains, earrings, rings, and straw of all kinds, shapes, and sizes. Straw handbags, straw-lace skirts, leather bags, gloves, fine sweaters, silk ties and scarves at modest prices will lure you.

Read the labels carefully, though, when you buy a scarf or tie. It may be polyester, which doesn't tie nearly as nicely as silk. Leather bookmarks are a great buy at twenty cents. Ask for a good price if you buy a dozen (sellers may ask as much as fifty cents individually). They are good send-home gifts that you can tuck in a card or envelope, as are scarves.

Don't be afraid to bargain for anything you buy along the street. Shop awhile before you decide. It doesn't hurt to ask for a better price in a small shop, but larger fine shops have fixed prices, usually higher than on the street. Decide which meets your needs, for sometimes the fancy shop merchandise is not much different from that on the street.

Go to the outdoor **straw market** near the Ponte Vecchio for some good haggling practice.

For reproductions of artworks, try **Alinari** on lungarno Amerigo Vespucci. With a mammoth range to choose from, you can also browse in peace as long as you don't drag a backpack in with you. Incidentally, most shops do not allow packs inside. They are unwieldy, tend to block traffic, and are too handy for shoplifting. If you plan to do a lot of shopping, try to stow your pack for the day. Check it at the train station if necessary.

## VENICE

Often described as a tourist trap, Venice has several points of interest, particularly her renowned endless canals, piazza San Marco, Doges' Palace, and the **Accademia Museum**. The Accademia has a magnificent collection of Venetian paintings by Titian and Tintoretto and others. You can ride canal boats for 100 L a ride, and you can enjoy the city's sidewalk cafes. An old hand at the tourist trade, Venice is an easy city to walk in. On flat ground, it has 120 islands and 400 bridges spanning over 150 canals.

The **Doges' Palace** contains one of Europe's remarkable galleries, a cluttered yet breathtaking courtyard, and a grand and glorious stairway called the Staircase of the Giants. If pink and white marble, frescoes, and gilt don't impress you, the art treasured here undoubtedly will. Don't miss the **Bridge of Sighs**, which links the palace to the grim jail, where prisoners had their last glimpse of freedom. You can take a tour with an English-speaking group, and entry to the palace costs 200 L for students. Open daily from 9 AM to 6 PM.

There are hundreds of churches and palaces in Venice, and even the churches charge a 100-L admission fee. Two art-filled churches from the early 1400s are: **Santa Maria Gloriosa dei Frari** and **Santi Giovanni e Paolo**. The latter was founded by the Dominican Order, and both are masterpieces of architecture.

Of course, the **Basilica of San Marco** on piazza San Marco, is called the heart and soul of Venice. Titian's *Last Judgment* is here, as is the incredibly rich golden altarpiece studded with precious gemstones. Guides can give you a good knowledge of the detail in this church.

Other Venetian churches with outstanding works are:

**San Giorgo**, at Campo san Vio, is an Anglican church of beautiful

*a canal in Venice*

Renaissance lines. Over the front door, you can see the bas-relief of St. George slaying the dragon.

**San Stefano's,** one of the liveliest churches in Italy, is a Gothic beauty with paintings by Tintoretto. The intricately decorated ceiling is remarkable.

Many tourists take the lagoon trip to the island of **Murano**, an ancient center of glass blowing. There's a glass museum here, and you can watch the interesting process firsthand. It's quite commercial, but then so is Venice.

For accommodations, check with the **tourist board** at the railroad station, or at piazza San Marco, Ascensione 71/c. Tel. 26356.

## SARDINIA

If you hanker for a respite from city touring, you can reserve a ferry ticket to Sardinia while you tour Rome. Sparkling waters perfect for snorkling await you in midsummer, and it's easy to get off the beaten path on this sleepy isle. In fact, two students who arrived there during siesta almost turned around and went back to the mainland because it seemed so deserted. They stayed and loved it.

Ferries run daily and cost 6500 L. They depart from Civitavecchia, one hour by train north of Rome, and arrive in Olbia, Sardinia. The trip takes seven hours and can be booked in Rome at via Bissolati 41, Tel. 481753. Reservations are suggested in summer. When you arrive in Olbia, a train will take you through the countryside to **Alghero** and a pleasant hostel. There are also more expensive tourist beaches at **Costa Esmeralda**, which is full of jet setters, casinos, and posh hotels. However, no one seems to be too fussy about who belongs on what beach.

There's a **youth hostel** at via Zara 2, in Alghero, with eighty beds and enough amenities to make a pleasant stay.

The town has much appeal. Of interest is an underwater cavern called the **Grotta di Nettuno,** with a twice-daily boat trip for 2000 L, student rate. Always ask if a student discount applies. Even if it doesn't, a kind-hearted guide will often cut the price for young people.

## SKIING

The Dolomites offer fantastic skiing on some world-famous slopes, at a fraction of the price you would pay on the other side of the mountain in Switzerland. **Cortina D'Ampezzo, Val Gardena**, and villages of **Selva-Wolkenstein** and **St. Ulrich** are ones we know well. Lift passes, hotels, and restaurant facilities are modest in cost. You can ski long runs at an altitude of over 3000 meters, and a lift pass for thirteen days will cost you about $6 a day and is good on over 100 lifts. Single-day passes are more expensive. For a list of pensions, write to the visitors' bureau in Santa Christina or in Cortina. Most pensions require a two-week reservation at Christmas and Easter and require that you take your meals there.

For a list of major ski and hiking regions in the Dolomites, write to: **Italian Government Travel Office,** 630 Fifth Avenue, New York, New York 10020; or: **Associazione Pro Loco,** 39047 S. Christina, Val Gardena, Italy.

# 16 FOCUS ON LUXEMBOURG

Population: 355,000
Capital: Luxembourg City

Language: French and German
Currency: franc (fr.)

## THE LAND AND THE PEOPLE

Luxembourg is best known to many Americans as the jumping-off spot for their European sojourn, chiefly because the low fares of Icelandic Airlines and Air Bahamas bring thousands of visitors to the continent via Luxembourg each year.

A tiny grand duchy the size of Rhode Island, Luxembourg is squeezed in between Germany, Belgium, and France. With the finesse of France and with some of Germany's stoutheartedness, the natives have carved a special niche with their own cuisine. Famous smoked Ardennes ham and elegant pastries will tempt you, as will the local fresh trout.

More than 130 ancient castles grace the landscape, and the people have a high standard of living, with very little unemployment. Iron and steel are the most important industries.

Luxembourg is also a good place to buy a European rail pass, such as InterRail. With this pass you must pay half fare in the country where you buy it, so many students deliberately go to Luxembourg to buy a pass since this country is where they will do the least traveling. Train service in and out is excellent.

## LUXEMBOURG CITY

**Important Addresses**

- **United States Embassy,** 22 boulevard Emmanual Servais, Tel. 40123.
- **American Express,** 15 rue Notre Dame, Tel. 22931.
- **Grand Duchy National Tourist Office,** place de la Gare, Tel. 481199, can provide maps, information, and hotel reservations. Open 8:30 AM to 8:30 PM.

**Where to Stay**

Youth Hostel, 2 rue Fort Olizy, Tel. 26889, was described by our travelers as the nicest hostel they found. Very clean, central, and the only one with a really modern laundry. Also a disco. You can walk about thirty minutes or take bus 9 from the train station. Bed and breakfast, 95 fr., about $2.75.

Write ahead for reservations. If the hostel is full, ask the tourist board for help. Since you'll likely spend only a night or two in

Luxembourg City, it's probably simpler to let them find you a place.

## What to See, What to Do

The city itself looks like the setting for a medieval operetta, with castles, turrets, bridges, moats, and deep ravines cutting through the pleasant wooded valley. It is small enough so you can easily explore on foot. Begin at the ruins of the old fort, the **Bock Casemates,** where you can look down into the valley. The hostel is just at the bottom of this hill. You can imagine a time when this impregnable fortress guarded the city. There's a lovely walk along the **Walls of the Corniche** and by the **Castle Bridge,** high above the Petrusse River. The **Grand Ducal Palace** dates back to the 1500s.

Near the **Hôtel de Ville** (city hall) there's a pleasant **Gothic cathedral.** Another interesting area is around the fish market called the **Marché aux Poissons,** where some of the capital's oldest buildings can be found. You might wander onto a Sunday-afternoon concert in the vicinity of the **National Museum,** as we did. The band concert was portable—hauled around on the back of a large fire engine. It was quite fine. At that time the museum had a modern tapestry exhibit and a showing of Russian icons.

So if your travels plunk you into Luxembourg City for a day or two, take heart. The people are friendly and the setting impressive. You won't be disappointed in the first city you see in Europe.

# 17 FOCUS ON THE NETHERLANDS

Population: 13,600,000
Capital: The Hague

Language: Dutch
Currency: guilder (written as f, or ff for florin, another name for guilder)

## THE LAND AND THE PEOPLE

A heavily populated country, with an average of 900 people per square mile, nearly half of Holland has been reclaimed from the sea. Yet you will not notice the density when you travel through the open green countryside, over flat, canal-bordered, tree-lined roads. Holland is a trim and tidy country of tulip-bulb fields, 950 windmills, and the head offices of industrial giants.

Since the national life in the Netherlands has been spent in an endless struggle to keep the sea at bay, no one is surprised to find the Dutch a tough, determined, and hard-working people, serious yet usually quite open and friendly. A favorite description of the Dutch people's ideal behavior was given to me by a young dental assistant working in Germany, "We like to be proper and very relaxed, both at the same time. We can be proper, but not stuffy."

Young travelers are always amazed at how helpful and accommodating Europeans are, and the Dutch seem to outdo most other peoples in this respect. They publish *Holland Loves You, Youth in Holland*—enough to make you want to go! The National Tourist Office, the VVV, will inundate you with maps and free information about student and youth facilities all over Holland. There are some 400 hostels in Holland. Ask for a young-people's list, *Camping Homes and Camping Farms*. Hostels charge f 9.25 per night with breakfast, about $3.30. Camping homes and farms charge from f 25 to f 50 per person per week, about $13 to $19. Hostels are better suited for overnight stays, while farms and camping homes take week-long visitors, particularly groups.

The National Tourist Board has a system of what they call Tourist Hotels and Tourist Menus. They will give you a complete list of both on request. For the Tourist Menus, they have designed a system that enables you to eat in a wide variety of places, from a castle to a farmhouse, restaurants simple or elegant, for a standard price of f 12.50, about $5, including service. You are served a three-course meal, with first course or appetizer, main course, and dessert. Meals differ from place to place, but they must meet certain standards. The emblem for these places is a large fork wearing a hat and camera on a blue background with white letters in English announcing "Tourist Menu."

Tourist hotels are also identified as such and rates begin at about $10.

## TRANSPORTATION

Dutch trains are fast, efficient, comfortable, and dependable. There are also many intercity, nonstop trains. Eight-day, unlimited-train-travel tickets are sold in Holland or at authorized rail offices abroad. To buy them you need a passport photo. Distances within cities are not great, so exploring on foot is recommended. If you are in a hurry, buses are frequent and cost little. You will probably see more bicyclists in Holland than in any other country. There are bicycle lanes in cities, and motorists are quite accustomed to cyclists. In most cities you can rent bicycles at the central railroad station or ask at the tourist office.

You can rent bicycles at Amsterdam's **central station** and at **HEJA,** Bestavaerstraat 39, Tel. 129211, and at **Fiet-O-Fiets,** Amstelveensweg 880-900, Tel. 445473.

There are several bike tours you can take for day-long trips out into the countryside. One is **Ena's Bicycle Tour,** Tel. 143797. The usual daily departure is 10 AM, and you will visit a cheese farm and see a windmill at work. The trip costs f 20 including bike rental and lunch. You will be back in Amsterdam by 7 PM.

## FOOD

The Dutch breakfast will be welcome after the hard roll and coffee served all over Europe. Most Dutch breakfasts include cheese, boiled eggs, several kinds of bread, including rusks (round, crisp toasts about a half inch thick), butter, jam, and often several sliced meats. Special native cheeses are Gouda (pronounced *How-da*) and Edam.

Lunch in Holland often consists of *Broodje,* a sandwich you can buy along the street, in cafeterias, and in restaurants. They are made on small, soft buns with meats and cheese and are not expensive.

Typical Dutch dishes appear in season, with fresh asparagus and new herring in spring. *Rodekool met Rolpens,* a heartier fare in autumn, is red cabbage and rolled, spiced meat with sliced apple. The famous Dutch pea soup can be found year round but more often in cold months, when it is made with ham chunks and sausage or bacon. This soup is wonderful on a foggy, cold day in Amsterdam, where the seaside proximity makes it chilly indeed along the canals in December.

What's more, the Dutch like international foods. Amsterdam is said to have more foreign restaurants than any city on the continent. You can eat couscous, shish kebab, hamburgers, *canard à l'orange*—plus the best Indonesian food outside of Indonesia. Amsterdam and other Dutch cities boast of their *rijsttafel*—literally rice table—where you are served heaping bowls of steamed rice and twenty or so side dishes of meats, seafood, and vegetables in bite-sized morsels, with zesty sauces on the side.

Department stores in Holland have an incredible display of well-known Dutch chocolate, in every size and shape, even to a whole wall full of alphabet letters made from chocolate, from three-inch ones to some twenty-inchers.

## SHOP HOURS

Stores are generally open from 9 AM to 5:30 PM, except on Mondays when some stores do not open until 1:30 PM. Others may close Wednesday afternoons. Banks are open from 9 AM to 4 PM, closed Saturdays and Sundays. Post offices are closed on Saturdays.

## AMSTERDAM

_____ **Important Addresses**

- **United States Consulate,** Museumplein 19, Tel. 790321.
- **American Express,** Damrak 66, Tel. 62042.
- **Tourist bureau,** VVV, central station, Tel. 221016, or at Rokin 5, Tel. 266444. (Tourist bureaus are identifiable in each town by the upside-down triangle, with three white VVV's on blue background.)
- **NBBS, Dutch student travel association,** Dam 17, Tel. 237686 or 234737.

If you arrive by train, you will quickly see that the central station is right in the middle of everything. Although by daylight the famous canals may look a bit green and run-down with small houseboats and clutter along their edges, at night they are quite appealing, with tree-lined banks and gabled houses adding to their charm. The **Dam Square** near the huge Krasnapolsky Hotel is still a scene of much action, both by day and night, and young people and students gather here from every country. Drugs are widely available in Amsterdam. While the Dutch are a broad-minded people in many ways, they are not with drugs. Arrests and penalties are frequent, and so are undercover agents.

## Where to Stay

The following are youth hostels or another Dutch specialty for youth called Sleep-Ins, which are usually dormitory-style places, where you can stay cheaply. All accommodations in this list are priced from f 8 to f 12 per person, including bed and breakfast. All are open year round.

**International Youth Hostel,** Kloveniersburgwal 97, Tel. 246832. Take bus 4, 9, or 16 from central station.

**Vondelpark Hostel,** Zandpad 5, Tel. 141744. Take bus 1, 2, or 3.

**Adolesce,** Nieuwe Keizersgracht 26, Tel. 263959. Pleasant setting with garden.

**COK,** Jan Luykenstraat 44, Tel. 720526. Has a laundry room.

**Hans Brinker Stutel,** Kerkstraat 136, Tel. 220687. Games and TV.

**Eben Haezer,** Bloemstraat 179, Tel. 244717. Mostly dormitory style.

**Kabul,** Warmoesstraat 42, Tel. 237158. Dormitory style; breakfast extra.

**Amad en Eva,** Sarphatistraat 105, Tel. 246206, 108 beds, nine dorms.

**NBBS Student Hotel,** Keizersgracht 15, Tel. 251364. Near central station, open summer only.

If you strike out on this list (you can write ahead for reservations), ask the VVV to make a reservation for you. There are many other student hotels, and some are open only from March to November.

There are also private families who accept guests. Some female travelers report that they were urged to take a room aboard a houseboat along the canal. By all means, keep away from any such arrangement, no matter how tempting. The red-light district is flourishing and well known.

## Where to Eat

Generally, the closer the restaurant is to the Dam Square, the more expensive, but some places are competitive, so read the menus posted outside before entering.

**Oliver Hardy,** Vijslstraat 95, sells hamburgers and other simple fare.

**La Cave Internationale,** Harengracht 561. With a student ID, you can get a good meal in this usually more expensive spot. Ask for it, at about f 5, but student cards are not valid on weekends, we are told.

**Sassafras,** Leidsegracht 68, from f 6, open daily from 5 PM to 10 PM.

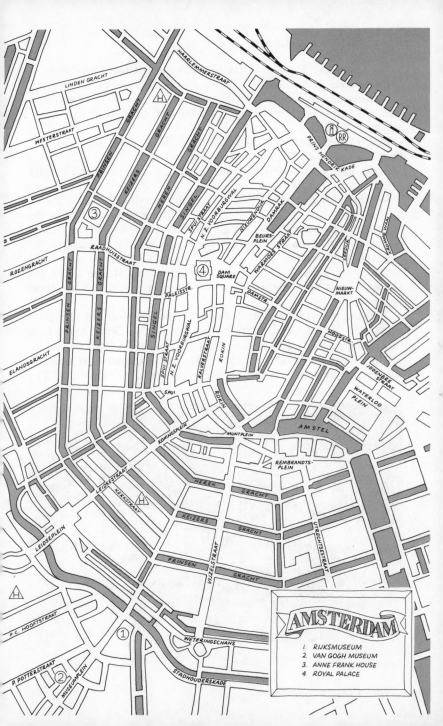

**De Lantaarn,** 2 e Const. Huygensstraat 64. Closed weekends.

**Cantharel,** Kerkstraat 377. Meals from f 5 daily, evenings only.

**Roosterplaetse,** Singel 359. Open noon to 3 PM, 6 PM to 11 PM. Very nice, gas lamps, dark wood and brick interior, cozy. More expensive, about $8 to $10.

**Bali,** Leidsestraat. A fantastic *rijsttafel.* Expensive, but good. The small dishes of sauces are super spicy.

**Fong Lie,** P.C. Hoofstraat 80. Great Chinese food, moderately priced.

**Surabaya,** N.Z. Voorburgwal 272. Hearty servings, medium prices.

_____ **What to See, What to Do**

Take a **sight-seeing tour** in a glass-roofed canal boat either from a pier near central station or along the Rokin and Stadthouderskade, near the Rijksmuseum. The ride costs about $1.50 an hour, and the multilingual guide will tell you some interesting stories about the skinny houses lining the canals and the people who have made them famous.

The impressive seventeenth-century **Royal Palace** on the Dam Square could be an easy starting point for touring. Open from 1 June to 31 August, daily 10 AM to noon, 1 PM to 4 PM. Closed weekends.

The **Rijksmuseum,** at Stadthouderskade 42, is the national museum, where paintings by world-famous masters are exhibited. The

*a typical Dutch canal scene*

collection ranges from the fifteenth to the nineteenth century and contains many Rembrandts, including *The Night Watch.* This painting has been recently under repair, after a knife slashing in 1976, and you can watch the repairmen at work behind a glass shield, as well as read a narrative about the restoration process. You can buy very fine reproductions, posters, and cards. Hours, daily 10 AM to 5 PM. Sunday and holidays 1 PM to 5 PM. Closed New Year's Day. Entry, f 2, f 1 on Sunday; people under twenty-one pay f 1. Take bus 26, 65, or 66.

**Vincent van Gogh Museum,** Paulus Potterstraat 7-11, open daily from 10 AM to 5 PM, Sunday and holidays 1 PM to 5 PM. Closed New Year's Day. Take bus 26, 65, or 66. Near the Rijksmuseum. Admission f 2.5.

The **Stedelijk Museum,** Paulus Potterstraat 13, houses contemporary art in both permanent collections and temporary exhibits. Collections include paintings, sculpture, graphics, posters, and industrial design. Highlights are works by Cezanne, Matisse, Picasso, and Chagall. Reproductions are for sale here at modest cost. Hours are from 9:30 AM to 5 PM daily. Sunday 1 PM to 5 PM. f 1.75 entry.

**Anne Frank House,** at Prinsengracht 263, is a monument to the young girl who wrote *The Diary of Anne Frank* while she hid here from the Nazis with her family. Hours, 9 AM to 6 PM daily, Sunday 10 AM to 4 PM. Entry f 2.50.

The Dutch are avid film fans, and foreign films appear in their original language with Dutch subtitles. VVV puts out a tip sheet on what's happening in town for the month or week. Check with them for movie schedules. There's also a **National Film Museum** at Vondelpark 3, where special screenings take place.

**Cafés** and **small jazz clubs** as well as cozy "brown pubs" are dotted all over Amsterdam. Most are not expensive and do not get lively before 10 PM. Young people cluster around **Leidesplein.** Ask the students you meet in hostels and around the Dam Square what the popular student places are at the moment; such spots tend to fade in and out rather rapidly. Some are more for rap sessions and serious discussions, while other are a combination restaurant-theater with a light-and-sound-show atmosphere. Some have dancing; others feature films and jazz.

## UTRECHT

Other tour spots could include Utrecht, a half hour by train from Amsterdam, a city with a very old sector that appeals quite strongly to Europeans, perhaps less so to Americans. It is interesting, yet somber. There are several museums here, including a **Gold, Silver, and Clock Museum.** There is also a castle in a park and a cathedral. General hotels are expensive, but the visitors' bureau can direct you to less costly accommodations, including student hostels and private homes.

## THE HAGUE

The seat of the Government, this is lovely and has a very different flavor from Amsterdam's. It has smart restaurants, intimate cafés, and pedestrian areas. You will find small, appealing shops and old bookstores and antique dealers worth your browsing time. The Hague is closely linked to a popular and lively beach resort, **Scheveningen.** If the pace of Amsterdam was not to your liking, you may prefer the Hague and environs. A special museum, the **Gemeentemuseum** (Municipal Museum), houses the largest collection of art by modern Dutch painter Piet Mondrian. It's located at Stadhouderslaan 41, open daily 10 AM to 5 PM, except on Wednesdays, when hours are from 8 AM to 10 PM. Sunday 1 PM to 5 PM. Free entry.

Here are some hostels in the area:

**Gruno,** Sweelinckstraat 49, Tel. 632277. Small, but open all year.

**t'Seehuys,** Zeekant 45, Tel. 559585. Near the beach, open all year. 120 beds, costs f 8 to f 14.

**Heemskerk,** Tolweg 7-9, Tel. 32288.

The **VVV** is located at the main train station, and they can find you a room. Bureau hours are from 8:30 AM to 8 PM, Sunday 10 AM to 7 PM. Hotels are expensive in this Government-oriented city.

In Scheveningen, be sure to take in an enchanting little wonder called **Madurodam,** the most complete miniature city in existence. The community includes castles, churches, airport, and 46,000 lights, all at one twenty-fifth scale. Well worth a side trip to see. Open April to October daily from 9:30 AM to 10:30 PM, including Sunday. Admission $1.50, cheaper if you buy your ticket at the visitors' bureau.

## ARNHEM

Near the German border is the town of Arnhem, with a marvelous museum, **Rijksmuseum Kröller-Müller,** where you can see much of van Gogh's work in a very different setting from a city museum's.

The museum is set in a park, where deer and rabbits abound. There are white bicycles that you can ride free through the heather, and then return to the museum for another look at van Gogh's *The Potato*

*Eaters, The Bridge at Arles, The Postman Roulin,* and *Haystacks in Provence.* There is also a sculpture garden.

Hours here are Monday to Saturday 10 AM to 5 PM, Sunday and public holidays 11 AM to 5 PM. Entry for adults is f 4, and there's a student discount. From June to September, you can reach the museum by bus from Arnhem's central railway station.

You can book **bicycle tours** from Arnhem in two- to seven-night arrangements. Write to **Provinciale VVV Gelderland,** Stationsplein 45, Arnhem, or Tel. 452921. You cycle twenty-two to twenty-eight miles per day, and prices range from f 85 to f 336, depending on the length of trip you take. Arnhem is located in one of the Netherland's loneliest provinces.

# 18 FOCUS ON SCOTLAND

Population: 5,607,000
Capital: Edinburgh

Language: English
Currency: pound sterling (£)

## THE LAND AND THE PEOPLE

For some of the finest scenery in all of Europe, go to Scotland. Pure, unadulterated magnificence can be found in the uncultivated, noncommercialized Scottish Highlands. Just a few hours away from Glasgow, itself a friendly industrial city, you can be in the different world of the Loch Lomond region, which is not unlike Norway's fjords.

You won't find high-rise hotels or even much of a tourist industry in parts of the Highlands, but you will find plenty of places to stay. Youth hostels and cottages everywhere seem to hang out the bed-and-breakfast sign. From the Scottish Highlands, abloom with heather in August and September, to lovely, quiet outer islands, where artisans toil at ancient crafts to produce stunning tweeds, Scotland will capture you in its medieval spell. The summer days are long in Scotland, with as much as nineteen hours of sunlight in these northern latitudes. You can play golf or tennis easily until past 10 PM and watch the sun slip lazily into the water as the peat fires begin to burn in the crofter's cottages.

Both the Outer Hebrides to the west and Orkneys to the north can be reached easily by ferry. The Hebrides have alternately the fairest and the foulest weather in all of Britain. Raised like a shield to protect the face of Scotland from the Atlantic's fury, this chain of islands has a quiet allure. Fishing, farming, gathering seaweed for industry, cutting the turf (peat), and weaving Harris tweed, their most famous work, are basic industries to the islanders. Yet the 100,000 tourists who visit must also be cared for. If you plan to visit the islands, write to the Scottish Tourist Board, 23 Ravelston Terrace, Edinburgh, and ask for the booklet *Getting Around in Highlands and Islands*. Enclose seventy-five cents in international-reply coupons for mailing. This pamphlet lists all means of transport.

The most important city in Scotland is Edinburgh, a gracious, understated gem. If you have only a short time for Scotland, visit Edinburgh and the Highlands. If time allows, saunter down the west coast to Ayr and Troon, beach resorts in Robert Burns country and a golfing paradise, where the British Open was held at Turnburry in 1977. Or go north to Inverness via Loch Ness to have a look for Nessie (the well-commercialized monster), or you can zero in on the Cairngorm region, the mountains, and the Spey Valley.

## FOOD

Scottish breakfasts are hearty, with a fried egg or two, bacon and sausage, scones or toast, and plentiful tea. Although the sausage in much of Britain is quite different from the American-style product, try it anyway.

When you see the *Stockpot* sign outside Scottish restaurants, it means that they are one of the more than 250 places participating in a tourist-board venture to provide menus of Scottish food prepared in traditional ways. Scotland's most famous dish is haggis, made from the heart, liver, and other parts of the sheep that are cooked and chopped, mixed with oatmeal and seasonings, then stuffed into the sheep's stomach and boiled. Are you brave enough? It's served with Chappit Taties and Bashed Neeps (mashed potatoes and turnips). Happily, most of the traditional dishes on menus are translated into English beside the Scottish version. Finnan haddie, haddock, kippers, smoked herring, and fresh salmon and trout are the special treats. Hotchpotch, which is mutton broth thickened with new vegetables, and Cock-a-leekie, chicken soup with cut leeks, are good soups to try. Rumbledethumps (with such a funny name, you have to try it!) is boiled cabbage and mashed potatoes mixed with butter and chives. Scottish beef is very fine indeed, generously served and not too expensive. And such a sweet tooth the Scots have. They are mad for pastries and their jug of cream. Pour the thick cream (not whipped) over a fresh apple or blackberry tart.

High tea in Scotland is a light evening meal, served from 5 PM to 7 PM. Teas announced on a sign outside a restaurant or hotel means pastries and sandwiches are served in late afternoon around 4 PM.

## SHOP HOURS

Usual hours are 9 AM to 5:30 PM, Monday through Saturday.

## SHOPPING

Good buys include Shetland sweaters, which cost about £4, far less than they do at home. You can also buy beautiful cashmeres for about £15, Scottish plaids of all types in scarves, long kilts, short kilts, caps and vests, or sport jackets. Caithness glassware, etched with thistle or heather, is also reasonable, although heavy to ship.

## EDINBURGH

_____ **Important Addresses**

- **United States Consulate,** 3 Regent Terrace, Tel. 5568315.
- **American Express,** 139 Princes Street, Tel. 2257881, open from 9 AM to 5:30 PM Monday through Friday, 9 AM to noon on Saturday.
- **Tourist Information Bureau,** Waverly Bridge Information Center, Tel. 2257120. Open Monday to Saturday 8:30 AM to 9 PM, Sunday 11 AM to 9 PM. The charge for finding accommodations is 20p (about thirty-four cents).
- **General post office,** 2 Waterloo Place.
- **Police,** Parliament Square, High Street, Tel. 2251212. Emergency number: 999.

The city is impressive, with Edinburgh Castle sitting like a crown above the Old Town. You will see a mélange of architecture, from Norman to Victorian. Mary, Queen of Scots, literary giants such as Sir Walter Scott and Robert Burns, and many characters in Scottish history—Queen Margaret, John Knox, Robert Louis Stevenson— have left their mark on the character of Edinburgh.

_____ **Where to Stay**

Accommodations are not a problem, except during the Edinburgh International Festival in August. First off, head for the visitors' bureau at Waverly Bridge for a good map, brochures on what's happening in Edinburgh, and information on the rest of Scotland.

There are several hostels, but you should phone ahead to be sure that they have space available:

**Carlyle Hall,** East Suffolk Road, Tel. 6672262. Open July through September.

**University of Edinburgh,** Pollock Halls of Residence, 18 Holyrood Park Road, Tel. 6674331, ext. 139. Bed and breakfast for £4 per night.

**YWCA of Scotland,** 14 Coates Crescent, Tel. 2253608, open all year. £2.50 for breakfast and a bed, weekly rates also.

**Edinburgh YMCA International Center and Hostel,** 14 South St. Andrew Street, Tel. 5564303. One hundred yards from Waverly Bridge Station, £3.20 per night with breakfast.

**International Youth Hostel,** 7 Bruntsfield Crescent, Tel. 4472994. Four kilometers from Waverly Bridge Station; take bus 11, 15, or 16.

**International Youth Hostel,** 18 Eglinton Crescent, Tel. 3371120. Two kilometers from Waverly Bridge Station; take bus 3, 4, 12, or 13.

When hostels are full, the visitors' bureau can find you a room at a

B and B for about £2.50 to £3.50 and slightly higher at Festival time. If you walk down the street in a neighborhood where the B-and-B shingle hangs out, you can hardly go wrong if you choose one that looks good. There's not much variation in price or quality.

## Where to Eat

Try the pubs, as they are many and not expensive. Along Rose Street and also on St. Stephen Street, you'll find some lively places. Hanover Street has many low-cost restaurants.

**The Scottish Fare,** 129 Rose Street, is a self-serve restaurant with pastries as well as full meals for about £2.

**Henderson's Salad Table,** 94 Hanover Street, features meals for £1.50 with vegetarian specialties. Open Monday through Saturday.

**Sik Tek Fok,** 97 Hanover Street. Costs about £2 for an adequate Chinese meal.

**Laigh Coffee House,** 83 Hanover Street. Excellent food, including truly Scottish fare at medium prices. Closed Sunday.

## What to See, What to Do

The **Edinburgh International Festival** is held annually from early August to early September, and the city sparkles with music, drama, art, films, and the **Military Tattoo.** This spectacle features music, precision marching, and military exercises full of all the pomp and ceremony a monarchy can muster. Reservations should be made well in advance. Write to: **Festival Box Office,** 21 Market Street, Edinburgh.

Edinburgh is a good city for walking, although bus transportation is cheap and excellent. The **Old Town** south of Princes Street is the area that includes most of the historic monuments and museums. To the north of Princes Street is eighteenth-century New Town, containing stores and private homes. Along Princes Street are fashionable shops, several fine department stores, a park, and monuments.

The **Royal Mile** begins at the **Castle,** overlooking the gardens of Princes Street. Rebuilt in the seventh century by Edwin, King of Northumbria, the Castle includes a lovely Norman Chapel, the royal apartments, Great Banquet Hall, the crown, scepter, sword of state, and other Scottish treasures. There are also some outstanding war memorials of the world. Open daily from 9:30 AM to 6 PM, Sunday 11 AM to 6 PM. Entry 30p.

**St. Giles's Cathedral,** or the High Kirk, a lofty Gothic structure; Scotland's **Parliament House,** now the home of Scotland's supreme courts; **John Knox's House,** built in 1490; and **Palace of Holyroodhouse** are other visitors' targets along the Royal Mile. The palace is the official residence of Her Majesty the Queen when she is in Edinburgh. In Holyroodhouse you'll find the room where Lord Darnley, husband of Mary, Queen of Scots, murdered the queen's friend David Rizzio.

The **Scott Monument** in East Princes Street Gardens is the most conspicuous monument, with a 200-feet-high Gothic spire. You can climb up 287 steps for a wonderful view of the city.

**Canongate Tolbooth,** (open daily from 10 AM to 5 PM, closed Sunday) is a city museum featuring Highland dress. **Acheson House,** not far from the Tolbooth, is an interesting old house built in 1633, which now houses the **Scottish Craft Center.** The unusual **Museum of Childhood** at 38 High Street, almost opposite John Knox's House, (same hours as Canongate) has a large collection of things relating to childhood—toys, dolls, and books of the past. Entry is 10p.

Some galleries you should consider visiting: **National Gallery of Scotland,** at the Mound, has collections by English masters and important Scottish artists. Open daily 10 AM to 5 PM. The **Scottish National Gallery of Modern Art,** at Inverleith House in the Botanic Garden, has graphics, sculpture, and other modern art. It is open daily from 10 AM to 6 PM and Sunday from 2 PM to 6 PM. The **Royal Scottish Academy,** at the Mound, Princes Street, has its annual exhibit to promote fine arts from April through August. Open daily 10 AM to 9 PM, Sunday 2 PM to 5 PM. There are special exhibits and extended hours during Festival. Entry fee 15p.

**Portobello Open Air Pool** beyond Regent Terrace allows 3000 (!) swimmers to cool off in summer, with a wave-making machine for extra fun. Hours, Monday to Friday 10 AM to 6:45 PM. Saturday and Sunday 10 AM to 5:30 PM. Entry 25p.

In the **Pentland Hills** you can visit the largest artificial ski slope in Britain, the **Hillend Ski Center,** featuring a chairlift and cafeteria. Open year round, Monday to Saturday 10 AM to 5 PM, Sunday 2 PM to 5 PM. Entry 50p. There is grass skiing in the summer. Bus 4 will get you there in about twenty minutes.

There are many theaters in Edinburgh that charge modest prices. For example, the best seats for a recent series, including *The Marriage of Figaro, The Nutcracker,* and *Giselle,* cost £4.50 for each production. The cheapest were £1, about $1.75.

**Concerts** can be booked for 75p. to £2.

## THE COUNTRYSIDE

A highly recommended brochure is *Break Away,* published by **Scottish Youth Hostels Association** (7 Glebe Crescent, Stirling FK 8

2 JA, Scotland). It describes in detail, including costs, the varied tours and sports courses you can enjoy with a group. You can sail or canoe on **Loch Morlich** and at **Ullapool** on the west coast, or take a cycle tour, or go mountaineering in the **Highlands** to learn gem hunting, rope management, and how to cope with weather exposure. At many of the hostels you can enroll in sports instruction on a per-hour basis. Prices vary, but one example is the week-long cycle tour for £23 that covers meals, accommodations, and guide.

Such a tour could be an ideal way for young travelers to get off into the countryside of Scotland, without the concern of mapping out routes. Some students who have managed very well on their own say that once in a while they don't mind going with an organized group if it has a special-interest program that appeals to them.

While the cities may offer a cultural feast—as Edinburgh does, especially during the Festival—the people are often less friendly than those in the country. In smaller towns along the seacoast and in villages, we have found the Scots to be delightful. One man endeared himself to me forever. In dreadful trouble with my hacking golf game, a canny Scot came to my rescue. He blithely trampled down the seaside grass to all but tee up my ball. "Golf was meant to be enjoyed, lass," he said gruffly.

## SOME SCENIC ROUTES

Hosteling in Scotland is excellent, with numerous hostels situated in scenic areas from the Highlands to the coastal regions and islands. Expect to pay £2 for overnight bed and breakfast. If a hostel is not convenient, choose a B and B and the price will be only slightly higher. If prices are the same, however, student travelers say they'd choose the B and B because you have a key for your own room, your belongings are safer, and you can hang up laundry.

Don't try to tour all of Scotland, but zero in on one or two areas. Save the rest for another time. You could head for **Aviemore,** which is the gateway to the Cairngorms. Train service is good, and the area is great for walking and climbing in summer and skiing in winter. Summer weather can be capricious, so be prepared for storms and chilly days. You can take the chairlift in Aviemore to the top of the **Cairngorm** or walk the woods in the **Spey Valley.** The hostel at Aviemore is seven miles from the train station.

The train to Inverness is pleasant, and you may stop wherever the country pleases you. Inverness is a tourist trap, but you can head toward the **Kyle of Lochalsh** via one of Scotland's scenic train routes. There's a hostel at Kyle called **Ross-shire,** and in this region you can explore the **Eilean Donal Castle,** which majestically watches over the Meeting of the Three Waters—Loch Duich, Loch Long, and Loch Alsh.

Farther northwest is **Ullapool** (population 600) with a good hostel on Shore Street. Ullapool is a convenient starting point for the **Outer Hebrides.** (You can catch a car ferry to Starnaway.) Fishing is excellent, and European sea-angling championships have been held here. The village perches on a promontory jutting into Loch Broom, and you can see some dramatic landscapes, steep peaks, and loch-fretted moors.

# 19 FOCUS ON SPAIN

Population: 33,600,000            Language: Spanish
Capital: Madrid                  Currency: peseta (ptas.)

## THE LAND AND THE PEOPLE

No matter what else lingers in your memory of Spain, you will not forget the spirit of the people. In a land where time has a different meaning, you may be surprised to discover the Spanish sense of pride and independence.

A hot-tempered American recently blew up when he encountered what he considered an inefficient hotel system. He threw his credit card across the desk in an attempt to pay his account. Calm, cool, and looking directly at the towering man, the clerk commented, "That's no way to present your card," and refused to pick it up. You may not always agree with Spanish business methods, but you will admire Spanish dignity.

The coastline and the borders of Spain, like a giant picture frame, hold much of her attraction, with some major exceptions such as Madrid, Seville, and Cordoba. For the most part, inland Spain is barren and rocky, arid and uncultivated.

Spain is a travel bargain, especially since the peseta was devalued in the late summer of 1977. Hordes of vacationers flock annually to Spain, one of the most popular countries in Europe for tourists. As John Masefield wrote, "Spanish waters, you are ringing in my ears like a low, sweet piece of music...." And indeed, Spanish waters are part of the understated grandeur of the Mediterranean.

Spanish life revolves around the simple pleasures of family, devotion to the Catholic faith, food, fun—and siesta! The tempo is most surely *lento*. There's a feeling of never-never land, where the worrisome world quickly fades into the distance. No one hurries about anything. Spanish clocks run slowly, several hours so by American standards. A young American tried on shoes in a Malaga shop last summer. "*Buena, buena.* They're good, I'll take them," he said.

The salesman shook his head, pointing to his watch. "Siesta, siesta," he said with a smile. "We close now. You come later." The tourist had to return later to pick up the shoes.

Every day traffic grinds to a halt by one in the afternoon. By five in the evening the streets are crowded again. Spaniards cherish their traditions, and a *paseo,* or evening stroll, is a highlight of the day for many families. The plazas and fountains are lively places, where you can see young girls walking arm in arm, or old men in animated conversation, arms linked almost at armpit level. Sidewalk cafés and flower-draped balconies characterize the street scene. The time taken for a glass of wine with friends, for reflection, for daily ceremonies helps preserve the peculiar rhythms of Spanish life. And in a very short time you feel comfortable in this aura. *Olé!*

## TRANSPORTATION

Spanish trains are in tune with Spanish clocks—slow. You *must* change trains at all Spanish borders because the track sizes in Spain are different. There are two exceptions to this rule on the Madrid-to-Paris run: the *Talgo* and the *Ter.* For some reason, Eurailpass holders must reserve seats in advance, even though travelers can usually hop on a Spanish train and pay the fare on board. If you can't suffer through the trains, try the night flights in and out of the country. Also check on special student flights through CIEE offices or student-travel offices in major cities.

City buses are reasonably reliable and very cheap, but crowded. Buses along the coastline of the Costa del Sol between Málaga and Gibraltar are inexpensive and pleasant, although they stop everywhere. Taxis are also inexpensive, so consider doubling up with other travelers for a taxi across town.

## ACCOMMODATIONS

The Spanish National Tourist Board has instituted a rating system for accommodations, from one to five stars, and the rating must be posted. The price must also be posted in each room. Ask to see a room before you decide to take it, and also find out if you must take meals there. One-star hotels and one- or two-star hostels may increase the room rate by 20 percent if you do not eat there. A *residencia,* which usually serves only breakfast, is not permitted to increase the rate from the posted one. Ask if there are any surcharges on the room, or you may find your tab jumping skyward. If you have any problems when you settle your bill, ask for the complaint book, which must be passed on to Government authorities. Don't pay for the room in advance, and always ask if the outer entry door is locked at a specific hour.

The **Brujula** is an official room-finding service, which has a booth at train stations and at the airport. For a small fee, they can find you a super-cheap room, from 135 ptas. upward.

Something very special you can find in many Spanish cities is the *sereno,* a man who has keys to all the doors in a four- or five-block area. He walks the street of residential neighborhoods from about 10 PM to 6 AM and is never very far away. If you need help, clap your hands loudly, and he will find you. The clanking of his large ring of keys and his loud call *"Voy!"* (I'm coming!) will let you know he is on the way. He knows which families may have room, which pensions have space, and can help you in any need, including a doctor or a drugstore. He received the title of *sereno* a hundred years or so ago when his forerunners sang out every hour to tell the conditions of the night. When the sky was clear and calm, he would sing, *"Sereno."* He is paid by city hall, but if he opens doorways for you or finds you a place to stay, you should tip him or offer him a drink. According to a most gracious *señora* from the Spanish National Tourist bureau, his job is not actually to find rooms for tourists, but Spanish people are so friendly and helpful that you can look to the *sereno* for help if in need. She also cautioned that *serenos* are a fading breed and are no longer found everywhere.

## FOOD

Breakfasts are simple in Spain, with large cups of coffee, tea, or chocolate. The chocolate is recommended, as the coffee tastes quite peculiar to American palates. Hard rolls and butter and marmalade complete the meal.

Eating hours are even later in Spain than in most of Europe. Many restaurants do not open their doors for dinner until 9 PM or even 10 PM. Early evening finds Spaniards at street-side cafés enjoying wine and *tapas,* small snacks of seafoods, artichokes, or sardines. Along the shore you can buy a generous handful of fresh sardines grilled over a charcoal fire—excellent and unusual.

Spanish specialties include *gazpacho*—a smooth, cold soup made with cucumbers and tomatoes, the best of it giving only a hint of olive oil. A wonderful concoction you should try is *paella,* a saffron-rice dish laced with chunks of chicken, shellfish, and seasonings, sometimes topped with a whole baby lobster. While the fish is excellent, the beef should not be attempted; it's like shoe leather. Roast lamb baked in earthenware casseroles is outstanding, especially in Madrid.

Service is always included in the price. Most restaurants have a tourist menu, serving soup, fish or meat, dessert, bread, and wine. Wine is cheap and good—except for a super-sweet raisin wine popular along the coast.

Unfortunately, many tourists are afflicted with dysentery when they travel in Spain. It may be brought on by the water or by the difficulty of adjusting to olive oil in much of the cooking. Severe stomach cramps and diarrhea are the symptoms. Avoid tap water, and have medicine handy. Reach for it at the first signs of stomach cramps.

## SHOP HOURS

Shops are open from 9 AM to 2 PM and from 5 PM to 8 PM. They are closed on Sundays. Banks are open from 9 AM to 2 PM.

Expect to bargain for goods in tourist areas, at street and roadside shops, but not in indoor shops.

## MADRID

**Important Addresses**

- **United States Embassy,** calle de Serrano 75, Tel. 2763600.
- **American Express,** plaza de las Cortes, Tel. 2221180.
- **Tourist offices,** Toree de Madrid, Tel. 2412325; calle de Jesús de Medinaceli 2, Tel. 2211268; plaza Mayor; Barajas Airport, Tel. 2054222.
- **Police,** Puerta del Sol, Tel. 091.
- **Post office,** plaza de las Cibeles, Tel. 2218195.
- **Student travel office,** calle Fernando el Católico 88, Tel. 2430008; branch office, 71 José Ortega y Gasset, Tel. 4019501.
- **Laundromat,** calle de las Infantas, near calle des Leon and plaza de las Cortes, wash and dry for 100 ptas.

**Where to Stay**

**International Youth Hostel Casa de Campo,** plaza Isabel II Tel. 4635699. Near city swimming pool and park. Take Metro to El Lago or bus 33. Good and cheap food, too.

**Josefina,** avenida de José Antonio 44, Tel. 2218141.

All along avenida de José Antonio you will find rooms to let, pensions, and hostels. An overnight room costs from 160 to 225 ptas. They can be noisy and hot, so choose a high room with windows.

**20 calle San Mateo** is very clean and has showers for 50 ptas. extra. Some rooms have balconies overlooking the street.

Here are some university residences with rooms for students. For about $4 daily students can have a room and three meals. They may require that you eat meals there—or at least pay for them.

**Colegio Mayor José Miguel Guitarte,** calle Amaniel 2, Tel. 2212990. Near Metro stop plaza de España, or take bus 1 or 2.

**Colegio Mayor Santa Maria de Europa,** Cea Bermúdez 17, Tel. 2336200. Can be reached by bus 1, 2, 4, or 15 to Quevedo.

**Santa Maria de la Almudena,** Paseo Juan XXIII, Tel. 2347207. Females only. Metro stop Cuatro Caminos. Low tariffs here also.

_____ **Where to Eat**

Spanish menus use MT (*menu turistica*) to indicate fixed-price meals. While Madrid has some outstanding restaurants, there are also many good low-cost ones, where you can look in and read the menu. The student restaurants around calle Princesa, calle Alberto Aguilera, calle San Bernardo, and avenida de José Antonio feature food, sandwiches, and pizzas at low prices.

**Restaurante Valencia,** avenida de José Antonio 44, serves up hearty portions of paella for 150 ptas., as well as seafood and chicken.

**Restaurante Risol,** calle Altamiro 13, has daily specials and good meals for 70 to 100 ptas.

**Restaurante Madrid,** calle Cruz 35, offers great food on the MT for 100 ptas., including beverage and free water.

**El Criollo,** 21 calle Barbieri, is very cheap. A full-course meal and delicious sangria (a wine drink with slices of fresh fruits) costs 60 ptas. for the meal and 50 ptas. for the sangria. Friendly, helpful manager.

For a change of pace from student fare:

**Casa Botín,** one of Hemingway's haunts at calle de Chuchilleros 17, is in a seventeenth-century building in a charming quarter behind the plaza Mayor. It has great food (excellent roast lamb) and atmosphere. Reservations are needed, and you will probably see fellow tourists here. Costs about $6 for dinner.

**Méson de San Javier,** calle de Conde 3, is wonderful for a special evening. Intimate, small, with a lovely setting and good service. Difficult to find, but worth the search. About $8 for dinner.

_____ **What to See, What to Do**

The **Prado** is Madrid's special place to visit. One of the world's finest art museums, it houses works by El Greco, Goya, and Velasquez. With over 3000 paintings to choose from, concentrate on the Spanish masters. If you can return for another visit, look at the Flemish and Italian works on display here. Hours are from 10 AM to 6 PM daily, 10 AM to 2 PM on Sunday. Students are admitted free.

**Plaza Mayor,** built in the seventeenth century, is an interesting and vivacious square, where people come to watch other people, to collect and trade stamps in the Sunday-morning philatelic market, and to browse in shops and sip wine in nearby cafés. You can savor Madrid's pulse by watching the smartly dressed and spirited people on the avenues and tree-lined parks.

The **Royal Palace,** sometimes called the National Palace, has an extensive armor collection, tapestries, the royal pharmacy and chapel, porcelains, and also portraits by Goya and Velasquez. Hours are from 10 AM to 12:45 PM, 4 PM to 6:15 PM daily. Entry fee is 200 ptas.

**Archeological Museum,** calle Serano 13, has collections of vases, porcelains, Moorish art objects, mummies, and navigation tools.

**Retiro Park,** easily found on your tourist map, has 300 acres of trees, flowers, fountains, and Roman-style temples. There's a large lake where you can rent a rowboat and find space to throw a frisbee. A visit makes a pleasant break from museum touring.

SPORTS

When you think of Spain, you may think of **bullfights.** You should go to one, though you may not care for a repeat performance. During March through September the confrontation between good and evil is played out in towns all over Spain in the Plaza de Toros. Ask for seats on the *sombra* (shade) rather than on the *sol* (sun). They cost slightly more, but the five-o'clock sun can be beastly. Bullfights take place every Sunday and sometimes on Thursdays. The schedule of who is fighting and in what ring is posted on the streets on large billboards, usually only a few days to a week in advance. If you are lucky, you may get to see Manuel Benitez, El Cordobes, Spain's most celebrated matador, in the ring.

In Madrid bullfights are held at **Plaza de Toros de Las Ventas.** You can purchase tickets on Saturday at calle de Victoria 9 from 10 AM to 1 PM, 5 PM to 9 PM. Sundays 10 AM to 5 PM. Ticket prices start at 100 ptas. Better ones go for 600 ptas.

**Soccer** (or football to Europeans) is played from September to May. Check with the visitors' bureau for exact schedules. Spanish soccer is among the best anywhere.

_____**Side Trips**

**El Escorial,** thirty-nine kilometers from Madrid, was the country palace of King Philip II. It can be visited daily from 10 AM to 1 PM, 3 PM to 7 PM, entry 50 ptas. There's an imposing basilica at the **San Lorenzo el Real Monastery,** with uncemented granite in Doric style. Take the train from Atocha or Charmentin.

**Avila** is a charming eleventh-century walled city, which can be reached by train from Madrid for less than 250 ptas. round trip.

**Toledo** is one and a half hours by bus from Madrid and has a

spectacular setting on a hill overlooking the Tagus River. Called the Imperial City, Toledo has been occupied by foreign powers many times. Her strategic location brought the Romans, who built a grand aqueduct. The Visigoths arrived around the middle of the sixth century and gave Toledo the name of Royal City. The Moslems followed, leaving behind beautiful mosques and elegant buildings. In 1085 King Alphonso of Castile reconquered Toledo and made it his capital. Today the city is undoubtedly touristy, but still imposing.

In Toledo the **El Greco House,** where the famous artist lived until his death in 1614, houses many of his finest works and is definitely worth seeing. **The Church of Santo Tome** should be on your list as well. Here you can see El Greco's most famous painting, *The Burial of the Count of Orgaz.* Some art scholars say that one face in the painting has never been identified, and speculation continues as to whether El Greco has hidden himself in the painting. It is in the front row and looks directly at the viewer.

Another building you may want to visit is a fourteenth-century synagogue now called the **Church of Santa Maria la Blanca.** With its horseshoe arches, it is considered a fine example of Mudejar handwork.

In this crowded city, many dissimilar monuments were built side by side, and you can often see Arab, Mudejar, Gothic, and Renaissance structures blending together, which gives Toledo its unique character. In fact, the entire city has been designated a national monument.

Toledo's **tourist office** is at Puerta de Bisagra, Tel. 220843, and a National Parador called **Conde de Orgas** is at Cerro del Emperador, Tel. 221850. *Paradores* are specially maintained accommodations for travelers at very low cost; sometimes they are in old castles, monasteries, or fortresses.

There's also a youth hostel at **Colegio Castillo de San Servando,** Tel. 226850.

## BARCELONA AND THE COSTA BRAVA

Situated on a beautiful gulf and harbor, **Barcelona** is a big, sophisticated port city, with a population of nearly two million people. The **Gothic quarter** is the nucleus of the old city, where a single itinerary can cover more than a dozen places of interest, including the **Cathedral, Cloisters,** and towers of the **Roman wall** at plaza Nueva. In this quarter of interesting small shops and medieval stone houses, you will also find lively night life. Here, as in much of Spain, unaccompanied girls should be careful.

**Tourist bureau,** avenida de José Antonio 658, Tel. 2221135, has a list of budget-rate accommodations.

**Alberque Juvenil J.M. Pina,** avenida Virgen de Montserrat 136, Tel. 2364746. Take bus 27, 46, or 47.

**Colegio Mayor Universitario San Jorge,** calle Maestro Nicolau 13, Tel. 2501419, is centrally located.

**Colegio Mayor Virgen Immaculata,** calle Copernico 88, Tel. 2176282, for women only. Good location in suburbs. Take bus 16 or 17.

Northeast of Barcelona begins the **Costa Brava,** an extraordinarily beautiful stretch of shoreline that extends for ninety miles of sun-drenched coves and sandy beaches toward France. The Costa Brava Express Company runs luxury coaches daily from Barcelona, or you can ride the cheaper *coche de linea,* which runs twice daily. The many fishing villages along the jagged coastline have fiestas honoring their patron saints, and you are likely to run into one of these colorful processions.

**Sitges,** a beach resort about forty-five minutes south of Barcelona, is a quiet coastal town, a welcome break from the city noise and dirt. Little cafés, pubs, and discos abound here. Two travelers stayed at the **Pension Bristol,** at calle de Rafael Llopart 3, a half block from the beach, for 200 ptas. with shower and breakfast. The owner speaks English and keeps the place spotlessly clean.

Sitges also has dozens of two-star hotels and five campsites. Golf, tennis, boating, and fishing are available. If you plan to be there in midsummer, write ahead to the **Sindicat d'Initiative,** plaza Maristany s/n Sitges or telephone to 8941230 for a list of hotels. You can also ask them to make you a reservation. Give specific dates and your price range. For $4 or under you should be able to get an adequate room.

## COSTA DEL SOL AND MÁLAGA

Spain's sunny southern coast, the **Costa del Sol,** has several boomtown resorts. You will find glamorous night life and beaches that attract visitors from all over the world. Prices have skyrocketed here over the last five years, but like most of Spain it's still a bargain, particularly since overbuilding is currently a problem. You will see empty high-rise condominiums in some crowded areas like the popular resort of Torremolinos.

**Málaga** is also a lively town, but has retained its fishing village atmosphere in palm-lined parks, lighted fountains, and quaint side streets with small cafés where wine and *tapas* are an important part of the day.

In addition to dozens of two-star hotels, Málaga has a youth hostel and two *paradores*. The hostel is **Colegio Mediterraneo,** plaza Pio XII, Tel. 234409.

Some recommended eating: The **El Boqueron de Plata,** at Alarcon Lujan 6, is a neat place for shellfish snacks and early-evening sipping. For a fine meal and a view, try the **Parador Nacional de Gibralfero,** near the castle. The special of the day costs about 250 ptas. for four courses.

There's also a fair amount of history in Málaga. The **Alcazaba,** a restored Moorish castle, is set high above the city in beautiful gardens. **Gibralfero Castle** has a fantastic view if you're willing to climb up the hillside. Málaga also has a **bullring,** which you can tour.

Down the coast toward Gibraltar is **Marbella,** forty kilometers west of Torremolinos. It's a quieter town, less crowded, and with a nicer beach. There's a youth hostel here called the **Alberque Juvenil Africa.** Of note is the stunning Marbella Club, owned by Prince Alfonso Hohenlohe, whose dining terrace overlooking the Mediterranean is full of jet setters.

## TOUR TO TANGIER

From Málaga or Algeciras you can take a ferry to Morocco and step into another world. Unless you are an experienced traveler, however, I would not recommend that young people do so on their own. Book a day trip—the ferry takes about one and a half hours each way from Algeciras—or a one-nighter to Tangier for a truly fascinating experience. Your InterRail pass will give you a discount on the ferry, so you can get there for about 145 ptas. The customs officials at Tangier will probably not worry about people who are with a tour. Drugs are plentiful, but so are undercover agents.

In Tangier you will see the old and the new side by side—veiled women in purdah mingling with those who are fashionably dressed. You will also see a degree of poverty that you may never forget.

The **Casbah,** or old city, with Woolworth heiress Barbara Hutton's Pink Palace set in the middle of incredible squalor, is a striking example of a fascinating and totally different culture. You will see women with buckets coming to water trucks to get a daily ration of water while others are on their way to communal ovens to bake their bread. Tiny children in cavelike dwellings chant the Koran. Old men live, work, and sleep in cramped caves in the walls.

At every turn you will be hounded to buy every kind of junk you can imagine. There are good things to buy, however, and they can be had cheaply. Leather goods, jewelry, brocade caftans, and Berber rugs can be found. Bargain for anything you want, and never pay more than one third of the asking price. If you have any watches, jeans, or shoes you can part with, bring them along. Ask five times what you want, but settle for about three.

If you go over only for the day, leave Spain as early as possible since some places close down after lunch. Your guide will try to direct you to those stalls in the Casbah that give him a kickback. Unfortunately, you had better stay with your guide, as getting lost in the Casbah is very easy.

## SEVILLE AND GRANADA

**Seville** is important for its charm alone—flamenco guitars, lovely walkways, fountains and plazas, and its Spring Feria during Holy Week. Andalusian in spirit, its people burst into song and strum guitars softly; romance is everywhere. **Granada** shows frequent evidence of its Moorish influence, especially in the haunting beauty of the Arab palace, the **Alhambra,** with its stunning Muslim art, mosaics, and gardens.

The **tourist bureau** in Seville, at avenida Queipo de Llano 9B, Tel. 221404, will give you a map of the city and can suggest accommodations, although there are no youth hostels or special student residences here. The old part of the city, the Santa Cruz quarter, is the best place to look for rooms in private residences. A building with a sign that says *Camas y Comidas* is a good place to try. Unescorted women should not walk in the old quarter at night.

Granada does have a youth hostel called the **Colegio Emperador Carlos.** It is located at Carretera de Ronda, Tel. 231600, and in this hot country its swimming pool is a welcome sight. The **Granada Tourist Bureau** is located at Casa de los Tiros, Pavaneras 19, Tel. 221022.

## SAN SEBASTIÁN

San Sebastián, in the northern Basque country near the French border, has a beautiful beach called **La Concha** at the end of calle de Victor Pradera, but the weather is cooler here than it is farther to the south. During the hottest summer months, this fashionable city houses the official Spanish Government. Although there are excellent restaurants and picturesque fishing-village streets, prices in San Sebastian are fairly high. Hotel rooms cost about 300 ptas. for a double. The youth hostel, **Anoeta,** is located at Cuidad Deportiva Anoeta, Tel. 452970.

Restaurants such as the **Casa Anastasio,** calle de Victor Pradera 19, offer complete menus with wine for 110 ptas. Special cider of this region costs 45 ptas. per liter, and local cheeses are excellent.

Another restaurant we liked is **Restaurant Bar Basarai,** F. Calbeton 17. Even if you're not a fish lover, try the fantastic fish soup. Special of the day goes for 190 ptas., with wine and dessert.

A disco with free admission is the **Hollywood Club,** calle de Blas de Lezo 9, off the wharf and beach and around the corner from the Hotel Orly.

Enjoy the beach early in the day because by four in the afternoon it becomes very crowded. Later, as waves chisel at the rocks and chase little children with their thunderous spray, watch the beach lights come on in the evening, white and fluorescent.

### PAMPLONA

After this peaceful interlude, you could make your way to a different kind of Spanish holiday, the **Festival of San Fermin,** well known as the running of the bulls at **Pamplona.** Ninety-two kilometers from San Sebastián, Pamplona is accessible by train. In *The Sun Also Rises,* Hemingway called this event "a damned fine show." Perhaps you will agree. The spectacle begins on 7 July and lasts for a week. Each morning the young men of the city (and any others crazy enough to join them) race through the street ahead of the bulls from the corrals to the bullring. You can get a good view of the frenzied activity from many safe vantage points. The indomitable spirit and courage this feat symbolizes can be seen in the statement by a woman whose seventeen-year-old son was killed by the bulls. When asked if she thought the running of the bulls should be stopped, she said, "If we do not have the bulls, we are not Navarros."

The **tourist office** is at Duque de Ahumada 3, Tel. 211387, and they can find you rooms in a private home. There are several campsites, and a **youth hostel** at Julio Ruiz de Alda, avenida Galicia, Tel. 235200.

# 20 FOCUS ON SWITZERLAND

Population: 6,863,000
Capital: Berne

Language: French, German
Currency: Swiss franc (SF or fr.)

## THE LAND AND THE PEOPLE

Nearly everyone has a fairy-tale image of Switzerland—mountain villages scattered high above broad meadows laced with wild flowers—and the Swiss have done nothing to shatter these preconceptions. Their country resembles a meticulously planned little Christmas-tree village, immaculate, manicured, and highly civilized, much the secret envy of other countries who can't quite forgive such success. A prosperous people, the Swiss prize quality and thoroughness. Given the diversity of people who populate the country—German-speaking Swiss in the east near Basel, the livelier Francophones in Geneva and Lausanne, and those influenced by Italy in the south—it seems surprising that such a thing as Swiss character emerges.

The complexities of each background contribute something to this tourist-oriented country. There are ultra-efficient transportation systems, beautiful and well-made manufactured goods (Swiss watches and toys, clothing, leather goods), immaculate cities, hotels, and restaurants. Traveling in Switzerland is not cheap, particularly in the cities. Visit them if you wish, but the best of Switzerland is in the mountains and the villages that huddle in their midst.

For economy, stick to the excellent hostel system, the rooms in private homes (Zimmer Frei), and try to buy your food in grocery stores.

Berne, Geneva, and Zurich are the major cities of Switzerland. Basel, near the German border, is worth seeing, as well as Lucerne, with its magnificent setting. Basel has some fine museums, and Berne is a picturesque medieval city as well as a university town. Geneva, hugging the French border, is an international center. As the headquarters for the United Nations in Europe, it is alive with diplomats from all over the world.

## FOOD

Swiss food combines French, German, and Italian cooking, and what you get often depends on which border country you are closest to. Sausages of all kinds are local specialties reminiscent of German cuisine. Most are made with pork and have names that vary from *Knackerli* and *Bantli* to *Salsiz* (small salami) and *Engadiner Wurst.* Geneva specializes in pig's feet, exotically called *pieds de porc au madere.* Perhaps more appealing is the wafer-thin dried beef, called *viande sèche* or *Bunderfleisch,* which is dried in Alpine barns. It is served for a first course, or with thin slices of buttered brown breads. Thinly sliced veal in a cream sauce, *Geschñetzeltes nach Zurcher Art,* is one of Switzerland's best offerings.

Popular in ski resorts are thick soups made even more delectable by chunky slices of *Wurst* floating on top. Lentil soup is served this way with crusty *Brötchen.*

In Basel you will find spiced honey cakes called *Leckerli.* And any confectionary worth its salt will have high, bunlike cakes called *Gugelhupf,* filled with freshly whipped cream. Cakes and pastries are light and airy and generally excellent.

*Apfelsaft,* fresh apple cider, Swiss beer, and white wines are plentiful.

Swiss fondue should be tried. It is a bubbling hot pot of melting cheese into which you dip chunks of crusty bread. Another specialty is beef fondue, chunks of meat cooked in a pot of hot oil, then dipped into four or five different sauces. Try the *raclette,* fried slabs of cheese served with pickled onion and boiled new potatoes, which is usually cheap and always filling. Specialty cheeses include Emmental (what we call Swiss cheese here) and Gruyère. Swiss chocolates are special too.

Tips are now, by law, included in all restaurant, hotel, and café bills.

## SHOP HOURS
Normal hours are from 8 AM to 12:15 PM, 1:30 PM to 6:30 PM. Banks 9 AM to 4 PM. Closed Saturdays.

## BERNE
One of Europe's best-preserved cities, Berne has a wealth of towers, sixteenth-century fountains, flower-decked, long, sandstone arcades, and a handsome natural setting. Surrounded by mountains and tucked into the bend of the Aare River, Berne is the capital of Switzerland, yet it is a small, compact city.

### Where to Stay
The main **tourist office,** located upstairs in the train station, is open daily from 8 AM to 7 PM and from 9 AM to 6 PM on Sunday; Tel. 227676. They will help you find a place to stay within your means.

And if you arrive after hours, you can help yourself by calling the hotels and guesthouses posted on the wall. If you feel hot and gritty after a long journey, the architects of the new station had you in mind: head for the excellent, spic-and-span shower facility, where you can suds up for 4 SF, including towel and soap.

**Jugendhaus,** Weihergasse 4, Tel. 226316. Ten minutes from the train station, good accommodations, including meals.

**Campground.** A first-class facility, according to Swiss rating system and firsthand information, located at Wabern, along the Aare, Tel. 031542602. Take tram 9 to Eicholzstrasse. Swimming, grocery store, and warm showers for 2 SF per camper.

## Where to Eat

**Migros** self-service restaurants, at Zeughausgasse 31, Marktgasse 46, and Hertensteinstrasse 26, have modest meals for modest prices, from 5 SF.

On **Bärenplatz** you will find a variety of small restaurants, cafés, and places to buy *Wurst* along the street. The street markets near the train station are also good places to buy cheese, fruits, bread, and *Wurst.*

**Pierrot Bar,** a small café tucked behind a deli counter at Marktgasse 7, serves good veal cordon bleu, French fries, and salad for 7 SF. Their daily menu special with soup is 6.50 SF. Closed Sunday.

The **Mövenpick** chain has three branches in the city, with pleasant surroundings and medium-priced food à la carte. However, the tab can add up surprisingly fast. You can probably still eat well for about $6. Check the daily specials rather than order a la carte.

## What to See, What to Do

You can visit the **Church of the Holy Ghost,** built around 1726, continue on to the 700-year-old **Clock Tower,** which was the city gate until 1250. Here at the astronomical clock small figures of bears—the city's heraldic animal—will entertain you every four minutes. Walk down Kramgasse to Kreuzgasse, where you can see the **Town Hall,** a Gothic building built around 1406, on to the **Fountain of Justice,** then to the **Bear Pit,** near the end of Nydegg Bridge. These living symbols of Berne are friendly clowns and will gladly accept your carrot offerings. From the nearby **Rose Gardens,** you will have the best view of the old part of the city. Notice the facades of the buildings along Junkerngasse. Then spend a moment in the **cathedral.** The stained-glass windows and carved choir stalls date from 1450 to 1523.

Berne has several museums you may wish to see, all of which are closed on Mondays:

The **Berne Historical Museum,** Helvetiaplatz 5, imposing even from the outside, has an impressive array of cannons, medieval costumes and armor, Flemish tapestries, and artifacts. Open from 9 AM to noon, 2 PM to 5 PM. Sunday 10 AM to 5 PM.

The **Swiss Alpine Museum,** Helvetiaplatz 4, will show you all sorts of climbing gear and mountaineering photos, perhaps enough to entice you to climb.

The **Kunstmuseum,** Hodlerstrasse 12, has a particularly large collection of Paul Klee's work as well as that of other contemporary artists. Hours are from 10 AM to noon, 2 PM to 5 PM.

## GENEVA

_____ **Important Addresses**

- **United States Embassy,** 80 rue de Lausanne, Tel. 327020.
- **American Express,** 7 rue du Mont Blanc, Tel. 326580.
- **Police and other emergencies,** Tel. 17.
- **Swiss Student Travel Office (SSR),** 72 boulevard de St. Georges, Tel. 299733, open daily from 9 AM to 5 PM, Saturday and Sunday from 10 AM to noon. Helpful for low-cost travel.
- **Post office,** 11 rue de Lausanne, open 6 AM to 11:45 PM.

_____ **Where to Stay**

**Auberge de Jeunesse,** rue des Plantaporrêts, Tel. 290619, reception open daily 6:30 AM to 10 AM, 2 PM to 10 PM. From the main station take bus 11 to boulevard Georges Favon, then bus 2 at quai de la Poste to Pont-Sous-Terre. Rates run 5 SF per night with hostel card.

**Centre Massaryk,** 1 avenue de la Paix, Tel. 330772. Take tram F to place des Nations. Rooms and dorms from 9 to 15 SF.

**Maison des Jeunes,** 5 rue du Temple, Tel. 322060. Take bus 7 or 11 from station. Not many beds, but they also have meals and entertainment catering to youth.

The **Geneva Tourist Office,** at the Gare Cornavin, the main train station, is open daily from 10 AM to noon, 2 PM to 9:30 PM, and it has a room-finding service, Tel. 322605. It may be your best bet, since there are about two-dozen student or university lodgings in Geneva, although most have only thirty to forty rooms available and at specific time periods. Usual cost is from 12 to 15 SF per day with breakfast. SSR can also find you a room, and they operate a service in the main train station in summer.

_____ **Where to Eat**

**Club International des Étudiants,** 6 rue de Saussure, attracts a friendly student crowd. Nothing fancy, but reasonable prices from 6 to 7 SF.

**Restaurant Universitaire,** 2 avenue du Mail, hours from noon to 2 PM, 6 PM to 8 PM. Nice food, good prices, daily specials at 5 SF. A meeting place for students.

**Buffet de La Gare Cornavin,** 3 place Cornavin, near main train station. Daily specials go for 12 SF.

The **Mövenpick,** a chain with at least four restaurants scattered about the city, offers daily specials for 8 SF, but the rest of the menu can tally much higher. Usually good Swiss food.

**Migros,** a supermarket chain with cafeterias, serves low-priced meals for about 6 SF. Two are located at rue des Paquis and place de la Navigation.

**Mr. Pickwick Pub,** 80 rue Lausanne, near the United Nations, has meals and sandwiches and a daily special for 8 SF.

**Au Viet-Nam,** 56 rue de Monthoux, serves a la carte. Oriental and Far Eastern specialties. Moderate prices.

## What to See, What to Do

In spite of its magnificent natural setting and its role as a center of politics, Geneva manages to retain a pleasant Old World, middle-class charm. While the hordes of diplomats, students, and businessmen come and go, the Old City spires and wrought-iron markers beckon visitors to come and enjoy the past. The austere home of John Calvin in the sixteenth century, Geneva today has a dedication to serve humanity. Nonetheless, it is a lively city, elegant, international, an all-season holiday resort—and quite expensive. You can find opera, theater, concerts, nightclubs, more night life than in most other Swiss cities.

One sight you can't miss is the **Jet d'Eau,** a stunning fountain that spouts 110 gallons of water per second to a height of 425 feet. The gossamer veil of water that shimmers down to the surface of the lake looks like a fine rain. The fountain had humble beginnings in 1886, when it was planned by Mr. Butticaz, an engineer in charge of Geneva's water supply who wanted to get rid of the surplus water near the Conlouvrenière Bridge.

The **Palais des Nations,** avenue de la Paix, is the United Nations' European headquarters. Take bus F or O from place Cornavin. Guided tours from 9:15 AM to 4:30 PM, entry 2.50 SF student rate. You can also be admitted to meeting sessions for a nonguided peek at world diplomacy.

The **Musée d'Art et d'Histoire,** rue Charles-Galland, is reached by bus 1 or 11 from place Cornavin. It is open daily except Monday, 10 AM to noon, 2 PM to 6 PM, free entry. In addition to a very worthwhile collection of works by van Gogh, Gauguin, Chagall, and Rodin, the

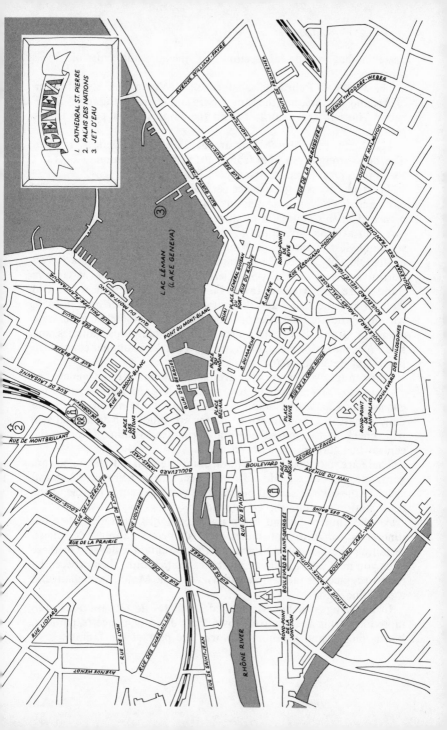

museum has a special section on the development of Swiss timepieces.

The **Musée de Petit Palais,** 2 Terrasse St. Victor, near the Museum of Art and History, has the same hours and charges students 3.50 SF entry. You can see paintings from the Impressionist period to the present.

The **Institut et Musée Voltaire** at 25 rue des Delices, is open Tuesday through Saturday from 2 PM to 5 PM and Sunday 2 PM to 6 PM. Free entry. Voltaire lived here for a decade.

The **Old City** is a good place for walking, with narrow streets and old mansions hovering around the **Cathédrale St. Pierre.** John Calvin preached in this church, a mixture of Norman and Gothic architecture. On a clear day, climb to the top of one of the towers for a stunning view of the lake and surrounding mountains. When you're in the Old City, go to the Cours St. Pierre at the top of the rue du Perron and rue du Puits-St. Pierre. The oldest house in Geneva stands here, the **Maison Tavel.** Cannons and towers near the **Old Arsenal** and the **Hôtel de Ville,** with the Baudet Tower built in 1455, will show you another facet of Geneva. From the Hôtel de Ville, walk along the Grand' Rue, where a crowd of antique shops, galleries, and boutiques make for pleasant shopping. There are summer concerts in the Hôtel de Ville's handsome courtyard.

You can take a steamer tour around **Lac Léman** (Lake Geneva) or a train to several small towns, including **Montreux** and the enchanting **Castle of Chillon,** which Byron wrote about. There are daily departures, and InterRail passes are valid. For details on side trips check at the **tourist office** at 2 rue des Moulins, Geneva, the central bus station, or a travel agent.

There are many **parks** in Geneva, complete with old-fashioned rose gardens and a clock made of flowers, accurate to the minute. You can swim in the lake at several points, and you can rent a bicycle at the train station to tour the countryside.

At the tourist bureau, pick up a pamphlet that describes ten itineraries for tours of under ten kilometers (about six miles), including the **Genevese Vineyards** and **mountain villages.** On these trips you may take a train or bus to a specific point, then proceed by foot for a picturesque ramble with views of the Mont Blanc chain and the Rhône Valley.

In mid-August a big bash called the **Fêtes de Genève** adds even more life to this already lively town. Folk dancing, concerts, parades, ballet, music, and gigantic fireworks are part of the fantasy.

## LUCERNE

Possibly Switzerland's prettiest city, Lucerne is perched on a dramatic Alpine lake. It still has Old World atmosphere of sixteenth-century houses, covered bridges, ancient city walls—enough to make you think you have been whisked back to the Middle Ages. Yet there is also lively interest in today's culture, with an international music festival in August and September that attracts many tourists.

_____ **Where to Stay**

**Youth Hostel am Rotsee,** Sedelstrasse 24, Tel. 368800, has 260 dormitory-style beds. Take bus 1 from the train station to the Schlossberg stop. From there it is a fifteen-minute walk. Not well located.

**Campground: Lido,** on Lidostrasse, Tel. 312146. A first-class facility near the city swimming pool, with sports activities, holiday camp, cottages, laundry, grocery store. Take bus 2.

**Hotel Alpenquai,** Alpenquai 42, Tel. 443343, is a SSR student center so it should be good. Singles and doubles go for 20 SF per night with breakfast. Open July and August; no reservations in advance unless you plan to stay a week or more.

**Hotel Kolping,** Friedenstrasse 8, Tel. 22901. Sterile, dorm-style beds for 15 SF; rooms a bit higher.

The **visitors' bureau** near the train station at Pilatusstrasse 14, Tel. 255222, can find you a room in a private home. Hotels are expensive.

_____ **Where to Eat**

There's a **Mövenpick** outlet here also, at Grendalstrasse, although we have found prices in this chain sharply escalating. You can probably still eat well for about $6, if you avoid steaks and order carefully.

**Migros Markt,** Hertensteinstrasse 46, is a cafeteria in a super-market where you can have simple meals—chicken, soups—from about 5 SF.

_____ **What to See, What to Do**

For a town tour, walk through the baroque **Jesuit Church,** visit the park near the **Richard Wagner Museum** (open daily from 9 AM to noon, 2 PM to 6 PM), where, if you are a music lover, you will want to see the Wagner memorabilia. Like many other European cities, Lucerne has a colorful old quarter with outdoor marketplaces along the River Reuss. The **Spreuer-Brücke** and the **Kapell-Brücke** should also be part of your strolling route. The Kapell-Brücke, which is the more famous, tells the history of the city through the paintings that line its walls. In the **Glacial Gardens** are giant glacial potholes that were discovered in 1872. They are open in summer, May to October, from 8 AM to 6 PM. In the same part of town is one of Lucerne's best-known sights, the **Lion Monument,** a dramatically sculpted beast whose unhappy death has been immortalized in stone. The Lion of Lucerne was dedicated to the Swiss Guards who defended French royalty in the Tuileries Palace at the beginning of the French Revolution. Summer-evening serenades are held nearby.

## ZÜRICH

### Important Addresses

- **United States Consulate,** Zollikerstrasse 141, Tel. 552566.
- **American Express,** Bahnhofstrasse 20, Tel. 211520.
- **Emergency,** Tel. 117.
- **Swiss Student Travel Office,** Leonhardstrasse 10, Tel. 473000.

### Where to Stay

**Youth Hostel,** Mutschellenstrasse 114, Tel. 453544. From the main railroad station, take tram 13 to Morgental.

**Touristenlager** (Tourist Hostel), Limmatstrasse 118, Tel. 423800.
Student accommodations are your best prospect, and these agencies can help find them. Cost is between 10 and 20 SF.

**Swiss Student Travel Office,** Leonhardstrasse 10, Tel. 473000.

**Student Housing Information,** Sonneggstrasse 27, Tel. 473317.

**Official Accommodation Office,** Stampfenbachstrasse 114, Tel. 265007.

**Zürich Tourist Office,** Bahnhofplatz 15, Tel. 2114000, at the main train station.

### Where to Eat

**Mensa,** student cafeteria at the University at Rämistrasse has several nice dining facilities, serves meals between 3 and 6 SF.

**Technische Hochschule** cafeteria on Leonhardstrasse near the University also serves breakfast and lunch.

**Silberkugel** chain at Bahnhofplatz 14 (central train station), at Löwenstrasse 7, and at several other locations has counter service with good hamburgers, light meals.

**Migros Markt,** five locations of cafeterias in these chain stores, has pastries and modest hot meals for 5 SF. A good in-town grocery store also.

### What to See, What to Do

You may have heard there's plenty of gold in Zürich, the center of Swiss banking. But would you be surprised to see gold rolling along the streets of Zürich? The **Goldtimer,** a gilded tram, gold inside and out, veteran from 1928, winds its way past historic buildings and landmarks, even along the central pedestrian zone, on four trips daily. The nostalgic little tram sports flower boxes and bright geraniums in added evidence of her city's pride in detail. The narrow cobbled streets, winding and steep, the many bridges, and the handsome natural setting at one end of Lake Zürich and the Limmat River give an Old World disguise to a modern commercial center. There are elegant shops and sidewalk cafés to enjoy. In August, Zurich hosts an annual **International Athletics Meet,** which attracts thousands of spectators to watch professional and amateur athletes compete in track-and-field events. James Joyce is buried in Zürich; he wrote part of *Ulysses* here, supposedly in the restaurant Pfauen.

There is ample city sight-seeing and culture here, and Zürich is also an exceptionally convenient base for side trips into villages and mountains. Here are some city sights:

**Schweizerisches Landesmuseum** (Swiss National Museum), on Museumstrasse near Walche Bridge, houses art, architecture, including complete rooms of different styles, local costume. Hours, Tuesday through Sunday 10 AM to noon, 2 PM to 5 PM. October to April, until 4 PM. Free admission.

**Kunsthaus** (Fine Arts Museum), at Heimplatz, has outstanding paintings, sculpture, fine arts, including changing exhibitions. Works by Chagall, Cranach, Giacometti. Hours, Tuesday through Friday 10 AM to noon, 2 PM to 6 PM. Thursday until 9 PM. Saturday and Sunday 10 AM to noon, 2 PM to 5 PM. Entry 3 SF.

**Grossmünster** (Cathedral), reputedly founded by Charlemagne, at Münster Bridge and Zwingliplatz, has elegant stained glass. The bronze statue of Ulrich Zwingli is in memory of the Reformation begun here when Zwingli defied the Pope in 1519.

**Fraumünster,** another church near Münster Bridge, has stained glass by Chagall.

**Beyer Museum of Time Measurement,** Bahnhofstrasse and St.-Peterstrasse will show you some of the precision movements the Swiss have made famous. Hours, Tuesday to Friday 10 AM to noon, 2 PM to 6 PM. Saturday and Sunday close at 5 PM. Entry 3 SF.

_____**Side Trips**

The Zürich tourist board boasts that every interesting place in the country can be reached within a day, and this claim is pretty accurate. You can go by organized tour or wander on your own, by motorcoach or by train.

Boat tours leave every thirty minutes from the Landesmuseum for a different view of the city scene and the ring of Alps that crown Zürich. A four-hour boat trip, leaving from Bahnhofstrasse/Burkliplatz, will take you to old Rapperswil, a lake tour popular with photographers.

A bus tour to Rhine Falls or to Lucerne are easy short day tours. By train, head for the Jungfraujoch, a spectacular 11,333 feet of mountain magnificence. A Swiss mountain train huffs and puffs its way beyond Kleine Scheidegg, and you can see views of the treacherous Eiger North Face. In winter you may choose to ski the Eigergletscher run, as we did, for a thrill of a lifetime.

Grindelwald and Interlaken are also on the route you would travel to the Jungfrau. Zermatt or St. Moritz/Pontresina are other possible one-day tours that will not disappoint you. Most one-day trips on organized tours leave about 7 AM and return to Zurich by 9:30 PM. Check with the Student Travel Office for schedules, rates, and possible discounts. Rail passes are usually valid for lake steamers.

## SKIING

Swissair has some fine package deals for skiing at famous and not-so-famous resorts, where you can stay at student hotels, sometimes dormitory style, three or four to a room. Two meals per day are generally included. This arrangement may be a good one if you are not experienced at travel and want to be with other young people. Most of these packages cannot be purchased in Europe. Rates vary, with those during the Christmas and Easter seasons the highest. Most run about $130 for hotel, two meals, and transfers to and from the airport. European half-pension or full-pension plans do not include beverages at meals other than breakfast. The period from 7 January to 1 February is considered shoulder season. Rates are lower then, and you can still have some fabulous ski days, perhaps even better snow, fewer snowstorms, more sun than at Christmas, and fewer crowds. Actually, Christmas is chancy, since snow is often found only at the highest elevations. Remember, too, that the villages are at one elevation, the ski runs at another.

### The Jungfrau Region

Here's a brief view of our absolute favorite, the Jungfrau Region, which includes Wengen, Mürren, Grindelwald, and Interlaken—Switzerland at its uncommercial best. **Interlaken** lies in the valley, between Lake Thun and Lake Brienz. A splendid mountain panorama surrounds the city, once considered only a place for summer tourists. There are many old hotels and tearooms in Interlaken, and the area is not cheap. Interlaken hosts a William Tell pageant in summer, and you can use your railpass for boat travel on the surrounding lakes. There are several hostels in the area—**Balmer's**

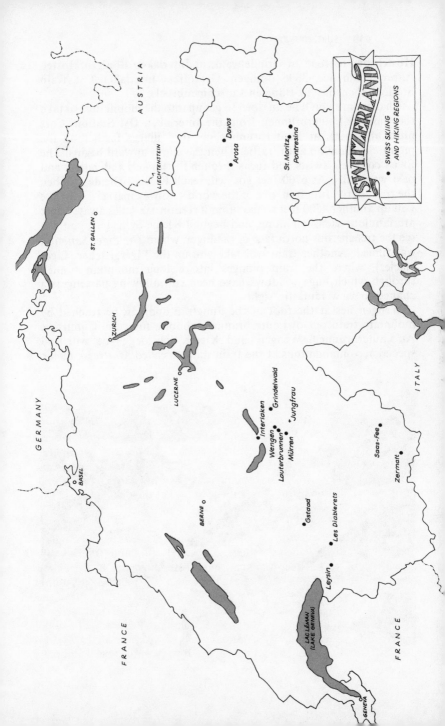

SWITZERLAND

SWISS SKIING
AND HIKING
REGIONS

AUSTRIA

LIECHTENSTEIN

Davos
Arosa

St. Moritz
Pontresina

ST. GALLEN

ZURICH

GERMANY

LUCERNE

ITALY

Interlaken
Grindelwald
Wengen
Lauterbrunnen    +Jungfrau
Mürren

BASEL

Saas-Fee

Zermatt

BERNE

Gstaad

Les Diablerets

FRANCE

Leysin

LAC LÉMAN
(LAKE GENEVA)

FRANCE

GENEVA

**Hostel,** on the road to Grindelwald, or **Interlaken Bönigen Hostel,** Aareweg am Sec, 3806 Bönigen. Get off at Interlaken Ost Train Station, then bus to Bönigen-Lutschinenbrücke..

Chances are you'll be anxious to get up into the mountains, so take the train to Lauterbrunnen from the Interlaken Ost Station. Cars must also park at Lauterbrunnen, as the villages farther up the mountain allow no auto traffic. Then the climb upward begins! The Swiss cog train twists and turns through the tunnels and valleys and past waterfalls. At 6700 feet you will reach **Kleine Scheidegg.** Then the train of the Jungfrau, one of the world's railway marvels, will take you up another 4500 feet to the summit station, six miles away. There are fabulous views all along, and beyond Kleine Scheidegg you can see the treacherous north face of the Eiger, where *The Eiger Sanction* was filmed. Another train will take you up the **Eigergletcher** (Eiger glacier), where the train plunges into a long mountain tunnel, through which huge windows have been cut, allowing passengers a chance to view fantastic sights.

**Wengen** lies at the foot of the Jungfrau and can be reached by mountain train out of Lauterbrunnen, about a fifteen-mile journey. At Lauterbrunnen, Wengen, and Kleine Scheidegg you will find special accommodations at the train stations called *Mattresse Läger.*

These are coed dormitories with eight or ten or more mattresses, blankets, and pillows. They cost more in ski season than in summer—about 12 SF in summer, 15 SF in winter, including breakfast. Ask at the train stations throughout Switzerland if there is a *Mattresse Lager*. Or look for a sign featuring a pictograph of a bed hanging near the station entrance.

The **visitors' bureau** in Wengen, Tel. 0363441, can find you a room, probably in a private home. If not, continue on up the mountain toward **Mürren**. Just below Mürren, in Gimmelwald, is an old chalet hostel near the Restaurant Schilthornbahn, which is popular with young people. Also here is **Chalet Brunner**, run by Frau Brunner, who will charge you 7 SF per night. In Mürren suggested restaurants are the **Staegstübel, Alpenruhe,** and **Pension Suppen Alp.** All charge about $3 for a good meal and are hospitable places, our ski travelers report.

In **Grindelwald**, there's a youth hostel called **Chalet die Weid,** Tel. 531009, about a twenty-five-minute hike from the train station. The **visitors' bureau** is near the station, on the main street, with hours from 8 AM to noon, 2 PM to 6 PM, and they can arrange for rooms in private homes. They will also provide a map of hiking areas in the region and a list of huts along mountain trails where you can stay for 12 SF a night. There are all levels of hikes. On some you can go part of the way by cable car; others have good trails that begin along the valley wall. Grindelwald also has a **Bergsteigerschule,** mountain-climbing school, and you can book a guided hike or rent equipment for your climb.

Some young skiers find Grindelwald too quiet, and they much prefer Wengen and Mürren for lively atmosphere.

## Other Ski Areas

**Zermatt** rates high for superb skiing and après-ski, although lift lines and crowds, as well as top prices, are minus factors. Of course, Zermatt boasts the **Matterhorn,** which towers over the village and is an awesome sight on days when you can see the peak. Zermatt is made for hikers as well as for skiers. Take the cable car up to Trockner Stegg, then hike to Gandegge Hutte, where you can marvel at some natural spectacles. A **youth hostel** near the town's edge, Tel. 77320, costs 8 SF. The **visitors' bureau** has the ever-changing list of rooms in private homes. Another possibility is a hotel by the train station, with dorms and private rooms from 14 SF.

At Switzerland's other ski areas you can also enjoy hiking in summer. **St. Moritz** is a prestigious resort, where, surprisingly enough, you can still find lodging within your budget. **Saas Fee,** one

valley to the east of Zermatt, has excellent runs and less busy lift lines. Good for experts, it has skiing until June. **Davos** and **Klosters,** a pair of towns with rather tame slopes, are in an old established Swiss ski area. **Gstaad** is very fine, very expensive skiing; **Arosa** and **Leysin** are becoming more popular all the time.

Lift passes in most Swiss ski resorts costs about $12 per day, a little less for one- and two-week passes. Evaluate your needs carefully before you buy, for you cannot get a refund should conditions keep you off the slopes.

There's a special **youth and student travel office**, the SSR, Limmatquai 138, P.O. Box 3244, CH 8023, Zürich, which will send you a comprehensive folder on youth and student travel, with packages that give discounts for individuals and groups at ski resorts, including Leysin and St. Moritz. Rates run about $12 per day with two meals, a room with three to four beds, and a shared bath. Ski passes cost about 80 SF per week; ski school for six days runs 55 SF. The SSR also offers mountain-climbing courses and a summer ski camp for good skiers only at St. Moritz. The SSR calls itself a nonprofit travel office that specializes in youth and student travel and is a member of the International Youth Travel Organization.

# Useful Words and Phrases

| ENGLISH | GERMAN | FRENCH |
|---|---|---|
| Thank you | Danke | Merci |
| Please | Bitte | S'il vous plait |
| Excuse me | Entschuldigen Sie | Pardon |
| Arrival | Ankunft | Arrivée |
| Departure | Abfahrt | Départ |
| Entrance | Eingang | Entrée |
| Exit | Ausgang | Sortie |
| To the platforms | zu den Bahnsteigen | Aux quais |
| How much? What is the cost? | Wieviel kostet es? | Combien? |
| A room | ein Zimmer | une chambre |
| Where is...? the toilet the railway station a doctor | Wo ist...? die Toilette der Bahnhof ein Artz | Où est...? la toilette la gare un médecin |
| I am ill. | Ich bin krank. | Je suis malade. |
| Can you help me? | Können Sie mir helfen, bitte. | Pourriez-vous m'aider? |
| I don't understand. | Ich verstehe nicht. | Je ne comprends pas. |
| Do you speak English? | Sprechen Sie englisch? | Parlez-vous anglais? |
| Tourist office | Verkehrsamt | syndicat d'initiative |
| Currency exchange | Wechsel | Bureau de change |
| When | Wann? | Quand? |

| ENGLISH | ITALIAN | SPANISH |
| --- | --- | --- |
| Thank you | Grazie | Gracias |
| Please | Per favore | Por favor |
| Excuse me | Mi scusi | Perdone |
| Arrival | Arrivo | Llegada |
| Departure | Partenza | Salida |
| Entrance | Entrata | Entrada |
| Exit | Uscita | Salida |
| To the platforms | Al binari | A los andenes |
| How much? What is the cost? | Quanto costa? | ¿Quánto cuesta esto? |
| A room | una camera | habitación |
| Where is...? the toilet the railway station a doctor | Dove si trova...? il gabinetto la stazione un medico | ¿Dónde está...? el servicio la estación un doctor |
| I am ill. | Mi sento male. | Me siento enfermo. |
| Can you help me? | Per favore, mi aiuti? | ¿Puede usted attender me? |
| I don't understand. | Non capisco. | No comprendo. |
| Do you speak English? | Parla inglese? | ¿Habla usted inglés? |
| Tourist office | Ente Provinciale per il Turismo | Información de Turismo |
| Currency Exchange | Cambio | Cambio |
| When | Quando? | ¿Cuando? |

# Clothing Sizes

In Europe as in United States, sizes vary somewhat among manufacturers. The following charts are a general guide.

## WOMEN'S

Dresses, Pants, Sweaters, Blouses

| U.S. | 8/30 | 10/32 | 12/34 | 14/36 | 16/38 |
|---|---|---|---|---|---|
| European | 36 | 38 | 40 | 42 | 44 |

Shoes

| U.S. | 5 | 6 | 7 | 8 | 9 |
|---|---|---|---|---|---|
| European | 36 | 37 | 38 | 39 | 40 |

## MEN'S

Suits, Jackets

| U.S. | 36 | 38 | 40 | 42 | 44 |
|---|---|---|---|---|---|
| European | 46 | 48 | 50 | 52 | 54 |

Shirts

| U.S. | 14 | 14½ | 15 | 15½ | 16 |
|---|---|---|---|---|---|
| European | 36 | 37 | 38 | 39 | 40 |

Shoes

| U.S. | 9 | 10 | 11 | 12 |
|---|---|---|---|---|
| European | 40 | 41 | 42 | 43 |

Glove sizes for men and women are the same in Europe as in the U.S.

# Measurements

## WEIGHTS AND MEASURES

Here are some commonly used metric measures and weights with their U.S. equivalents:

Weights
500 grams (g) = 1 lb
pfund (pfd) = 1.1 lb
    (pfund is an old form, yet widely used in Germany, Austria)
kilogram (kg) = 2.2 lbs
Volume
Liter (l) = 1.0567 liq. qt.
Length and Distance
centimeter (cm) = .3937 inch
meter (m) = 39.37 inches
kilometer (km) = .62 mile

**Note:** Europeans commonly buy grocery items in small amounts, i.e., 100 g salami, about enough for one generous sandwich.

## EUROPEAN TIME

Official time uses a 24-hour clock. Thus, after noon, hours are counted from 13 to 24. For example, 13.30 is 1:30 PM for us and 20.15 is 8:15 PM. At midnight time returns to 0, which means that 12:15 AM is written 0.15. Travel tickets are issued written this way.

## TEMPERATURE

The thermometer unit is Celsius. The Celsius thermometer has zero, 0°, as the freezing point and 100° as the boiling point. To change to degrees Fahrenheit, multiply degrees Celsius by 1.8 and add 32. To convert Fahrenheit into Celsius, subtract 32 and divide by 1.8. 20°C is about 70°F.

# Index

ABOUT THE AUTHOR

Born in Oakmont, Pennsylvania, Elizabeth McGough grew up in Pittsburgh and attended the University of Pittsburgh. In the following years she turned to both writing and teaching, and more than one hundred of her magazine articles have appeared in such publications as *Today's Health*, *Family Weekly*, *Family Circle*, *Teen*, and *Ingenue*.

While in Sacramento, California, where she lived for ten years, Mrs. McGough gave a course in writing magazine articles at the American River College. She has taught journalism for junior-high-school students in Richland, Washington, and she has worked with teen-agers in many activities from telephone crisis lines to communications courses. Mrs. McGough is presently living in Connellsville, Pennsylvania.